OUT OF THE DEPTHS

OUT OF THE DEPTHS

THE PSALMS SPEAK FOR US TODAY

3rd Edition
Revised and Expanded

Bernhard W. Anderson
with Steven Bishop

Westminster John Knox Press
LOUISVILLE • LONDON

Book design by Sharon Adams
Cover design by Mark Abrams

First edition
Published by Westminster John Knox Press
Louisville, Kentucky

This book is printed on acid-free paper that meets the American National Standards Institute Z39.48 standard. ∞

PRINTED IN THE UNITED STATES OF AMERICA

04 05 06 07 08 09—10 9 8 7 6 5

Library of Congress Cataloging-in-Publication Data
Anderson, Bernhard W.
    Out of the depths: the Psalms speak for us today/Bernhard W. Anderson, with Steven Bishop.—3rd ed.
        p. cm.
    Includes bibliographical references and index.
    ISBN 0-664-25832-8 (alk. paper)
        1. Bible. O.T. Psalms—Introductions. 2. Bible. O.T. Psalms—Textbooks
    I. Bishop, Steven. II. Title.

BS1430.5 .A53 2000
223'.206—dc21   99-054854

In memory of my mother
Grace Word Anderson

Upon You was I cast from my birth,
From my mother's womb You have been my God.
—Psalm 22:10

Contents

Preface

The book of Psalms has a unique place in the Christian Bible. One reason for its singular role, as noted by Athanasius, an outstanding Christian leader of the fourth century, is that most of scripture speaks *to* us
while the Psalms speak *for* us.[1] There is great truth in this observation.
Much of the Bible, in the conviction of the community of faith, is the
medium of God's speaking; it is "the word of God in human words," to
cite a well-known formulation. But the psalms of the Old Testament
have a different function. Here, for the most part, we find people addressing God in various ways—complaint in situations of distress and
perplexity, thanksgiving in moods of liberation and joy, and hymnic
praise in times of rejoicing in the goodness and wonder of God's creation and providential care. In this sense, the Psalms may speak "for"
us by expressing the whole gamut of human responses to God's reality
in our midst and thereby teaching us how to pray with others in the various times of our lives.

This book, which in its first edition was used experimentally as a
study guide, has served through the years as a brief introduction to the
book of Psalms. It is now being released in a new form, largely rewrit-
ten and thoroughly revised to take account of changing accents and new
developments in the study of the Psalms. As in previous editions, this
one also finds its way through the 150 psalms by means of the so-called
form-critical method, that is, the study of psalms classified according to
literary form and liturgical function. (See the appendices where the
classifications of the Psalms are given.) But in this edition we go beyond study of literary forms (that is, laments, thanksgivings, hymns,
songs of trust, royal psalms, wisdom psalms) into a more careful study
of the rhetorical (stylistic) features of the psalms and the new vistas that

Israel's psalmists open for us in poetic language. A new chapter is devoted to reading the Psalms as a whole, that is, a "book" of scripture; a subject that has increasingly engaged the attention of interpreters.

I am pleased that Steven Bishop, who engaged in graduate study with me at Boston University School of Theology, has joined me in the composition of this new edition. Employing his talents in literary criticism, he has expanded the discussion of poetic dimensions of the Psalter, has assumed special responsibility for translations used, and has effectively helped to bring the overall revision to a satisfying completion. Both of us profited from participation in the Psalms and Practice Conference (1999), held under the sponsorship of the Austin Presbyterian Theological Seminary and the Valparaiso Project on Education and Formation of People.

Since this is not a book *about* the Psalms but a guide *through* them, it is important that you read the designated psalms meditatively, following the study plan as it unfolds chapter by chapter. If you cannot read all the psalms listed in particular categories, read at least those recommended (marked with an asterisk in the lists given in the various chapters). Assuming that you cannot read a psalm in the original language (Hebrew), it will be helpful to consult more than one modern translation, such as:

> Revised Standard Version (RSV)
> New Revised Standard Version (NRSV)
> Tanakh: Translation of the Jewish Publication Society (NJPS)
> New Jerusalem Bible (NJB)
> New American Bible (NAB)
> Revised English Bible (REB)
> New International Version (NIV)
> The Psalter: A faithful and inclusive rendering from the Hebrew
>   into contemporary English (ICEL)

When a translation from one of these is used, the abbreviation of the version is given, for example, Psalm 22:10 (NRSV). Sometimes we have offered our own translation (marked BWA or SB). It is also appropriate to turn from time to time to the classic *King James Version* (KJV), now available in revised form, the *New King James Bible.*

Out of the Depths is designed for use in classes or study groups, or it could serve as a private *vade mecum* (Latin, meaning "go with me")—a medieval name for something one carried about as a guide or reference. Besides treating psalms that belong to a specific genre or classification, each chapter will raise important theological questions with which the community of faith wrestles as it rereads the psalms in its ongoing spiritual pilgrimage. These questions revolve around such topics as the enemies that threaten our faith, the power of death in the land of the living, the identity of God, and the coming of God's dominion (kingdom). The final chapter shows how the first two psalms provide windows into the book of Psalms as an edited whole: God's Torah or Teaching (Psalm 1) and the One Who Is to Come, the Messiah (Psalm 2; cf Luke 17:18–19).

Since the interpretation of scripture takes place within a community, not only a community of worship but a community of scholarship, I should like to thank the many persons who have influenced me, directly or indirectly, in church and academy. Besides thanking my assistant, Steven Bishop, for his supportive collaboration, I also extend thanks to the publisher, Westminster John Knox Press, for keeping this work available though the years. In particular, I want to thank executive editor, Stephanie Egnotovich, for encouraging me to produce this brand new edition.

Now that we stand at the beginning of a new century, I hope that the study of the Psalms will lead to a deeper understanding of the meaning of life in God's world and that these poems will speak *for us* "out of the depths"—to cite the opening words of Psalm 130—of our human experience.

BERNHARD W. ANDERSON

Princeton Theological Seminary
September 25, 1999

Acknowledgments

This page constitutes a continuation of the copyright page. Grateful acknowledgment is made to the following for permission to quote from copyrighted material:

Scripture quotations marked NRSV are from the New Revised Standard Version of the Bible, and are copyright © 1989 by the Division of Christian Education of the National Council of the Churches of Christ in the U.S.A. Used by permission. All rights reserved.

Scripture quotations marked RSV are from the Revised Standard Version of the Bible and are copyright 1946, 1952, and 1971 by the Division of Christian Education of the National Council of the Churches of Christ in the U.S.A. Used by permission. All rights reserved.

Scripture quotations marked JB are taken from *The Jerusalem Bible,* copyright 1966, 1967, 1968 by Darton, Longman and Todd, Ltd.and les Editions du Cerf, and Doubleday & Co., Inc. Used by permission of the publishers.

Scripture quotations marked NJB are taken from *The New Jerusalem Bible,* published and copyright 1985 by Darton, Longman and Todd, Ltd. and les Editions du Cerf, and Doubleday, a division of Random House, Inc. Reprinted by permission.

Scripture quotations marked REB are taken from the *Revised English Bible.* Copyright © 1989 by Oxford University Press and Cambridge University Press. Used by permission of Oxford University Press, Inc.

Scripture quotations marked NIV are from *The Holy Bible, New International Version.* Copyright 1973, 1978, 1984 International Bible Society. Used by permission of Zondervan Bible Publishers.

Scripture quotations marked NJPS are from *The Tanakh: The New JPS Translation According to the Traditional Hebrew Text.* Copyright 1985 by the Jewish Publication Society. Used by permission.

The English translation of Psalms 40 and 57 are from *The Liturgical Psalter* © 1995, International Committee on English in the Liturgy, Inc. All rights reserved.

Pritchard, James B., *Ancient Near Eastern Texts Relating to the Old Testament.* Copyright © 1950, 1955, 1969, renewed 1978 by Princeton University Press. Reprinted by permission of Princeton University Press.

Excerpt from *The Cocktail Party,* copyright 1950 by T. S. Eliot and renewed 1978 by Esme Valerie Eliot, reprinted by permission of Harcourt, Inc.

Excerpt from *W. H. Auden: Collected Poems,* edited by Edward Mendelson. Copyright © 1941 and renewed 1969 by W. H. Auden. Reprinted by permission of Random House, Inc.

Joan Anderson for permission to reproduce her illustrations found on pp. 110 and 112.

1

Songs of a Pilgrim People

In his book *Fear No Evil*, Natan Sharansky, the noted Jewish dissident who eventually became a member of the Israeli parliament, tells how the book of Psalms saved his life during a long nine-year imprisonment by the KGB, the Soviet secret police.

He spent just over one year in a punishment cell, a cold, damp basement room that measured barely six feet square. In a constant battle of wills with Soviet authorities, he went on hunger strikes and endured countless hours of interrogation. His one possession and constant companion during those hard years was a book of Psalms given to him by his wife Avital. Though not a particularly religious man, he began reading the psalms, even memorizing them. To his astonishment he found a striking affinity between his experience of bondage and the distresses articulated by many of the psalmists. Their prayers of lament became his own and their hope of deliverance became a gleam of light in his cell. After nine grueling years, several confiscations and reluctant returns of his book of Psalms, he was finally transported to an airport outside Moscow for his trip to East Germany and then to freedom.

Sharansky's release was choreographed by the Soviets to insure the most favorable exposure for the world press. An official car drove him to the Bykovo airport, then to a plane at the far end of the airport. Photographers were in place when he got out of the car; he was now minutes away from freedom and the end of his nine years of humiliation and suffering. His record continues:

> "Where's my Psalm book?"
> "You received everything that was permitted," answered the intellectual in an unexpectedly rough tone.
> He signaled to the tails to take me away.

1

I quickly dropped to the snow. "I won't move until you give me back my Psalm book." When nothing happened, I lay down in the snow and started shouting, "Give me back my Psalm book!"

The photographers were aghast, and pointed their cameras toward the sky.

After a brief consultation the boss gave me the Psalm book.[1]

On the plane ride to freedom, Sharansky opened his book of Psalms to keep a promise he had made to himself. While in prison he vowed that his first act in freedom would be to read Psalm 30. He turned the well-worn pages to the appropriate place and began,

> I extol You, O Lord,
>   for you have lifted me up,
>   and not let my enemies rejoice over me.
> O Lord, my God,
>   I cried out to You,
>   and You healed me.
> O Lord, You brought me up from Sheol,
>   preserved me from going down into the Pit.
>   (Ps. 30:1–4, NJPS)

In our troubled and traumatic times there are many people—even those who have not been in such extremity as Natan Sharansky—who have found deep meaning in the book of Psalms. When they have felt isolated, it has brought them an awareness of their interconnection with members of an invisible community of faith. When they have been in desperate circumstances or sickness unto death, it has given them comfort and hope. When they have been torn away from their homes and families, and subjected to cold and hunger, torture and rape, it has given them inner strength to bear up and to persevere with courage and fortitude. When they have been put in prison unjustly and under sentence of death, it has enabled them to believe that there is a God who will obtain justice for the oppressed.

Early Christians sang "psalms and hymns and spiritual songs" (Eph. 5:19) in prison (Acts 16:25) or in other difficult situations. Likewise, in our turbulent period of history, when the foundations are shaking (Ps. 11:3) and the world seems to be on the verge of chaos, many people testify that the psalms enable them to speak to God "out of the depths" in company with a community of faith, visible and invisible, past and present, local and worldwide. Participants in this community have learned to praise God anew, not just in times of God's presence but in those times when, to use an expression that frequently occurs in the psalms, "the face [presence] of God" is hidden (e.g., Ps. 10:11; 13:1; 30:7).

The book of Psalms had a special meaning for Dietrich Bonhoeffer, the martyred Christian whose writings have profoundly influenced contemporary theology.[2] One of his last writings in prison, before being executed for conspiracy in a plot to kill Hitler, was *Psalms: The Prayer Book of the Bible.* This tiny book began with the observation that the Psalter is a prayer book, containing the words that worshiping people address to God. How, then, can these prayers to God be, at the same time, God's word to the people? Bonhoeffer answers this question by saying that these are the prayers God gives us to pray in the name of Jesus Christ, who has brought every human sorrow and joy, every frustration and aspiration, before God. If we prayed out of the poverty of our hearts we might pray for only what we want to pray for; but God wants our prayers to be much fuller, encompassing not only our own needs but the life of the whole community of God's people. So just as the Lord's Prayer was given in answer to the request "Lord, teach us to pray" (Luke 11:1), so the book of Psalms teaches how we are to come before God in the proper way. It is therefore quite appropriate, in this view, for the New Testament and the Psalms to be bound together, for the Psalter is "the prayer of the church of Jesus Christ" and "belongs to the Lord's Prayer."[3]

The Psalter as a Christian Hymnbook

The bracketing together of the New Testament and Psalms, as in the case of the Lutheran edition just mentioned, emphasizes the important place of the psalms in Christian worship.

From the very first, Christians highly treasured the book of Psalms. As a matter of fact, the title "the book of Psalms" comes from the New Testament (Luke 20:42; Acts 1:20). In the Hebrew Bible the title is *tehillim,* which means "praises." The early Christian community, however, read Jewish scripture in the Greek version (Septuagint), where the prevailing title was *psalmoi,* referring to songs sung to the accompaniment of stringed instruments. One codex of the Greek Old Testament used the title *psalterion,* a term that referred basically to a zither-like instrument and secondarily to songs with stringed accompaniment; hence the alternate title "Psalter."

The early followers of Jesus of Nazareth expressed their faith in the singing of "a new song," yet this "new speech from the depths," as Amos Wilder puts it, drew deeply upon fountains that sprang up within Israel's worship.[4] The early church was profoundly influenced by synagogue practice in which psalms were read as scripture, recited as prayers, or sung as hymns. This style of worship prepared the way for the liturgical use of the psalms through the centuries to the present.[5]

The early Christian church not only drew upon the Psalter, it also composed its own "psalms and hymns and spiritual songs" (Eph. 5:19). Students of the New Testament have demonstrated the presence of hymnic fragments and other liturgical materials embedded in early Christian literature. For instance, in the magnificent portrayal of the humility of the Christ "who, though he was in the form of God, did not regard equality with God as something to be exploited, but emptied himself, taking the form of a slave" (Phil. 2:6–11), Paul made use of an early Christian song that was familiar to his readers. Fragments of Christian hymnody are contained in the "new song" of Rev. 7:9–14, which Handel transposed into the triumphal music of *Messiah* ("Worthy is the Lamb who was slain."). And the Gospel of Luke includes two complete Christian psalms: the Magnificat of Mary (Luke 1:46–55) and the Benedictus of Zechariah (Luke 1:68–79). The Benedictus calls people to "bless" ("praise" cf. Ps. 103:1; 104:1) the God of Israel:

> Blessed be the Lord God of Israel,
>   for he has looked favorably on his people and redeemed
>   them.
> He has raised up a mighty savior for us
>   in the house of his servant David,
> as he spoke through the mouth of his holy prophets from of
>   old,
>   that we should be saved from our enemies, and from the
>   hand of all who hate us.
> Thus he has shown the mercy promised to our ancestors,
>   and has remembered his holy covenant,
> the oath that he swore to our ancestor Abraham,
>   to grant us that we, being rescued from the hands of our
>   enemies,
> might serve him without fear in holiness and righteousness
>   before him all our days.

(Luke 1:68–75, NRSV)

Here the language echoes tones heard in the psalms, including the theme of God's promises to the ancestors (Ps. 105:7–11) and deliverance from Israel's enemies (Ps. 23:5), but this is *a new song,* pitched in the brilliant key of the good news that in Jesus Christ, God "has turned to his people and set them free" (v. 68, REB).

The Psalms and Jesus Christ

In the New Testament the Christian community has appropriated the whole body of Jewish scriptures (Law, Prophets, and Writings—in Christian terms, "the Old Testament"), and in so doing has "baptized the Psalter into Christ."[6] Along with the prophecy of Isaiah, the Psalter is one of the two Old Testament books most frequently drawn upon in the New Testament (see appendix C). Early Christians, who regularly used the book of Psalms in worship, wanted to say that these songs bear witness to Jesus Christ. Thus the royal psalm, Psalm 2, with its divine declaration, "Thou art my Son," was understood to refer to *the* Anointed One (Messiah), Jesus Christ; and Psalm 22, a song of lament beginning with a poignant cry of dereliction, "My God, why hast thou forsaken me?" was taken to be a portrayal of Christ's passion.

In saying that these and other psalms bear witness to Jesus Christ, the early Christian community was associating itself with the people of Israel—"the Israel of God" as Paul designates it (Gal. 6:16)—whom God had formed and consecrated. Christians confessed then, as they do now, that the Old Testament is indeed part of "the story of our life," as H. Richard Niebuhr once put it,[7] a story of God's involvement in the life story of Israel that leads to and is illumined by God's visiting the people in the event of Jesus Christ: his life, death, and resurrection. In this perspective it may be said that the entire Psalter—not just those psalms that are interpreted christologically in the New Testament—is illumined by the Christ event. This conviction is beautifully illustrated in Luke's postresurrection story of the walk of two disciples from Jerusalem to the nearby village of Emmaus (Luke 24:13–35). As they walk, a stranger joins them and encourages them by interpreting recent events in the light of "the law [teaching] of Moses, the prophets, and the psalms" (v. 44). Later, after they recognize the stranger to be Jesus, they exclaim: "Were not our hearts burning within us while he was talking to us on the road, while he was opening the scriptures to us?" (v. 32, NRSV).

It is important to keep in mind, however, that the native setting of the psalms was the community of ancient Israel and, in particular, Israel's service of worship in temple or synagogue. There the tones of Israel's praises were heard as the people remembered and celebrated the sacred story. Even though Christians hear the psalms in a different liturgical setting, they express in their own way the sonorities of Israel's worship. Perhaps this matter may be clarified by a figure of speech that musicians will readily appreciate. The same notes may have a different tone quality when the sounding board is changed, for instance, from violin to cello, or from harpsichord to piano. Even so, to Christian ears the notes of the psalms have a fuller and deeper resonance when played against the sounding board of the Christian liturgy, which celebrates God's saving activity and presence through Jesus Christ. Christian worship services often conclude the responsive reading or the chanting of a psalm with the ancient Christian hymn, the Gloria Patri, or by the invocation of the Trinity.

The Psalms in the History of Christian Worship

Our discussion of the role of the early Christian community in composing and interpreting psalms leads to a very important point. The psalms of the Bible are not individualistic poems such as a modern person might compose to express personal thoughts and feelings. Rather, the psalms show that the individual finds his or her identity and vocation in the community that God has created, "the Israel of God." Within that community of faith one has access to God in worship, and within that community one participates in a great historical pilgrimage. As we are reminded in the documents of Vatican II that deal with the church, the Bible presents the story of "God's pilgrim people."

Psalms outside the Psalter

It should not be surprising, then, to discover that the songs of this pilgrim people are not confined to the Psalter but are found in connection with the whole unfolding story of the Bible—not only in the New Testament, as we have noticed, but throughout the Old Testament as well. Many of the materials in the Old Testament, such as the story of creation in Genesis 1:1–2:3, were shaped by liturgical usage, perhaps in connection with one of the great temple festivals. In addition, numerous psalms are scattered throughout the Old Testament. As a preface to our concentrated study of the book of Psalms, it would be helpful to glance over some of these Old Testament psalms. The list includes:

- The Song of the Sea (Ex. 15:1–18), composed to celebrate Yhwh's ("the LORD's," in many English translations) deliverance of the people Israel from Egyptian bondage. This Mosaic song is based on the Song of Miriam (Ex. 15:20–21).
- The Song of Moses (Deut. 32:1–43), which contrasts God's faithfulness with Israel's unfaithfulness.
- The Song of Deborah (Judg. 5:1–31), a victory song that celebrates God's coming to the rescue of the embattled "people of the Lord" (v. 11) in a great military crisis.
- The Song of Hannah (1 Sam. 2:1–10), a psalm of thanksgiving inserted into the story about Samuel at Shiloh.
- David's Song of Deliverance (2 Sam. 22:2–51), a psalm of thanksgiving, preserved also as Psalm 18.
- A song of thanksgiving (Isa. 12:4–6) used to conclude the first section of the book of Isaiah.
- King Hezekiah's song (Isa. 38:9–20), a psalm of thanksgiving for use when presenting a thank offering in the Temple.
- The prayer of Habakkuk (Hab. 3:2–19), a hymn praising God for deliverance of the people Israel from foes described in mythical language.
- Jonah's prayer from the belly of a fish (Jonah 2:2–9), actually a psalm of thanksgiving.
- Hymns embedded in the prophecy of so-called Second Isaiah (e.g., Isa. 42:10–12; 52:9–10) that summon people to sing "a new song."
- Hymns (e.g., Job 5:8–16; 9:4–10; 12:7–10; 12:13–25) and complaints or laments (e.g., Job 3:3–12, 13–19, 20–26; 7:1–10; 7:12–21; 9:25–31; 10:1–22) in the book of Job.
- Psalms of complaint in Jeremiah (e.g., Jer. 15:15–18; 17:14–18; 18:19–23) and in Lamentations, especially chapters 3 and 5.

If we were to consider literature belonging to the expanded Greek Old Testament (i.e., including the books often called the Apocrypha), other psalms could be added to the list. For instance, in Ecclesiasticus (otherwise known as the Wisdom of Jesus the Son of Sirach) from the early second century B.C., we find the thanksgiving of Sirach (51:1–12) and superb hymns of praise (39:14b–35; 42:13–33). Also, in the popular story of Tobit, from around the second century B.C., there is a magnificient hymn of praise (chapter 13). And though we cannot go into all the relevant literature outside the scope of the Hebrew Bible, special mention should also be made of the beautiful songs found among the Dead Sea Scrolls (second century B.C.), apparently composed by members of the Qumran monastery for use in their worship services. In accordance with liturgical styles in vogue in the synagogue, these hymns fall into two main categories: thanksgiving ("I give thee thanks, O Lord . . .") and blessings ("Blessed art thou, O Lord . . . ").[8]

Even this cursory review shows that the psalms preserved in the Psalter represent only a small selection of the many psalms that once were composed and sung in Israel. The Bible as a whole is not only the story of God's dealings with a particular people, but also this people's response in thanksgiving and adoration, in lament and petition, along the way of its historical pilgrimage. The sounds of Israel's praises are heard, to one degree or another, in practically every book of the Bible, from Genesis to Revelation. It is in the Psalter, however, that the praises of God's people resound clearly as nowhere else.

The Psalms in the History of Worship

On first glancing through the Psalter we discover that the 150 psalms are divided into five parts, or "books." This fivefold arrangement (to be considered in chapter 10) was made relatively late in the biblical period and was undoubtedly patterned after the five-book Torah (Pentateuch), Genesis through Deuteronomy. In its present form the Psalter comes from the period of the Second Temple—the temple of Zerubbabel, which was rebuilt in 520–515 B.C. (the time of the prophets Haggai and Zechariah) and stood until it was superseded by the temple of King Herod (begun about 20 B.C.), the stones of which may still be seen in the famous Western Wall of Jerusalem.

Musical Recitation of the Psalms

We wish that we knew more about the place of music in the temple services. Various indications are given that psalms were to be sung to the accompaniment of musical instruments or temple choirs. A small clue to musical recitation of psalms may be the enigmatic word *selah,* which appears here and there (e.g., Ps. 3:2, 8; 9:16, 20). Possibly the term indicated a break or interlude in the recitation of the psalm, at which time the choir or instrumental accompanists would provide an intermezzo. Musical notations are also provided now and then in the superscriptions to certain psalms. Perhaps an example is the notation at the head of Psalm 22: "To the choir leader: according to the Deer of the Dawn." The curious words, "the Deer of the Dawn," may refer to the tune to which the psalm was to be sung.

In recent years the work of a Parisian composer, Suzanne Haïk-Vantoura, has opened up exciting possibilities for understanding what the cantillation of the psalms may have sounded like in ancient times. Basing her work on the standard (Masoretic) text of the Hebrew Bible, she believes that she has discovered a key to the melodic recitation of the Hebrew scriptures. Her view assumes that biblical texts were recited to various melodies in the period of temple worship and later in synagogue services. These melodies, she believes, were captured by rabbinical interpreters known as the Masoretes, who in the ninth century A.D. fixed and notated the text with a system of signs. The purpose of those notations was to help one hear the phrasing of the text and thereby appreciate its meaning more deeply. Using this approach, she has produced melodies of astonishing power and beauty.

This theory is unique in that it attempts to integrate musical notations to the text with a grammatical study of the lines (syntax). Of course, Haïk-Vantoura is not without her critics. Two major reservations are that her work is dependent on subjective hunches regarding melody and is also dependent on Western harmonic tradition. Undoubtedly these matters will be debated for some time. Nevertheless, her work sheds some light on a once impenetrable mystery: how the psalms were used musically. It provides a channel, as it were, on which we may hear how the earliest cantillation of the psalms sounded.[9]

The Hymnbook of Temple and Synagogue

Sometimes the Psalter is called "the hymnbook of the Second Temple." This is proper insofar as the Psalter was given its final shape during this period. Yet this was also the period when the synagogue was emerging as the focal point of prayer and scriptural interpretation. Therefore the Psalter, with equal justification, may be called the prayer book of the synagogue, especially since it opens with a psalm that reflects the piety based on the study of the Torah. We are coming to realize that many of the psalms were used to nurture piety in the home and for scriptural recitation in the synagogue.

In a form-critical analysis of the psalms, Erhard Gerstenberger has suggested that the Israelite tradition of psalm use was an aspect of community and family life in ancient times. Occasions for ritual recitations, he observes, were twofold: seasonal and spontaneous. The seasonal occasions were predictable, marking agricultural rhythms such as seedtime and harvest, or social events such as weddings, circumcision, and other rites of passage. There were also spontaneous occasions characterized by unforeseen good and bad fortune. Illness, threat of war, loss of crops by storm or drought, and other "acts of God" would evoke expressions of lament and complaint; experiences of good fortune such as recovery from illness or victory over enemies would prompt songs of thanksgiving. In Gerstenberger's view, these literary forms emerged apart from a prescribed liturgy or national sponsorship. Only after Israel became a state were these traditional expressions adapted and transformed for use in the national temple cult.[10]

The rise of the synagogue was a major factor in keeping alive the faith and tradition of Israel in a time when Jewish colonies were springing up outside Palestine. Alexandria in Egypt came to be one of the major centers of the Jewish dispersion in the postexilic period. About 250 B.C. the Alexandrian Jews began to translate their sacred scriptures into the vernacular, the common (*koine*) Greek of the Hellenistic world in which the New Testament was also written. This Greek version of the Old Testament (known as the Septuagint) contains a Psalter that differs in several interesting respects from the Hebrew tradition followed by the Protestant Reformers. For one thing, the Greek Old Testament (like the scriptures of the Dead Sea community of Qumran) contains an extra psalm (Psalm 151), which is attributed to David.[11] The Greek Bible also differs somewhat in the determination of where a particular psalm begins and ends; for instance, what is regarded as one psalm in the Greek Bible may appear as two in the Hebrew Bible (e.g., Psalms 9–10; 114–115).

The early Christian community, being Hellenistic in complexion, read its Old Testament in Greek vernacular. Accordingly, the structure of the Psalter in the Greek Bible has influenced Christian usage, as may be seen from translations formerly used in Roman Catholic and Eastern Orthodox communities. In this study, however, we shall follow the generally accepted numbering of the New Revised Standard Version, which has been accorded the status of "the Common Bible" by Protestant, Roman Catholic, and Eastern Orthodox representatives. Even this

numbering will have to be questioned at points, for some psalms reckoned as two in the Hebrew Bible (and hence in the Common Bible) actually constitute one literary unit (e.g., Psalms 42–43); and vice versa,
a psalm that is considered as one may actually consist of two literary
units (e.g., Psalm 27). In other words, the numerical determination of
the psalms does not always coincide with the literary units. (See the
listing in Appendix B.)

Collections of Psalms

Let us return to our consideration of the Psalter as a hymnbook. A
closer look at the fivefold structure of the Hebrew Psalter reveals that
this symmetrical organization was superimposed upon previously cir-
culating collections of psalms, just as modern hymnbooks are based
upon previous editions. Evidence of this is found in the editorial notice
at the end of Psalm 72: "The prayers of David, the son of Jesse, are
ended." This postscript is rather surprising when one discovers that
psalms of David, according to their headings, are found later on:
Psalms 108–110 and Psalms 138–145. This can only mean that at one
stage in the history of the formation of the Psalter a Davidic collection
ended here.

Looking over the psalms up to Psalm 72 (minus Psalms 1 and 2
which are introductory to the whole Psalter), we find that this list actually includes two groups of psalms that, by their headings, are ascribed
to David—namely, Psalms 3–41 and Psalms 51–72.

> [Note: Two of the psalms in the first Davidic collection, Psalms
> 10 and 33, are not explicitly ascribed to David. Psalm 10,
> however, is actually the second half of an alphabetical psalm (i.e.,
> one in which every second verse begins with a successive letter
> of the Hebrew alphabet). The first half of the alphabetical
> sequence is Psalm 9 (ascribed to David), and thus Psalms 9 and
> 10 should be considered one psalm, as in the Septuagint. The
> other psalm in question, Psalm 33, is ascribed to David in the
> Septuagint.]

In between these two Davidic collections we find a group of psalms
ascribed to Korah (Psalms 42–49), and just after the second Davidic
collection we find another group ascribed to Asaph (Psalms 73–83).
We gather from the book of Chronicles (written about 300 B.C.) that
Korah and Asaph were leaders of musical guilds during the period of

the Second Temple (see, e.g., 2 Chron. 20:19). It seems likely, then, that the original nucleus of the Psalter was the Davidic collection found in Psalms 3–41. In the course of time this core group was supplemented with other Davidic collections (especially Psalms 51–72), and with various collections composed and used by the choirs of the Second Temple (Psalms 42–49; 73–83; 84–88). Eventually the collections now found in Psalms 90–150 were added. In this last section of the Psalter we find, for instance, a group of psalms that celebrate God's enthronement as king over the earth (Psalms 93–99, except 94). Another group is characterized by the exclamation "Praise the Lord [Yhwh]," which in Hebrew is *hallelujah* (Psalms 111–118; 146–150). Still another group bears the superscription "Song of Ascents" (Psalms 120–134), an expression that probably means "a pilgrimage song," that is, a song used when pilgrims ascended to Jerusalem to worship at the Temple. Psalm 122, for instance, expresses the pilgrims' joy on having arrived at their destination.

> I rejoiced that they said to me,
>> "Let us go to the house of Yahweh."
> At last our feet are standing
>> at your gates, Jerusalem!
>> (Ps. 122:1, NJB)

In summary, we find embedded within the present edition of the Psalter the following collections:

1. An original Davidic collection (Psalms 3–41)
2. Psalms of the Korah musical guild (42–49)
3. A second Davidic collection (51–72)
4. Psalms of the Asaph musical guild (73–83 + 50)
5. Additional psalms of the Korah guild (84–88, except 86)
6. Various other collections (90–150), including:
   a. Psalms of Yhwh's kingship (93–99, except 94)
   b. Songs of praise (103–107)
   c. Psalms of pilgrimage (120–134)
   d. A third Davidic collection (138–145)
   e. Hallelujah psalms (111–118; 146–150)
   f. Other important psalms have been put in this section too.

The Elohistic Psalter

The collections shown with a brace in the above outline (nos. 2, 3, 4)—the so-called Elohistic Psalter—at one time must have circulated as a separate hymnbook. This is evident only from the text of the original Hebrew Bible, in which all these psalms show a decided preference to use the general name "God" (Elohim) instead of the special divine name (Yhwh) usually translated "the LORD." A computer search reveals that in this Elohistic Psalter (Psalms 42–83) the divine name "God" appears 200 times and "the LORD" only 43, whereas in the rest of the Psalter "the LORD" appears 642 times and "God" (Elohim) only 29. The best explanation for this striking phenomenon is that the collection once existed independently before it was included in the final framework of the Psalter. This would explain why two psalms appear in almost identical form: Psalm 14, which uses "the LORD" and Psalm 53, which uses "God."

It is appropriate, then, to speak of the Psalter as "the hymnbook of the Second Temple" if we keep in mind that, like a modern church hymnal, it is a relatively late arrangement based on previous collections and including hymns of many ages. This is true, for instance, of *The Methodist Hymnal* (1966). It includes hymns from the patristic period ("O Guide to Every Child" by Clement of Alexandria), from the Middle Ages ("Creator of the Stars of Night," anonymous), from the Reformation ("A Mighty Fortress Is Our God" by Martin Luther), from the period of the Enlightenment ("The Spacious Firmament on High" by Joseph Addison), from the great Wesleyan revival ("O for a Thousand Tongues to Sing" by Charles Wesley), to say nothing of modern hymns that reflect the pietism of the nineteenth century or the theological renaissance of the mid-twentieth century. Similarly, the Psalter, though it received its final form three or four centuries before Christ, reflects a long history of worship, reaching back at least to the time of David and, in some instances, including forms of worship used by Israel in the early period of the settlement in the Land of Canaan. It may cover as much as a thousand years of the history of worship.

Invocation of the Name of God

The so-called Elohistic Psalter, discussed above, calls our attention to the question of the name of God. Generally speaking, two words for deity are used in the Psalms: *Elohim* ("God," prominent in the Elohistic Psalter) and *Yhwh,* (the so-called Tetragrammaton), a personal name most often translated "the LORD."

Recall that in the story of the burning bush (Ex. 3), when Moses received a commission from God to lead the people out of Egypt, he asked for the name of God who was speaking. He wanted to divulge the identity of the deity who was about to act to liberate the Israelites from bondage. The pressing question was (as in a profound sense it is even today) Who is God? The translation of the Jewish Publication Society reads this way:

> God [Elohim] said to Moses: "Ehyeh-Asher-Ehyeh" ["I Am That I Am"]. He continued: "Thus shall you say to the Israelites, 'Ehyeh sent me to you.'" And God said further to Moses, "The Lord, the God of your fathers, the God of Abraham, the God of Isaac, and the God of Jacob, has sent me to you. This shall be My name forever." (Ex. 3:12–14, NJPS)

It can be seen from this translation that the answer to Moses' question about God's name (signifying God's identity or self) is given cautiously if not evasively.[12] Scholars believe that originally the divine name (consonants plus vowels) was spelled Yahweh. Eventually, however, the personal name came to be considered as so sacred that it was withdrawn from ordinary usage and the word *Adonai* (Lord) was pronounced instead. This was the practice in the late biblical period when scripture was read in the synagogue.

Jewish reverence for the Name has influenced modern translations. One Catholic version, the New Jerusalem Bible, boldly uses "Yahweh," but most modern translations, following ancient synagogue practice, substitute "Adonai," rendered "the LORD" in English. In its preface to the Psalter, the Anglican (Episcopal) book of worship known as *The Book of Common Prayer* (1977) introduces an explanatory note, pointing out that the synagogue practice is to be followed except in two passages (Ps. 68:4 and 83:18–20) where "the context requires that the Divine Name be spelled out."

It is appropriate for Christians to join with the Jewish community in the attitude of reverence to God, refusing to use the name of God lightly. We should be aware, however, of difficulties that stand in the way of adopting the synagogue usage. For one thing, *the Lord* (Adonai) is a title, not a personal name appropriate for an I-Thou relationship.

[handwritten in left margin: the original vowels are lost forever]

Also, *the Lord* is a masculine title, the use of which only aggravates the dominance of masculine speech in the Bible. In English this language problem is not immediately evident, for the title Lord (as well as Lady) is somewhat archaic, but the problem leaps to attention in other languages where the title is a common masculine address: in German "der Herr," Spanish "El Señor." No wonder that in recent revisions of hymnals serious questions have been raised about following the synagogue practice.

In this book our policy will be to follow the lead of the Elohistic Psalter and use "God" wherever appropriate. Often in modern usage this general term for deity has come to be a name, filled with the content of personal relationship. In the beautiful Psalm 27, to take one example, many people would experience no loss of spiritual meaning if "God" were to replace the frequent reference to "the Lord [Yhwh]." When quotations are made from modern translations, we shall follow the synagogue usage when adopted by the particular translator, though sometimes putting the Tetragrammaton in parentheses. Often in discussion of psalms we shall use the Tetragrammaton without further ado, leaving it to the reader to decide whether to read "God," "Adonai," "Yhwh," or even the archaic term "Jehovah."

The Composition of the Psalms

In one respect the comparison of the Psalter with a modern hymnbook does not hold. Most of the songs in our hymnbooks are assigned to definite composers of words and tunes, whose dates are usually given on the same page. Relatively few modern hymns are anonymous; indeed, numerous books have been written about the authors of our great hymns. In the Psalter, however, the situation is just the opposite. The authors of the psalms are unknown, and practically nothing can be learned from the psalms about the time or circumstance of their composition.

This statement may sound surprising in view of the traditional belief that the book of Psalms contains the very words of David. Since the beginning of the Christian era, and indeed right to the nineteenth century, David has been regarded as the author of the Psalter. This view is reflected, for instance, in Mark 12:35–37, which reports Jesus' dispute with the scribes over the lineage and identity of the Messiah. The argument assumed that "David himself, inspired by the Holy Spirit," wrote Psalm 2, although in the Psalter this psalm, unlike many others, does not have a heading that attributes it to David. Jesus' argument, however, was *ad hominem,* that is, it was addressed to the prejudice of the scribes and was not intended to be a critical view of the authorship of the psalm. When it is assumed elsewhere in the New Testament that the Psalter is Davidic (e.g., Acts 4:25–26; Rom. 4:6–8), the writers merely adopted the contemporary way of referring to the hymnbook of Israel. In the same manner people of the time identified the Torah (Pentateuch) with Moses or the wisdom literature with Solomon.

The Sweet Singer of Israel

Even on critical grounds, however, the association of David with the Psalter is substantially valid. There was an ancient tradition, to which the prophet Amos appealed in the eighth century B.C. (Amos 6:5), that David was skillful with the lyre. It was this skill that brought him into the court of King Saul, according to a well-known story (1 Sam. 16:14–23). Moreover, David gave great impetus to Israel's worship by bringing the ark of the covenant to Jerusalem (2 Samuel 6) and by laying plans for the building of the Temple (2 Samuel 7). Further, there must be some truth in the view expressed in the relatively late Chronicler's history that David sponsored the composition of psalms and was active in organizing the music and liturgy of Israel's worship (1 Chronicles 13–29). In the light of all this it may be assumed that embedded in the Psalter are poems or poetic fragments actually composed by David or by those in his court. An example is Psalm 24, especially its concluding portion with its address to the gates of Jerusalem to lift up their heads (arches) so that the "King of glory" may enter—an antiphonal ritual that reenacts David's bringing the ark into his new capital.

> O gates, lift up your heads!
> Up high, you everlasting doors,
> so the King of glory may come in!
> Who is the King of glory?—
> the Lord, mighty and valiant,
> the Lord, valiant in battle.
> O gates, lift up your heads!
> Lift them up, you everlasting doors,
> so the King of glory may come in!
> Who is the King of glory?
> the Lord of hosts,
> He is the King of glory!
>   (Ps. 24:7–10, NJPS)

Not all the psalms, however, are attributed to David. The Psalter contains psalms attributed to the choir leader Asaph (12 psalms), to the Sons of Korah (11), to Moses (1), to Solomon (2), to Heman (1) and Ethan (1). Moreover, in the Hebrew Bible thirty-four psalms have no title at all, and for that reason they are known as "orphans." In all, seventy-three psalms bear the title *leDawid,* translated in the NRSV as "of David." Unfortunately, it is not clear what the preposition *le* means in this combination. It could mean "for David" or "concerning David," in which case one would think of a poem dedicated to the great king. David was "the favorite of the songs of Israel," to quote a marginal translation at 2 Samuel 23:1 (RSV, NJPS) rather than the adopted translation, "the sweet singer of Israel." On this view the psalms are Davidic in the sense that David was the favorite figure in the minds of composers, or perhaps they were composed at his orders or under his sponsorship. It may well be that in the earliest period of the collection of the Psalms the superscription *leDawid* designated psalms that were used in the royal (Davidic) cult, specifically "those psalms which the king was authorized to recite in the festival cult of the Temple."[13]

It is quite clear, however, that eventually the superscription *leDawid* was taken to mean "belonging to David" in the sense that the songs in question were composed by Israel's great king. Clearly this view was held at the time thirteen of these psalms were introduced with notes indicating when David supposedly composed or recited the psalm (Psalms 3; 7; 18; 34; 51; 52; 54; 56; 57; 59; 60; 63; 142). A good example is the well-known penitential Psalm 51, which bears this superscription: "A psalm of David, when Nathan the prophet came to him, after he had gone in to Bathsheba" (cf. 2 Samuel 12). Since the conclusion contains a prayer for rebuilding the walls of Jerusalem (vv. 18–19), the psalm in its present form must come from a time much later than David. In the late Old Testament period there was a tendency to ascribe various psalms to situations in David's life, and eventually, as we have seen, the whole Psalter was associated with the great name of David.[14] For Israel, this ascription did not necessarily indicate authorship; rather, it signified that the community identified itself with David as it came before God in worship. David was an archetypal figure whose career portrayed both the misery and the grandeur of the people of God. Therefore, as Christoph Barth points out, the people remembered "the king, pursued and abandoned in innocence and guilt, but always delivered and restored to power by the faithfulness of God, in whom their own existence as the People of God had found an expression that was valid for all time."[15] In a troubled time when Israel had no king, the people found in the story of David not only the archetype of their own existence but also the prototype of the coming king who would inaugurate God's dominion.

Poetic Vistas in the Psalms

This discussion leads to a conclusion for the use of the psalms in worship today. The main question to ask about any psalm is not about the situation in the life of David or in the life of some unknown individual that occasioned the composition. Nor is it necessary to discover the historical situation in the life of the people Israel in which the psalm was composed, for with the exception of Psalm 137, which clearly presupposes life in Babylonian exile, there are very few historical hints for dating individual psalms. Nor is it essential to recover the original liturgical use of the psalms in the worship of the Jerusalem temple, perhaps in some great festival.[16] These considerations are important and often illuminate our understanding of a psalm, but the most important question has to do with the psalms as literature, or, better, as poetry. These poems "create a world," to use the language of contemporary interpreters of literature. As Walter Brueggemann observes, "They create, evoke, suggest, and propose a network of symbols, metaphors, images, memories and hopes."[17] The poets of Israel invite us into a world, quite different from the world of ordinary daily life, in which God is taken seriously as sovereign, judge, and redeemer.

The purpose of all great poetry is to open up an alluring vista, to catch sight of a strange, new world. That is true, for instance, of the poetry of the great British poet, William Wordsworth (1770–1850). Recently at the University of California at Santa Cruz, this author experienced an orchestral and choral rendition of Wordsworth's "Intimations of Immortality," by the composer Gerald Finzi (1907–1951). In this marvelous performance we were brought into a metaphorical world, quite different from the world of getting and spending that is "too much with us," as Wordsworth puts it in another poem.[18] It is a world in which the beauties of nature intimate that the "soul" comes from and returns to God, "our home."

> Our birth is but a sleep and a forgetting;
> The Soul that rises with us, our life's Star,
>   Hath had elsewhere its setting,
>   And cometh from afar;
>   Not in entire forgetfulness,

And not in utter nakedness,
But trailing clouds of glory do we come,
From God, who is our home.

Similarly, the psalms bring us into God's world, which often clashes
with the marketing, materialistic, militaristic world in which, most of
the time, we have our being. Biblical poets use human speech
metaphorically to portray a world in which God is related covenantly
to a people, Israel, and through them to all peoples. It is a world in
which our relation to God, whether in times of divine presence or apparent absence, is expressed creatively in language of great power.

It is no wonder, then, that down through the ages people have made
the words of the psalms their own. All that is required, as Roland Murphy reminds us, is "a certain sensitivity to poetry, a yielding to the imagery." Quoting a statement of the noted Catholic theologian Karl Rah-
ner to the effect that "the poetic words and the poetic ear" are the
prerequisite for hearing the word of God in the human words of the
Bible, Murphy goes on to say, "The poetic is 'prerequisite' in that there
is an innate poetic potential in all of us to react to reality by means of
imagery."[19] The deep within them calls out to the deep within us. They
articulate the human cry of every person "out of the depths."

2

The Poetry
of Prayer and Praise

The psalms, as we have seen, are the songs that accompany the people of God on their journey through history. In the Hebrew language these songs are called *tehillim,* "praises." Strictly speaking, this title should be reserved for the type of psalm labeled "hymn" (to be considered in chapter 5). Indeed, the one time the title occurs in the superscriptions to the psalms it is applied to a hymnic form (Psalm 145). Yet in a larger sense it is appropriate that the title "songs of praise" was finally applied to the Psalter as a whole, which includes various types of psalms: hymns, laments, thanksgivings or various classifications (songs of trust, royal psalms, wisdom psalms, and Torah meditations), and others. For every psalm, whatever its typology or classification, is actually a song that extols and glorifies God. In one of the most poignant laments of the psalter, Psalm 22, the psalmist affirms that God is "enthroned on the praises of Israel" (v. 3, NRSV).

Considering that the psalms were intended to be recited and sung to musical accompaniment, it is not surprising that they are cast into a poetic form, whose exalted style, rhythmic cadences, interplay of imagery, and emotional overtones are evident even in English translation. In ancient Israel the rhythm of worship involved not only poetic expression but bodily movement, as in the case of Miriam and her companions who "with timbrels and dancing" celebrated the people's liberation from bondage (Ex. 15:20–21) or David who with "all the house of Israel" danced and sang to the accompaniment of musical instruments as the ark, symbol of the throne of God, was escorted into Jerusalem (2 Sam. 6:5; cf. Ps. 24:7–10). Contemporary expressions of worship in the style of a dance, to the accompaniment of guitar or singing, are quite in harmony with the worship expressed in the psalms.

[handwritten margin note: but not to the same extent]

Reading the Psalms as Poetry

The proper place to begin our study of the book of Psalms, then, is with the fact that every one of the 150 psalms is composed in poetry. In his little book of reflections on Psalms, C. S. Lewis observes that

> The Psalms must be read as poems; as lyrics, with all the licences and all the formalities, the hyperboles, the emotional rather than logical connections, which are proper to lyric poetry.[1]

It may be going too far to call the psalms "lyrics," except in the basic dictionary sense that they are to be sung to the accompaniment of a lyre, but Lewis's high estimation of their poetic quality deserves attention:

> It seems to me appropriate, almost inevitable, that when the great imagination which in the beginning, for its own delight and for the delight of men and angels and (in their proper mode) of beasts, had invented and formed the whole world of Nature, submitted to express itself in human speech, that speech should sometimes be poetry.

Lewis sums up his estimate of biblical poetry in one pithy sentence:

> For poetry too is a little incarnation, giving body to what had been before invisible and inaudible.[2]

In the light of this testimony, it is surprising to discover that it is fairly recently that the poetic character of the psalms has been appreciated and suitably represented on the printed page, as in all modern translations. At first when the Hebrew texts were written on scrolls, usually the lines were run together to save space. Early Christians were not interested in the literary quality of the psalms but in their theological—or rather, their christological—meaning. Even when poetic interest in the psalms was awakened, these poems were understood—or rather, misunderstood—by comparison with classical poetic canons, as when Josephus, the first-century Jewish historian (ca. A.D. 37–95) alleged that David composed the psalms in classical meter, such as hexameter. In the subsequent centuries the genius of Hebrew poetry, and the poetic form of the psalms, was not fully appreciated.

Though the poetry of the Bible had been discussed in some detail by early commentators such as Philo and Augustine, it was not until the mid-eighteenth century (approximately the time of Mozart!) that the pervasiveness of parallelism was emphasized. The leading figure in the breakthrough observation was a bishop of the Anglican Church, Robert Lowth of Oxford. In 1753 he published (in Latin) his pathbreaking *Lectures on the Sacred Poetry of the Hebrews* (the English translation did not appear until sixty years later). Turning away from attempts to understand Hebrew poetry according to classical meter, he perceived that the Hebrews were more interested in a rhythm of sense, expressed in balance of sound and expression. We have learned much about Hebrew poetry since then, but the foundation for esthetic appreciation of the psalms was laid by Bishop Lowth.

Poetic Parallelism

Bishop Lowth called the Hebrew rhythm of meaning *parallelismus membrorum,* "parallelism of lines." This literary phenomenon is quite familiar to worshipers who are accustomed to chanting or reading psalms responsively. Generally the poetic lines are constructed symmetrically, so that there is a balance or correspondence between two lines, A and B, or even three lines, A, B, C. A good example is the opening of Psalm 103, in which the psalmist invokes his or her being (self) to praise God:

A. Bless [praise] Yhwh, O my being,
B. all that is within me, praise God's holy name. (BWA)

Psalm 24 opens with an invocation that intensifies the thought by moving from "everything" to all beings who dwell in the earth.

The earth belongs to Yhwh, and everything in it,
the world and those who dwell in it.

(BWA)

Sometimes, as Bishop Lowth pointed out, the parallelism balances the meaning by stating the opposite, so-called antithetic parallelism. A good example is found in Psalm 1:

For Yhwh knows the way of the righteous,
but the way of the wicked will perish.

(Ps. 1:6, BWA)

The entire psalm is built on the structure of contrast. From beginning to end, the righteous and the wicked are contrasted with one another. Parallelism allows the contrast to become part of the fabric of the poem, built into the structure of its sentences.

At other times the second (or perhaps third) line continues the thought of the first line by ascending toward a climax or completion.

> For Yhwh is a great God,
>   and a great King above all gods.
>   (Ps. 95:3, BWA)

This sort of parallelism has a narrative quality, that is, a story unfolds as parallel lines follow one another in succession.[3] Notice too that the psalm just quoted presents an example of "gapping," that is, in the second line the verb is omitted. This ellipsis enables the narrative to move forward with an economy of language.

Rhetorical Style

Building on the insights of Bishop Lowth, subsequent studies have sought to understand the various ways in which parallelism creates poetic effect.[4] Biblical poetry is not "art for art's sake," the use of poetic devices for purely esthetic delight. Rather, it is "poetry with a purpose," the purpose being to communicate a message.[5] As we have seen previously, biblical poetry reflects concrete experiences and ponders on those experiences, whether they be joyful or sorrowful, whether occurring in times of God's presence or when God's "face" is hidden.

Following the lead of Bishop Lowth, most studies focus on semantic parallelism, the heightening of expression through similarity or contrast.[6] One scholar, for instance, observes that the correspondence between the lines is not that of "reduplication," as though A = B, but rather the function of the second line is to continue, expand, and reinforce a single thought, that is, A + B. The second line, he says, "typically supports the first, carries it further, backs it up, completes it, goes beyond it." It is as though the poet makes a statement, pauses to add "what is more," and then continues with a statement that carries the momentum of thought further, "echoing it, defining it, restating it, contrasting with it," in short, emphasizing or "seconding" the thought introduced in the first line.[7] An illuminating study by Adele Berlin breaks new ground by demonstrating that poetic parallelism is even more pervasive than scholars have realized.[8]

This and other linguistic studies show that parallelism is evident not just at the semantic level but at other levels too (grammatical, syntactical, morphological, phonological). This pervasive parallelism enhances the unity and movement of the poem even when literary parallelism is not strongly evident.

Bible translations are hard pressed to retain all these poetic features since their primary concern is to be faithful to content, not to delineate poetic features. Indeed, no recent translation of the Psalms has managed to capture the pervasiveness of parallelism at all levels.[9] In the study of biblical poetry, however, it is impossible to separate content from form.

Since most of us read biblical poetry only in English translation, the most helpful discussions are those that focus on examples of easily translatable literary parallelism in which a parallel line does not merely repeat the meaning of the previous line, but heightens it. As Robert Alter has pointed out, often the second noun used in a parallel sentence has a more literary, idiosyncratic quality. Thus the poetic movement is from a general term to a more specific, descriptive expression, as well as toward greater specificity and enhanced meaning.

> In you our ancestors trusted;
>   they trusted, and you delivered them.
> To you they cried, and were saved;
>   in you they trusted, and were not put to shame.
>   (Ps. 22:4–5, NRSV)

Here the word "trusted" tolls like a bell three times. In a situation of great danger, the psalmist speaks to God about the effectiveness of trust. Following the second tolling of the bell a new verb is used, "to cry," which pushes the sense of trust beyond an inward, passive state—in which sense it is often understood today—into active trust, faith in action. Of course, "trust" and "cry" are not synonyms, though the structure of the verses gives the impression that they are. Here poetic parallelism moves the action forward and intensifies the expression.

In addition to parallelism, terseness of formulation contributes to energy of expression. In the above example, the last two lines consist of six words in Hebrew. The Hebrew language allows this terseness, for in Hebrew the subject-verb-object often constitutes just one word, and the direct object may be indicated without the particles found in prose (e.g., "the," "which"). Compactness of expression contributes to the effect of the poetry on the audience, heightening the emotional impact. A word-by-word translation of the Hebrew words quoted above may help to make this point clear.*

> In-you they-trusted our-fathers,
>   they-trusted and-you-rescued-them.
> To-you they-cried and-they-were-delivered,
>   in-you they-trusted and-not-they-were-ashamed.

In these verses, the mounting or intensifying verbs are verbs of rescue, escape, vindication (to be unashamed). In trust the psalmist cries out to God in order to be rescued and not experience the shame of trusting in an impotent or indifferent God.

The purpose of this brief introduction to biblical poetry is to emphasize that reading Psalms requires of each of us some poetic sensitivity. We have to overcome the bad habit, instilled in us since the rationalism of the Enlightenment in the eighteenth century, of treating scripture as prose that sets forth a literal meaning or supports doctrinal truths. In the book of Psalms, faith finds expression in poetry. To echo C. S. Lewis, quoted above, the poetry of the psalms is a kind of "incarnation" which "gives body" (and we may add, beautiful body) to truth which, before its expression in words, "had been invisible and inaudible." God's word, and our human words in response to God, are incarnated ("made flesh") in literary form (cf. John 1).[10]

Influences from Israel's Environment

Thanks to the light that archaeology has cast upon the culture of the ancient Near East, we have become increasingly aware of Israel's profound indebtedness to the literature and mythology of its neighbors. When the Israelites settled in the land of Canaan during the two centuries before David (ca. 1200–1000 B.C.), they became part of an advanced culture where forms of worship were already firmly established. This was true especially at places like Shechem, Bethel, and Jerusalem, which had been home to Canaanite sanctuaries for centuries before they were taken over by Israel and converted to the worship of Yhwh. Beth-el, the name of one of these shrines, literally means "house of El." El was the high god of the Canaanite pantheon, the "Father" of the gods, and the "Creator of creatures," as we know from mythologi-

---

* In this translation, English words bound together by hyphens constitute one Hebrew word.

cal tablets found on the coast of Syria at Ras Shamra (ancient Ugarit), dating from about 1400 B.C.

The Canaanite texts discovered there display similarities in language, imagery, and poetic structure to biblical Hebrew poetry. The similarities are so striking that some scholars have advocated improving or even revising the Hebrew text of the Psalms on the basis of the Ras Shamra texts. In his three-volume commentary on the Psalms, Mitchell Dahood offers a bold, new translation of each psalm, often with startling changes.[11] He does not hesitate to replace words in the Hebrew text when, in his opinion, the Ugaritic offers a similar and superior word. The value of the Ras Shamra texts for the study of Hebrew literature is indisputable, but Dahood's bold reworking of passages has been widely criticized.[12] What is clear is that Hebrew is a cousin of Ugaritic and as such has helped us to understand the ways in which biblical writers creatively reworked inherited mythic imagery and poetic style.

An example of the reworking of Canaanite tradition, one that is very important in the study of the Psalms, is the appropriation of the ancient myth of the sea monster (known variously as Tiamat, Rahab, Leviathan, Yam) who threatens the ordered creation with a return to chaos. In the Canaanite (Ugaritic) version, Yam ("Sea") threatens to overthrow Baal, the god of fertility and storm, aided by the god of the underworld, Mot ("Death"), and a monster sea serpent called LTN (Lotan), the Leviathan of the Bible. Baal is triumphant in the struggle with Death and deals a mortal blow to the seven-headed serpent:

> When you killed Lotan, the Fleeing Serpent,
>   Annihilated the Twisty Serpent,
>   The Potentate with Seven Heads,
>   The heavens grew hot, they withered.[13]

In Psalm 74 an Israelite poet has appropriated this myth:

> By your power you cleft the sea monster in two
>   and broke the sea serpent's heads in the waters,
>   you crushed the heads of Leviathan,
>   and threw him to the sharks for food.
>   (Ps. 74:13–14, REB)[14]

In an apocalyptic section of the book of Isaiah this mythical imagery is used effectively to portray the ultimate conquest of Yhwh, the Divine Warrior, over the forces of evil.[15]

There is ample literary evidence, then, that Israel was profoundly influenced by the advanced culture into which it entered. Israel's interpreters did not say a flat No of repudiation to the culture of the ancient Near East, but rather said both No and Yes. Faith in Yhwh, the God of Israel, demanded turning from other "gods" of the ancient world, whether imported from Mesopotamia or Egypt, or indigenous in Canaan (Josh. 24:14–15) and, consequently, challenging the theological presuppositions of the religions of the environment. These religions, with their elaborate myths and rituals, enabled people to find meaning and security within the natural order, which moves in cycles of creation, chaos, and recreation. The modern counterpart would be a religion that diverts people from the conflicts and terrors of history and promises the peace of nature, which moves serenely in rhythms of seedtime and harvest, summer and winter, life and death (Gen. 8:22). Israel's prophetic interpreters, on the other hand, perceived divine reality primarily in the dynamic arena of social change, where slaves are freed from their oppressors, where empires rise and fall.

Hence, the first response to the religions of the environment was critical. There could be no compromise between faith in Yhwh and the gods of paganism. However, Israel's No at this deepest level was usually accompanied by a Yes of appropriation, that is, by taking over forms of worship (such as sacrifice) and literary forms (such as psalms of lament and praise) and converting them to the service of Yhwh. The three great agricultural festivals of the Canaanites were adopted and eventually adapted to decisive events in Israel's historical experience. "Three times in the year you shall keep a feast to me," was the command from Yhwh in Exodus 23:14, and as the context shows, these were the festival times of the Canaanite agricultural calendar (on the festivals, see chapter 6).

The situation that Israel faced in Canaan was like many situations faced by the Christian community as it has moved into alien cultures and has had to decide whether to adopt native forms of religious expression. This problem was vividly illustrated some years ago when the author was teaching for a summer in a theological institute in Ghana. A heated discussion arose on whether the Christian churches should admit into their worship the rhythms of African drums and folk dances that were part of the native religion and communal life of the people. Some of the older generation, under the influence of the first missionary churches, opposed this radical step, knowing that the African drum "talks" its own languages (war, sex, native religion, etc.). Members of the younger generation, however, believed that the risks of using the drum and dance in worship were worth taking for the sake of letting the Christian faith become indigenous. Thus, in ever new ways the people of God have had to face the problem of re-expressing faith in the forms provided by different cultures.

This problem became crucial in the Old Testament period when Israelite leaders made the fateful decision to ask for a king to rule them "like all the nations" (1 Sam. 8:4–22). The step was risky, as the prophet Samuel pointed out, for concentration of power in a king would deprive the people of their cherished liberties. But there was also a theological danger, for, as recent studies in the "sacral kingship" of the ancient Near East have shown, the king was thought to be endowed with divine talents and to enjoy a special relationship with the deity. To adopt kingship, then, was not only to run a political danger; but to take the chance the court poetry of the ancient world would erode the Israelite faith in Yhwh, which received its classical and most vigorous expression in the time when Israel had no king. Liberal elements, however, insisted that Yhwh was leading the people forward into the new way of life and thought represented by the monarchy (see chapter 6). Thus the kingdom established by David and consolidated by his son Solomon was characterized by a new openness to cultural influences from Egypt, Mesopotamia, and elsewhere.

Israel's Debt to Its Neighbors

It follows from this discussion that the songs used in the worship services of the Jerusalem temple should be viewed in the wider context of the psalm literature of the ancient Near East: that of the Sumerians, Babylonians, Canaanites, and Egyptians. The psalms in Israel's psalter are similar in form, and often in content, to the hymns and laments composed by Israel's neighbors.

As an example we may take the following passage from a hymn to the Moon-God, *Sin,* which archaeologists found at the site of Nineveh, an ancient capital of the Assyrian empire. In its present form it dates from about the time of Jeremiah (seventh century B.C.), but the tablet states that it was copied from an older edition.

> O Lord, decider of the destinies of heaven and earth, whose
> word no one alters,
> Who controls water and fire, leader of living creatures, what
> god is like thee?

In heaven who is exalted? Thou! Thou alone art exalted.
On earth who is exalted? Thou! Thou alone art exalted.
Thou! When thy word is pronounced in heaven the Igigi†
    prostrate themselves.
Thou! When thy word is pronounced on earth the Anunnaki‡
    kiss the ground.
Thou! When thy word drifts along in heaven like the wind it
    makes rich the feeding and drinking of the land.
Thou! When thy word settles down on the earth green
    vegetation is produced.
Thou! Thy word makes fat the sheepfold and the stall; it
    makes living creatures widespread.
Thou! Thy word causes truth and justice to be, so that the
    people speak the truth.
Thou! Thy word which is far away in heaven, which is
    hidden in the earth is something no one sees.
Thou! Who can comprehend thy word, who can equal it?
O Lord, in heaven as to dominion, on earth as to valor,
    among the gods thy brothers, thou hast not a rival.16

Compare the language of this hymn with passages from Israel's psalms
that raise the question: "Who is like thee, O Yhwh, among the gods?"
(Ex. 15:11; Ps. 86:8–10; and especially Ps. 89:5–14).

The Borrowing of Hymns

We may take a step farther. Not only are there striking formal similarities to the songs of Israel's neighbors, but in a few instances Israel
has taken over hymns from the Canaanite environment (just as the
church has borrowed pagan or "secular" melodies and poetry) and used
them in the praise of Yhwh. Psalm 29, for instance, is an adaptation of
a Canaanite hymn originally sung to Hadad, the god of the storm. In the
modified form of the old hymn it is Yhwh whose "voice" is heard in the
thunderstorm and who is enthroned above the tumult of nature's forces.
The change of divine names, from Baal Hadad to Yhwh, makes all the
difference in the world!

Because all is true of yhwh

---

† Igigi are the great gods of heaven.
‡ Anunnaki are the gods of the earth and netherworld.

The voice of Yhwh is over the waters,
   the God of glory thunders,
Yhwh over the mighty waters.
The voice of Yhwh is powerful,
   the voice of Yhwh is majestic.
The voice of Yhwh breaks the cedars,
   Yhwh breaks the cedars of Lebanon.
He makes Lebanon skip around like a calf,
   and Sirion [Mount Hermon] like a young wild ox.
The voice of Yhwh stirs up flames of fire.
The voice of Yhwh makes the wilderness tremble,
   Yhwh causes to tremble the wilderness of Kadesh.
                          (Ps. 29:3–8, BWA)

The poem reaches a climax by announcing Yhwh's kingship over the flood (*mabbul*), the mythical waters of chaos (a theme to which we shall return in chapter 6).

Yhwh is enthroned over the flood,
   Yhwh is enthroned as king forever!
                    (Ps. 29:10, BWA)

Another striking example of the borrowing of hymnic elements is the superb creation hymn, Psalm 104. It has long been recognized that this psalm, both in form and content, is related to the beautiful "Hymn to the Aton," which was found in a tomb at Tell el-Amarna, Egypt, the capital of the reforming Pharaoh Akhenaton (Amenhotep IV, ca. 1380–1362 B.C.). The Egyptian hymn expresses the universal beneficence and re-creating power of the sun disc (the Aton). Some scholars maintain that the new style of worship introduced by the iconoclastic pharaoh was monotheistic. Compare the following excerpt, for instance, with Psalm 104:24:

How manifold it is, what thou hast made!
They are hidden from the face (of man).
O sole god, like whom there is no other!
Thou didst create the world according to thy desire,
Whilst thou wert alone:
All men, cattle, and wild beasts,
Whatever is on earth, going upon (its) feet,
And what is on high, flying with its wings.

According to the Egyptian poem, each day is a new creation (a thought that is echoed in Psalm 104:27–30):

> The world came into being by thy hand,
> According as thou hast made them.
> When thou hast risen they live,
> When thou settest they die.
> Thou art lifetime thy own self,
> For one lives (only) through thee.[17]

During the period of the Davidic monarchy this hymn came to be known in Jerusalem, probably through wisdom circles, and was adapted to the worship of Yhwh, the sole Creator and Lord.

We shall have more to say in chapter 6 about how the great worship festivals in Jerusalem were influenced by the festivals of Israel's neighbors, such as the New Year festival celebrated in Babylonia. First, however, it is important to focus on what was distinctive in Israel's worship, for when Israel borrowed literary forms and cultic practices, it did not merely imitate its neighbors. Borrowed forms were transformed, religious practices were converted. This is evident from the examples cited above in which hymns or hymnic motifs appropriated from the religions of the cultural environment have been recast for Israel's liturgical use.

Response to God's Initiative

It would not be surprising if modern people would attempt, like Akhenaton, to turn to the sun disc or some other cosmic phenomenon to symbolize their worship of the Power behind the whole cosmic order. In modern times the notion has developed—perhaps in a more radical fashion than at any other time in human history—that "God" is outside our historical world. Few people who go to synagogue or church today expect God to be actively involved in the human world: the civil rights struggle, the war against poverty and oppression, the tragic suffering in Africa or India, or the harsh political realities of the strife between the great world powers. The popular notion is that God is, if not "up there," at least "out there" somewhere—a transcendent deity located in some never-never land beyond the universe. For all practical purposes, this God is estranged from the human situation, distant from the places where historical beings are living, suffering, and deciding.

Israel's praise, by contrast, did not begin by extolling the Creator who is before, behind, beyond, and above the whole created order. True, the Psalter contains magnificent creation psalms, such as Psalm 104 which has just been mentioned, showing that Israel shared a creation faith with other ancient peoples. It is not proper, however, to begin our study with creation psalms, for the reason that Israel's worship was not grounded primarily in creation faith. Rather, the invocation to worship was based fundamentally upon a "root experience" of liberation from bondage that was enshrined in the memory of the people (to be considered more in the next chapter).

Israel's praise is a reflex to the prior action of God that moves people, as one psalmist testifies, to seek God's "face" (Ps. 27:8) in worship. The prevenience of God's grace, which motivates worship, is beautifully expressed by Augustine at the beginning of his *Confessions.*

> Thou movest us to delight in praising Thee;
> for Thou hast formed us for Thyself,
> and our hearts are restless till they find rest in Thee.[18]

3

Narrative Praise

Stories and Storytelling

Storytelling is a human art, as old and as universal as language itself. Whether a story is told for entertainment, to celebrate a victory, to explain the origin of a common experience, or for some other reason, the narrative creates a world and invites the audience into it. A story or "history" is appealing when it stirs our curiosity about something that happened "once upon a time" and touches upon, even illuminates, our human adventure in the present. Usually it rehearses a sequence of events that move from a beginning to what comes next, and it moves toward an end, when the plot is resolved or the tale is told. Thus it reflects the tenses of human existence: past, present, and future; yesterday, today, and tomorrow—or, in other terms, remembrance, reflection, and hope. Because a story creates a world, in whose perspective we may see the ordinary world anew, it has affinities with lyric poetry (discussed at the end of chapter 1).[1]

From early times Israel confessed its faith characteristically by telling the story of its life. Storytellers recalled a crucial event, a "root experience"—the deliverance from Egyptian bondage.[2] "We were once slaves of the mightiest emperor of the day but the Holy God intervened, freed us from oppression and gave us a future." The ancient confession of faith opens, like a symphony pathetique, in a minor mode that expresses sorrow and lamentation, but these heavy minor chords modulate into the major key of praise to the God who opens a way into the future out of a no-exit situation.

Celebrating a Crucial Experience

This root experience of the exodus from Egypt was celebrated in worship from the very beginning of Israel's existence as a people. The astonishing wonder of the event provides the motive for praise in a poetic couplet known as the Song of Miriam, one of the oldest verses of poetry in the Old Testament. Indeed, this ancient poem may have been composed by one who witnessed the *wonder-full* event of the crossing of the sea (not the Red Sea, but a shallow body of water farther north in the area of Lake Timsah, in Hebrew called "the Sea of Reeds").

> Sing to Yhwh,
> for Yhwh has triumphed gloriously,
> the horse and its rider
> God has hurled into the sea.
> (Ex. 15:21, BWA)

Here we find the literary genre of the "hymn"—indeed, the oldest example of it in the Old Testament. (See chapter 6 for a fuller discussion of this literary type.) Miriam's hymn begins with an invitation to the community (the verb "sing" is plural imperative in Hebrew) to join in praise to the liberating God. The transitional word "for" (Hebrew, *ki*) gives the motive for praise: God's saving action in a time of great distress. Significantly, this call to worship is not based on a general awareness of God's greatness or on God's universal power as creator, as in Psalm 24, the well-known psalm that calls people to join a processional ascent to the temple of Jerusalem where the Lord is enthroned over the ark. Rather, Miriam's call to worship is based on the demonstration of God's saving presence in a situation of distress when, humanly speaking, there was no way out, no exodus. Israel's history of worship, which reached its climax in the praises of the Psalter, was initiated in that crucial hour at the beginning of the tradition when women, under the leadership of Miriam, sang and danced to music, inviting the people to join them in hymnic praise.

We find the same kind of narrative praise in another ancient poem, the Song of the Sea, which is closely linked to the Song of Miriam in the present scriptural context (Ex. 15:1–18). Probably this hymn is later than, and dependent upon, Miriam's song. This longer poem, influenced by Canaanite literary style and mythical imagery, apparently

comes from the period of the tribal confederacy that flourished before
the rise of the Davidic monarchy (1200–1000 B.C.). In any case, the
Song of the Sea also issues a call to worship, based on God's historical
act of liberation.

> Who is like you in the heavenly council, O Yhwh?
> Who is like you, majestic in holiness?
> You who are awesome in deeds, who does wonders?
> You stretched out your right hand,
> Earth swallowed them.
> In your faithfulness you led the people that you redeemed,[3]
> You led them in your power to your holy abode.
>
> (Ex. 15:11–13, BWA)

From Humiliation to Exaltation

The jubilant note of Miriam's song of praise echoed again and again
from generation to generation as the story of Israel's liberation from
bondage was told and retold. The story, found in expanded form in
chapters 1–15 of the book of Exodus, displays the same movement
from oppression to deliverance, humiliation to exaltation, as noted previously. It begins with a poignant cry out of distress as it portrays
vividly the oppression of Jacob's descendants in Egypt. The turning
point in the story, God's intervention, comes in connection with the
episode of the burning bush.

> Then the LORD said, "I have observed the misery of my
> people who are in Egypt; I have heard their cry on account
> of their taskmasters. Indeed, I know their sufferings, and I
> have come down to deliver them from the Egyptians, and
> to bring them up out of that land to a good and broad land,
> a land flowing with milk and honey." (Ex. 3:7–8, NRSV)

The rest of the story is a narrative portrayal of how Yhwh, the God of
the ancestors, humbled the mighty and exalted those of low degree. In
its present form, the dramatic story reaches a climax with the Song of
the Sea, discussed above.

The saving event of the exodus is rehearsed in a striking manner in
Psalm 114, where the crossing of the Reed Sea is likened to the passage
through the Jordan into the promised land.

When Israel came out of Egypt,
the house of Jacob from a barbaric people,
Judah became God's sanctuary,
Israel his domain.
The sea fled at the sight;
Jordan turned back.
The mountains skipped like rams,
the hills like lambs of the flock.
(Ps. 114:1–2, REB)

Here the poet uses language that reverberates with mythical overtones of the Divine Warrior's victory over the powers of chaos ("sea"), suggesting that the saving event at the beginning of Israel's history was also a creative event. Israel, the people of God, was created *ex nihilo*— out of the nothingness of historical oblivion, the chaos of oppression. Therefore, Yhwh is praised as Israel's maker, and all the elements of nature, such as mountains and hills (cf. Ps. 96:11–13), join in rejoicing.

Contemporizing the Story

Thus the exodus story, from its distressful beginning to its jubilant end, is told to praise and glorify the God whose saving power was manifested in creating the historical community known as Israel and in giving the people a future. The story was probably shaped through repetition in liturgical ceremonies, chiefly the observance of the Passover festival. So crucial was the exodus for Israel's existence as a community of faith that the event was relived and reenacted in every generation. In the great festivals the story of the formation of Israel was told and retold: the deliverance from Egypt, the crossing of the Reed Sea, the entrance into Canaan. The story was not rehearsed as something "back there" in the past. Rather, the story had a meaning for persons here and now. It was a drama in which the present generation was involved. These "master stories," as Michael Goldberg terms the "root experience," are told and retold not only to *inform* us but to *form* us as a community of faith.[4] Even today the Passover ritual contains the reminder that believing Jews should confess that the God of the ancestors brought them, the contemporary generation, out of Egypt.

It was not alone our fathers whom the Holy One, blessed be He, redeemed, but also us whom He redeemed with them, as it is said, "And us He brought out thence that He might

lead us to, and give us, the land which He swore to our
fathers."[5]

The contemporaneity of the exodus story of liberation is evident in
a passage found in Deuteronomy, a book that received its present form
after the fall of Jerusalem in 587 B.C. The language, therefore, is col-
ored by the relatively late Deuteronomic style. Yet the content, in the
judgment of some scholars, is much older.

> A wandering Aramean was my ancestor; he went down
> into Egypt and lived there as an alien, few in number, and
> there he became a great nation, mighty and populous.
> When the Egyptians treated us harshly and afflicted us, by
> imposing hard labor on us, we cried to the LORD, the God
> of our ancestors; the LORD heard our voice and saw our
> affliction, our toil, and our oppression. The LORD brought
> us out of Egypt with a mighty hand and an outstretched
> arm, with a terrifying display of power, and with signs and
> wonders; and he brought us into this place and gave us this
> land, a land flowing with milk and honey. (Deut. 26:5–9
> NRSV; see also 6:20–23)

This "historical credo,"[6] as it has been called, is not a private prayer. It
is, rather, a confession of faith that is made in connection with an act of
worship: the presentation of the firstfruits at the sanctuary at harvest-
time (Deut. 26:10). The worshiper who engages in this liturgy of
thanksgiving is identified with the worshiping community, as indicated
by the plural pronouns ("the Egyptians treated *us* harshly," "*we* cried to
the LORD . . . the LORD heard *our* voice," etc.).

Even more important for our immediate purpose, the passage expresses the motive of Israel's praise—praise that modulates from a minor into a major key. It begins by portraying a situation of distress. "A
wandering Aramean" refers to the ancestor Jacob, and if one paraphrases the Hebrew more literally, Jacob's wandering is like the stray-
ing of an animal that has lost its way. The credo continues with a further portrayal of the people's distress in Egypt, out of which "we cried
to the LORD, the God of our ancestors." This cry out of the depths, however, is followed by the jubilant affirmation that "the LORD heard our
voice and saw our affliction" and marvelously opened a way into the
future. Thus the appeal out of distress and the jubilant cry of deliverance combine to express Israel's praise of God.

This movement—from distress to jubilation, from humiliation to exaltation—can be traced through the whole Bible, especially in liturgical materials. It is found, for instance, in the Song of Deborah (Judges 5), one of the oldest pieces of Hebrew literature of any length, which praises God for coming to the rescue of the people in a time of distress when they were threatened by the overwhelming forces of the Canaanites (ca. 1100 B.C.). It is found in the much later Song of Hannah (1 Sam. 2:1–10), a psalm of thanksgiving for the community's deliverance from deep troubles. And in the New Testament the language of Hannah's song is echoed in the Magnificat (Luke 1:47–55), in which Mary praises the God who exalts the humble and fills the hungry with good things. Mary begins by praising the God of Israel, the Mighty One:

> My soul magnifies the Lord,
>   and my spirit rejoices in God, my Savior,

In good hymnic style she gives the motive for praise:

> for he has looked with favor on the lowliness of his servant.
>   Surely, from now on all generations will call me blessed;
> for the Mighty One has done great things for me,
>   and holy is his name.

The poem continues by affirming that this grace (mercy) is also displayed to all generations:

> He has shown strength with his arm;
>   he has scattered the proud in the thoughts of their hearts.
> He has brought down the powerful from their thrones,
>   and lifted up the lowly;
> he has filled the hungry with good things,
>   and sent the rich away empty.
> He has helped his servant Israel,
>   in remembrance of his mercy,
> according to the promise he made to our ancestors,
>   to Abraham and to his descendants forever.

> (NRSV)

Meditations upon God's Acts in History

Israel was not alone in praising God for wonderful actions in the world. In the religions of other ancient peoples, such as the Babylonians, the gods were regarded as taking part in historical affairs.[7] One of the fundamental differences, however, between Israel's psalms and the songs of its neighbors is that in the context of worship Israel turned to its own sequence of historical experience to confess its faith. Furthermore, Israel's psalmists retold "the old, old story," not to pride themselves in believing that God was with them, supporting their values or their political agenda, but to confess humbly their failures to keep their covenant with God.

Storytelling Psalms

This confessional way of retelling the Israelite tradition provides a background for the study of a special group of psalms that express the shared history of the believing and worshiping community. These "storytelling" or "historical" psalms portray Yhwh's saving action in the history or story of Israel. The story/history is not related with detachment but is told as a drama that is true "for me" or "for us." Since the Christian community has appropriated the story of Israel as its own, it is important to consider what is involved in this kind of narrative praise. Some religions, as Amos Wilder reminds us, emphasize philosophical reflection, others mystical meditation, and still others didactic discourse, but "the narrative mode is uniquely important in Christianity."

> It is through the Christian story that God speaks, and all heaven and earth come into it. God is an active and purposeful God whose action with and for men has a beginning, a middle and an end like any good story. The life of a Christian is not like a dream shot through with visions and illuminations, but a pilgrimage, a race, in short, a history. The new Christian speech inevitably took the form of a story.[8]

The "narrative" mode is evident throughout the Psalter, especially in a number of psalms in which Israel's praise takes the form of recounting God's "deeds of salvation" (e.g., Ps. 66:5–7; 71:15–16; 75:1; 77:11–15; 98:1–3; 107:31–32; 145:4–6). In a group of storytelling psalms, sometimes called "salvation history psalms," the central subject is the recitation of the Lord's "mighty deeds" in Israel's history. One gets the impression from reading and contemplating these psalms that they have a strong didactic interest: History is recounted in order to *teach* people the meaning of their history. These psalms retell the story of the people of God to show God's *faithfulness*, even when the people "have erred and strayed" from the path "like lost sheep" and "have followed too much the devices and desires of [their] own hearts," to quote the well-known words of the Prayer of General Confession.

In the process of retelling, the Israelite story—centering on the exodus and Sinai experiences—was extended backward to include the period of the ancestors (Genesis 12—50) and the primeval times (Genesis 1—11). Eventually the story was extended forward into the time of the tribal confederacy (Joshua, Judges) and beyond that, into the time of the monarchy, when David became the "shepherd" of Israel and the Jerusalem temple became the central sanctuary to which all the tribes "went up" for worship of the God of Israel (Psalm 122). The expansion of the core Israelite story is evident in the so-called story-telling psalms. It is recommended that these psalms be read in the following order:

1. Psalm 105: A historical summary paralleling the Pentateuch from Genesis 12 forward.
2. Psalm 106: A similar summary recited in a penitential mood.
3. Psalm 78: A summary that carries the story up to the selection of David and the choice of Mount Zion (Jerusalem), again recited in a penitential style.
4. Psalm 135: A historical summary that includes a reference to God's power as creator (vv. 5–7).
5. Psalm 136: An antiphonal summary of the Lord's great deeds, beginning with the creation.

[Note: In the present form of the Psalter, Psalms 105 and 106 are regarded as "hallelujah psalms," that is, each begins and ends with the cultic exclamation, "Praise Yhwh." The hallelujah at the end of Psalm 104 actually belongs at the beginning of Psalm 105. Psalm 135 is also a hallelujah psalm, while Psalm 136 is a *todah* ("thanksgiving") psalm, as is clear from its beginning and end.]

In this discussion, however, we are not chiefly concerned with how these psalms were classified in the final edition of the Psalter or with their proper classification according to literary type (e.g., "hymn" or "song of thanksgiving"). The important thing is their subject matter. These five psalms recapitulate the unfolding drama of God's dealings with the people from the very beginning of Israel's history to the entrance into the Promised Land and—in the case of Psalm 78—as far as the raising up of David as "the anointed one." They recite events fundamental to Israel's self-understanding as a people and essential to Israel's knowledge of God's character.

God's Acts in History

This historical accent in the Psalter holds the possibility of bringing these songs of worship closer to where we live.[9] We too are historical beings, and if we are to know God at all, our knowledge will be a historical knowledge. As H. Richard Niebuhr has reminded us: "We are in history as the fish is in water and what we mean by the revelation of God can be indicated only as we point through the medium in which we live."[10] The Christian church has inherited this historical legacy, minus the nationalistic overtones that sounded at times in Israel's scriptures. In the New Testament, too, the church speaks of God primarily by telling the story of Jesus Christ, a story that is understood to be part of the larger story of God's dealings with the people Israel.[11]

The last two psalms (Psalms 135 and 136) have one noteworthy feature in common: each associates the story of the saving deeds performed on behalf of Israel with God's actions as creator in the beginning. This is true especially of Psalm 136, a historical recitation of "the mighty deeds of the Lord," in which the congregation makes an antiphonal response to each affirmation: "For his faithfulness endures forever!" (See 2 Chron. 7:3–6, where we find the worshiping congregation responding with this refrain.) Whereas in the first pair the recitation begins with the exodus (Psalm 106) or with Abraham, Isaac, and Jacob (Psalm 105—the only direct reference to the patriarchs in the Psalter), in Psalm 136 the community traces the actions of God right back to the beginning, to God's first work of creating the world (v. 4–9). This is Israel's way of saying that the meaning disclosed in its own historical experience ("the story of our life") unveils the meaning that underlies the whole of human history right from the start, and indeed of the entire cosmos. The "word" that Yhwh spoke to Israel is the same word by which the heavens and the earth were made, as affirmed in Psalm 136 (v. 6–9).

Is God with Us?

These psalms in the narrative mode show that the recapitulation of the story of God's action in the history of the people Israel was not just a paraphrase of the story found in the Pentateuch. Rather, in worship

the story was *retold* with a contemporaneous ring, so that it touched the
concerns of people in their present situation. The poetic form creates a
sense of immediacy, and as narrative it is a "direct address which is
heightened, made memorable and almost inexorable through the rhetorical resources of formal verse."[12]

It is one thing to affirm that God has done marvelous things in the
past. For many worshipers the problem that must be addressed is: If
God was marvelously active in the past, why is God apparently inactive
in the present, when people find themselves in deep distress? This is a
perennial problem for faith. In the Psalter such distress finds expression
in laments in which psalmists, perplexed about the meaning of the present, seek consolation by recalling God's mighty deeds in the past. This
is the case in an individual lament:

> Remembering Yahweh's great deeds,
> remembering your wonders in the past,
> I reflect on all that you did,
> I ponder all your great deeds.
> God, your ways are holy!
> What god is as great as our God?
> You are the God who does marvellous deeds,
> brought nations to acknowledge your power,
> with your own arm redeeming your people,
> the children of Jacob and Joseph.
> (Ps. 77:11–15, NJB)

The same note is sounded in community laments such as this one:

> We have heard, O God,
>   our fathers have told us
>   the deeds You performed in their time,
>   in days of old.
> With Your hand You planted them,
>   displacing nations;
>   You brought misfortune on peoples,
>   and drove them out.
> It was not by their sword that they took the land,
>   their arm did not give them victory,
>   but Your right hand, Your arm, and Your goodwill,
>   for You favored them.
> (Ps. 44:1–3, NJPS)

Some readers may discount the latter lament on the ground that Israel as a nation had experienced a humiliating defeat at the hand of a political power and was disillusioned because God had not come to Israel's rescue, as in days past when the people were victimized by Pharaoh's tyranny. Such a community lament, it is argued, could be raised by a modern nation that supposes naively that "God is on our side" and that feels let down in the political contests of history. Is the problem so simple, however? Even when we make due allowances for the nationalism in some of the psalms, there is the larger problem that the people of God (which is not essentially a nation) must live through times of uncertainty when history appears to be under the control of powers of evil and darkness. Even in the perspective of faith, the sovereignty of God is hidden, the meaning of human history unclear. Out of such experiences arises the poignant question of whether God has forgotten the people or disregarded human cries of suffering. Israel's lament, raised in a time of exile by an uprooted and despondent people, is typical of the cries raised by many people today in India, China, and the Balkans who feel the brutal weight of oppression and injustice. Just because Israel believed so firmly in God's presence in history, the people had to learn to sing praises, not only in times of God's presence but in trying times of God's absence.

Perhaps we can begin to understand, then, why so many of Israel's psalms are laments. More than one third of the psalms fall into the category of complaints to God in a situation of limitation and threat (see chapter 4). Indeed, it is striking that all the psalms that have superscriptions referring to episodes in David's life are laments! Just as Israel, in the time of Egyptian oppression, cried out for deliverance when opposing powers were formidable and hope was gone, so in the course of its historical pilgrimage Israel cried out to God from the depth of its distress in the name of David, the one in whom Israel found its existence before God portrayed.

Israel's cries out of the depths were not based on the philosophical kind of atheism that has come to be familiar in the modern period. Now and then psalmists speak about the "fool" who says in his heart, "there is no God" (Ps. 14:1; cf. 10:4). This is a practical, not a theoretical, atheism. The fool does not deny God's reality; he only denies that God's action affects his life. He thinks that God does not see and therefore he can live as he pleases (Ps. 10:11). Helmer Ringgren draws attention in this connection to the old Babylonian phrase "living *ina ramânishu*"—"living by oneself, on one's own resources, without dependence on God." This refusal to "let God be God" is "the essence of sin" and hence the fool and his folly will be exposed in the day when God judges the people.[13]

God's Faithfulness

As can be seen from the narrative psalms treated above, a fundamental theme of Israel's praise is God's faithfulness. One of the key words in the psalms is the Hebrew word *hesed,* which is rendered variously: "mercy" (KJV), "steadfast love" (NRSV, NJPS), "constancy, love" (NEB), "faithful love" (NJB). *Hesed* refers to the faithfulness that characterizes God's covenant relationship with the people or, vice versa, that should characterize the relationship of the people to their God. The term is filled with the rich content of personal relationship, as in the friendship between David and Jonathan, though it also suggests a relationship in which a stronger party can offer help and protection to the weaker (see the story in 1 Samuel 20, where David shows *hesed,* loyalty to his friend).[14] Notice that when the term is used of God in the psalms it is often paralleled with such words as "goodness" (Ps. 23:6), "salvation" (Ps. 85:7), "faithfulness" (Ps. 89:2; 100:5), "righteousness" (Ps. 103:17), "truth" (Ps. 25:5). Unlike the capricious gods of the ancient world, the God whom Israel worships is true to promises made, constant in faithfulness.

Yet in the complexities and perplexities of human life the purpose of God can be seen only dimly. There is no sure evidence to prove that God is in control beyond a shadow of a doubt. Hence the psalmists often cried to God out of their distress, remembering how God had manifested favor (*hesed*) in the past and hoping that God would once again "show his face" graciously. Their lament was a form of praise based on the conviction that God is concerned about the people's condition and answers the human cry in ways surpassing human expectation or understanding:[15]

> Make me to know your ways, O LORD;
>   teach me your paths.
> Lead me in your truth, and teach me,
>   for you are the God of my salvation;
>   for you I wait all day long.
> Be mindful of your mercy, O LORD, and of your steadfast
>   love [*hesed*],
>   for they have been from of old.
> Do not remember the sins of my youth or my transgressions;

according to your steadfast love [*hesed*] remember me,
for your goodness' sake, O LORD!

(Ps. 25:4–7, NRSV)

Many of the psalms, like the alphabetical (acrostic) psalm just
quoted, express the stance of waiting for God—waiting for the time
when the reality of God's presence and the sovereignty of God's purpose in the world will once again become clear. The present is often the
time of "the eclipse of God," to quote the title of a book by the Jewish
philosopher Martin Buber. In the time of the exile, when many Israelites thought that God had deserted them, a prophet echoed the note
of waiting struck in many psalms of lament:

Even the young may tire and faint
    and the strong may fall exhausted;
but those who wait for Yhwh will renew their vitality;
    they will mount on wings like eagles;
they will run without getting weary, they will walk and not
    faint.

(Isa. 40:30–31, BWA)

In our time, too, we can understand this waiting for God, this experience of God's apparent absence from the human situation. It is more
difficult for us to understand that Israel's lament out of distress was a
way of praising God in the time of God's absence.

In the following discussion we shall not begin with hymns that
praise God's greatness in general terms as the ruler of universal history
or the creator of heaven and earth. We shall turn first to Israel's speech
to God in the form of lament. Since this type of psalm quickly resolves
into the assurance that God hears the human cry, we shall turn next to
the songs of thanksgiving. Then in later chapters we shall study the
hymns that extol the greatness and glory of God, who is enthroned as
King over Israel, the nations, and the entire creation.

4

The Trials of Faith

Israel's praise was evoked by the action of the God who turned to a band of oppressed slaves and in a marvelous way opened to them a new possibility of life. Accordingly, the faith of the psalmists does not rest upon glittering generalities about the nature of God or upon a numinous awareness of God's transcendent majesty in the remote reaches of the cosmos. Rather, it is founded upon the good news that the Holy God intervenes in a desperate situation to help those who are oppressed. This fundamental note sounds out in various psalms.

Imperatives of Praise

The LORD works righteousness
and justice for all the oppressed.
He made known his ways to Moses,
his deeds to the people of Israel.
(Ps. 103:6–7, NIV)

Here the psalmist alludes to the story in Exodus 33 and 34, where, in a time of crisis, Moses asked for a manifestation of God's "ways" (Ex. 33:13) and received the assurance that, despite the people's fickle behavior, God would nevertheless go with them and give them a future. The marvelous demonstration of God's faithfulness (*hesed*), greater than anything expected or deserved, provides the motive for the imperatives that summon the people to worship: "Sing!" "O give thanks," "Make a joyful noise!" etc. Claus Westermann observes that, in contrast to Babylonian psalms, "something entirely new has been added to the psalms of praise in the Old Testament: the imperative exhortation to praise."[1] This is because Israel has a story to tell, a deliverance to celebrate.

The story of God's turning toward a people in distress, as found in the exodus tradition, is supplemented with the narrative of Israel's murmurings in the wilderness. According to traditions found in the books of Exodus (Ex. 16; 17; 32), Numbers (Num. 11; 14; 16; 20; 21), and Deuteronomy (e.g., Deut. 8), the wilderness sojourn was the time when Israel's faith was put to the test. To be sure, "signs" of the presence of the Lord were given, such as the manna that fell from the desert bushes, the quails that drifted into the area with the prevailing winds, or the water that was found in unexpected places. These signs, however, were indications but not proofs of God's presence and guidance. Indeed, the period in the wilderness was a time when the people longed for the "fleshpots" of Egypt and when they murmured, "Is the LORD among us or not?" (Ex. 17:7). Doubt lurks in the shadow of faith, as many faithful people know.

As we have seen in connection with the storytelling psalms (chapter 3), this narrative is not "history" in the strict sense but "story." This portrayal of Israel in the wilderness was a kind of mirror in which the people found its own history with God reflected. The pilgrim people of God in the New Testament period saw itself in the same mirror. Paul, for instance, did not dismiss the events of the wilderness as ancient history but insisted that "these things . . . were written down for our instruction, upon whom the end of the ages has come" (1 Cor. 10:11). The signs given to God's people by Jesus Christ were not proof of God's real presence and sovereign control of history beyond any shadow of a doubt; they were assurances given to faith. Still it must be said, even in the time that Christians mark as A.D. (i.e., after Christ), "We walk by faith, not by sight" (2 Cor. 5:7).

The Literature of Lament

Laments outside the Psalter

It is not surprising, then, that the Bible contains a great deal of literature of lament. Embedded in the book of Jeremiah are six "confessions" or laments in which the prophet complains to God in strong language, protests his innocence, and cries out for vindication over his enemies. These poignant outcries deserve cursory attention at this point.[2]

Jer. 11:18–12:6	"A lamb led to the slaughter"
Jer. 15:10–21	"I sat alone"

Jer. 17:14–18	"Be not a terror to me"
Jer. 18:19–23	"Is evil a recompense for good?"
Jer. 20:7–13	"A fire shut up in my bones"
Jer. 20:14–18	"Why did I come forth from the womb?"

A good example is the second lament. Like Hamlet, Jeremiah castigates his mother for having given birth to him (cf. Job 3, a similar passage), he cries out for vengeance upon his persecutors, he accuses God of having become like a "deceitful brook" that is full during the spring rains but dries up in the summer, and at the end he is given an oracle in which God assures him of deliverance.

The fact that Jeremiah voiced such cries of dereliction gave rise to the later tradition that he was the author of the mournful poems in Lamentations, composed in the shadow of the destruction of Jerusalem by the Babylonians in 587 B.C. Three of these poems (Lamentations 1; 2; 4) are really funeral dirges that open with the customary wail, *'ekah* (translated "how") and are cast in the "limping 3–2 meter" used in songs of mourning. A dirge is an expression of sorrow in a situation that cannot be reversed (e.g., death). The other two poems, however, are laments. A lament is an outcry in a situation that can be changed if God wills it and a person is responsive (e.g., sickness).[3] Lamentations 3 is an individual lament and chapter 5 is a community lament.

We should also mention the book of Job, a wisdom writing. Although the prose introduction and conclusion to this book portray a pious man who patiently suffered "the slings and arrows of outrageous fortune," the poetic sections depict a figure who, in language even stronger than that of Jeremiah, lashes out against God, protests his innocence, and cries out for vindication.

It is striking that the laments found in Jeremiah's confessions, the book of Job, and Lamentations have the same general form as the laments found in the Psalter. This suggests that these writers were following an accepted literary convention, as poets frequently do in our Western culture. The form was not confined to Israelite society but was known throughout the ancient Near East. Israel's psalms of lament display a formal resemblance to the songs of its neighbors, especially the Babylonians and the Assyrians.

Prayer of Lamentation to Ishtar

An excellent example is the magnificent "Prayer of Lamentation to Ishtar" which comes from the neo-Babylonian period (approximately the time of Jeremiah, seventh century B.C.).[4]

Address of Praise

The Babylonian psalm begins with a long ascription of praise to Ishtar, the Queen of Heaven, "who guides [humankind] aright" and who "regards the oppressed and mistreated."

Complaint in Distress

The second movement of the prayer is a lament in affliction to "the goddess of goddesses." Notice the cry "How long?" and the persecution by enemies, two typical elements of a lament. The prayer opens with an appeal for divine favor:

> Let the favor of thine eyes be upon me.
> With thy bright features look faithfully upon me.
> Drive away the evil spells of my body (and) let me see thy
> bright light.
> How long, O my Lady, shall my adversaries be looking upon
> me,
> In lying and untruth shall they plan evil against me,
> Shall my pursuers and those who exult over me rage against
> me?
> How long, O my Lady, shall the crippled and weak seek me
> out?
> One has made for me long sackcloth; thus I have appeared
> before thee.
> The weak have become strong; but I am weak.
> I toss about like flood-water, which an evil wind makes
> violent.
> My heart is flying; it keeps fluttering like a bird of heaven.
> I mourn like a dove night and day.
> I am beaten down, and so I weep bitterly.
> With "Oh" and "Alas" my spirit is distressed.

Protestation of Innocence

Another theme, often found in laments, is that the sufferer is not really to blame for what has occurred and does not understand why divine wrath has come upon him or her.

> I—what have I done, O my god and my goddess?
> Like one who does not fear my god and my goddess I am
> treated;

> While sickness, headache, loss, and destruction are provided
>   for me;
> So are fixed upon me terror, disdain, and fullness of wrath,
> Anger, choler, and indignation of gods and men.

In Israelite psalms we also find prayer for God's wrath to be averted (Psalm 6), but psalmists typically insist that, though God's ways are mysterious and past finding out, God is just in judgment (see Ps. 51:4) and that somehow both divine wrath and divine mercy are included under the "faithfulness" (*hesed*) of God.

Petition for Deliverance

After pleading faithful devotion to Ishtar, the suppliant cries out for vindication, which will demonstrate that divine wrath turns to divine favor. Notice the prayer for subduing enemies, a theme that resounds through the laments of the Psalter.

> Accept the abasement of my countenance; hear my prayers.
> Faithfully look upon me and accept my supplication.
> How long, O my Lady, wilt thou be angered so that thy face
>   is turned away?
> How long, O my Lady, wilt thou be infuriated so that thy
>   spirit is enraged?
> Turn thy neck which thou hast set against me; set thy face
>   [toward] good favor.
> Like the water of the opening up of a canal let thy emotions
>   be released.
> My foes like the ground let me trample;
> Subdue my haters and cause them to crouch down under me.

Concluding Praise

> Let my prayers and my supplications come to thee.
> Let thy great mercy be upon me.
> Let those who see me in the street magnify thy name.

As we shall see, the general structure of this psalm corresponds closely to Israelite psalms of lament. In fact, we may assume that this literary form, mediated through the Canaanites, influenced Israelite worship very early in the history of worship, providing a pattern for composers of psalms.

Prayer and Magic

There are, however, profound differences in content. The observation that the Ishtar psalm is polytheistic, while Israelite psalms are addressed to the one God, is true enough but does not go to the heart of the matter. The Babylonian psalm was to be accompanied by a ritual of incantation, that is, a magical spell over the evil spirits (demons). Thus prayer was tied up with magic, the release of a power believed to be effective in overcoming evil. People found themselves in a capricious situation, in which they were not sure what wrong had been done and not certain whether the deity could really deliver them from evil. They were apprehensive in the face of hostile powers that make life precarious. By contrast, the Israelite psalms of lament express the conviction that Yhwh is trustworthy and faithful. The God of Israel has displayed *hesed* (covenant loyalty) decisively in the saving experience of the exodus and has come to the aid of the people in the subsequent crises of their history. Human beings often fail to be true to their word, but God is the promise-keeper par excellence. Unlike the words of transient mortals or the promises of false gods, the word of the God of Israel is fraught with eternal power.

> The grass withers, the flower fades,
>   but the word of our God will stand forever.
>   (Isa. 40:8, NRSV)

Therefore the word of Israel's God can be trusted in all the ups and downs of human life, for it is laden with the power to accomplish its saving purpose.

> But as the heavens are high above the earth,
>   so are my ways high above your ways
>   and my thoughts above your thoughts.
> As the rain and snow come down from the heavens
>   and do not return there without watering the earth,
>   making it produce grain
>   to give seed for sowing and bread to eat,
> so it is with my word issuing from my mouth;
>   it will not return to me empty
>   without accomplishing my purpose
>   and succeeding in the task for which I sent it.
>   (Isa. 55:9–11, REB)

The practice of magic is found in parts of the world today, sometimes mixed with Christian piety. Perhaps there are passages in the Psalms that reflect the hostile use of magic in ancient Israelite society. But the voice of the psalmists of Israel sounds out loud and clear: it is unnecessary and wrong to use magic to assist or cajole God to rescue people from distress. The God whom we worship has the power to save and is near to those who "seek the LORD" in prayer (Isa. 55:6–7).

Living in the Interim

Nevertheless, the people of God find themselves again and again in the interim between God's promise and the fulfillment of the promise. That interim is the time when faith is put to the test, for there are no unambiguous proofs that God has spoken and that God is in control of the human situation. This is the problem with which God's people wrestle throughout the Old Testament period—and beyond. The hymns found among the writings of the Qumran monastery (the Dead Sea scriptures), which flourished at the beginning of the Christian era, contain the same notes of lament, the same motif of "the wilderness of isolation."[5] The New Testament, of course, proclaims that God has spoken decisively in Jesus Christ, thereby endorsing the promises made to Israel. But the Christian community also finds itself living in the interim between the inauguration of God's kingdom and its final realization, between the first break of dawn and the full light of day. This period of tension, between promise and realization, is sometimes referred to as the "already/not yet" paradox of Christian faith. It is articulated in Paul's statements that the old is already passing away and the new creation has been inaugurated in Jesus Christ (1 Cor. 7:31).[6] Therefore the church knows too the trials of faith that are poignantly expressed in the laments of the Psalter. Two of the three Gospels report that Jesus himself uttered the words of one of the laments as a cry of dereliction from the cross: "My God, my God, why hast thou forsaken me?" (Ps. 22:1; see Matt. 27:46 and Mark 15:34); and according to Luke he died with the words of another lament on his lips: "Into thy hand I commit my spirit" (Ps. 31:5; see Luke 23:46). Thus Israel's laments were drawn into the context of the passion story and thereby into the history of the people of God, which received a new beginning in Jesus Christ.

Community and Individual Laments

The first thing to notice about the laments in the Psalter is that they fall into two general groups: laments of the community and laments of the individual. The boundary between the two is uncertain, for some-times, as in Psalm 129, Israel speaks in the first person; at other times, as in Psalm 77, the individual identifies with the affliction of Israel and laments for and with the community. Nevertheless, the following out-lines of these two groups of psalms will be useful. Those psalms marked with an asterisk deserve special attention. Captions here and elsewhere are from the RSV.

Community Laments

*12	"On every side the wicked prowl"
*44	"For thy sake we are slain all the day long"
58	"Surely there is a God who judges on earth"
60	"Thou hast made thy people suffer hard things"
74	"O God, why dost thou cast us off for ever?"
79	"The heathen have come into thy inheritance"
*80	"The bread of tears"
83	"O God, do not keep silence"
*85	"That glory may dwell in our land"
89:38–51	"Wilt thou hide thyself for ever?" (A royal lament. The first part, verses 1–37, is a hymn.)
*90	"Teach us to number our days"
*94	"How long shall the wicked exult?"
123	"We have had more than enough"
126	"Those who sow in tears"
129	"Sorely have they afflicted me from my youth"
137	"On the willows we hung our harps"

(See also the community lament in Lamentations 5.)

All these psalms express the distress of the community in a time of threat, when people found it difficult to believe that "God is with us," a fundamental conviction of faith expressed pregnantly in the word *Immanuel* ("God with us," Isa. 7:14; Matt. 1:22–23). One psalm, Psalm 137, clearly reflects the time of the Babylonian exile (587–538 B.C.)

Beside Babylon's rivers we settled,
> there we wept
> when we remembered Zion,
there, upon the poplars, we hung our harps
for there our captors ordered us
> to sing a song,
> our tormentors a song of joy.
"Sing to us a Zion song!"
How can we sing Jahve's song
upon a foreign soil?

(Ps. 137:1–4, SB)

For the most part, however, the community laments are lacking in references to concrete historical situations. The language is so general that psalms of this type could be used on various occasions, especially the cultic "fast" held in a time of crisis. Various passages in the Old Testament allude to times of community mourning and soul-searching (e.g., Judg. 20:26; 1 Kings 21:9–12; 2 Chron. 20:3–19).

A Liturgy of National Disaster

One of the "situations in life" of the community lament is reflected in the book of Joel.[7] This prophecy was delivered at a time when a locust plague threatened the land, a disaster that farmers have experienced in that part of the world from time to time. Joel likens the invasion of locusts to an army that advances irresistibly, leaving devastation in its wake. At one point the prophetic message seems to presuppose a liturgy, consisting of a call to worship, the people's lament and petition to God, and the "oracle of salvation," which assures worshipers that their prayer has been heard. The liturgy would be appropriate for the terrible havoc wrought by a hurricane, an earthquake, a volcanic eruption or other natural disaster.

Call to Repentance (Joel 2:12–13)

> Yet even now, says the LORD,
> > return to me with all your heart,
> with fasting, with weeping, and with mourning;
> > rend your hearts and not your clothing.
> Return to the LORD, your God,
> > for he is gracious and merciful,
> slow to anger, and abounding in steadfast love,
> > and relents from punishing.

(Joel 2:12–13, NRSV)

Summons to Prepare for a Fast (Joel 2:15–16)

All members of the community, even nursing infants, are to take part in the ceremony of contrition.

The People's Lament (Joel 2:17)

Standing in the courtyard outside the Temple, between the entrance hall and the altar of burnt offering, the ministers of God are to lament on behalf of the people:

> Spare your people, O LORD,
>> and do not make your heritage a mockery,
>> a byword among the nations.
> Why should it be said among the peoples
>> "Where is their God?"
>
> (Joel 2:17b, NRSV)

The Oracle of Salvation (Joel 2:19–27)

God's gracious answer to the prayer comes in the form of words of assurance, including abatement of the plague.

Individual Laments

More numerous are the individual laments. Originally some of these laments were composed by persons who, in a time of need or anxiety, went to the temple to pray. Hannah is a case in point. Unable to conceive a child, she went to the temple, once located at Shiloh, and in "great anxiety and vexation" poured out her heart to God. In this cultic situation the priest, Eli, spoke "words of assurance" to her: "Go in peace, and the God of Israel grant your petition which you have made to him" (1 Sam. 1:17). We may assume that some of the individual laments presuppose a setting in worship something like this, though in the course of time they lost their cultic association and became only forms of literary composition. The superscription to Psalm 102, one of the "penitential psalms," is an appropriate introduction to all these laments: "A prayer of one afflicted, when he is faint and pours out his complaint before the LORD." The list is long; pay attention especially to the psalms that are marked with an asterisk.[8] Notice that laments are found throughout the Psalter but are clustered in the first three "books" (Pss. 1–89).

*3	"Many are rising against me"
*4	"In peace I will both lie down and sleep" (song of trust?)
5	"Their throat is an open sepulchre"
7	"Save me from my pursuers!" (prayer of one unjustly accused)
9—10	"Why dost thou hide thyself in time of trouble?" (In part a song of thanksgiving)
*13	"Wilt thou forget me for ever?"
14	"The fool" (same as Psalm 53)
17	"Keep me as the apple of the eye" (prayer of one unjustly accused)
*22	"My God, why hast thou forsaken me?"
25	"For thee I wait all the day"
26	"I walk in my integrity" (prayer of one unjustly accused)
27:7–14	"Let your heart take courage!" (the first part of this psalm is a song of trust)
28	"Take me not off with the wicked!"
*31	"Into thy hand I commit my spirit"
35	"Fight against those who fight against me!" (prayer of one unjustly accused)
36	"In thy light do we see light"
*39	"I held my peace to no avail"
40:11–17	"Evils have encompassed me without number" (cf. Psalm 70) (the first part of the psalm is an individual song of thanksgiving)
41	"Heal me, for I have sinned against thee!" (some regard this as a song of thanksgiving)
*2—43	"Why are you cast down, O my soul?"
52	"Why do you boast, O mighty man?"
53	A variant of Psalm 14
54	"Save me, O God, by thy name!"
55	"O that I had wings like a dove!"
56	"When I am afraid, I put my trust in thee"
*57	"I will awake the dawn!" (prayer of one unjustly accused)
59	"Thou, O God, art my fortress"
61	"The rock that is higher than I"
63	"My soul thirsts for thee" (very likely a song of trust)

64	"Hide me from the secret plots of the wicked!"
*69	"I have come into deep waters"
70	"Be pleased, O God, to deliver me!" (almost the same as Ps. 40:13–17)
*71	"Upon thee I have leaned from my birth"
*77	"I am so troubled that I cannot speak"
86	"In the day of my trouble I call on thee"
88	"Afflicted and close to death"
109	"They reward me evil for good"
120	"Those who hate peace"
*139	"Whither shall I flee from thy presence?"[9]
140	"By the wayside they have set snares for me"
141	"Let my prayer be counted as incense"
142	"When my spirit is faint"

(See also the individual lament in Lamentations 3.)

The Literary Form of the Lament

The term "lament" is not an altogether satisfactory label for these psalms. The term may suggest a pessimistic view of life, the whining complaint of self-pity, or "bemoaning of a tragedy which cannot be reversed, which is characteristic of a dirge."[10] But this is not the mood of the psalmists. What characterizes these psalms, with very few exceptions (notably Psalm 88), is the confidence that the situation can be changed if God wills to intervene. Perhaps we should distinguish between a "lamentation" and a "lament." "The lamentation," says Roland Murphy, "is an expression of grief over a calamity that is not reversible [i.e., a dirge], whereas the lament is an appeal to God's compassion to intervene and change a desperate situation."[11] The psalmists are not like Greek tragedians who portray a no-exit situation of fate or necessity; rather, they raise a cry out of the depths in the confidence that God has the power to lift a person out of the "miry bog" and to set one's feet upon a rock (Ps. 40:1–3). Hence the laments are really expressions of praise, offered in a minor key in the confidence that Yhwh is faithful and in anticipation of a new lease on life.

Here we can do little more than delineate the literary form of the lament in the hope that this will provide a basis for the reader to study the psalms individually, especially those psalms marked with an asterisk in the lists above. In the case of the lament, Israel, as we have observed, borrowed a literary form known in the ancient world and poured into it the content of its faith in God. While subject to variation according to the interests and creativity of the author, the form exhibits a definite structure:

Address to God

Sometimes this is a brief cry, though it may be expanded into an ascription of praise (Ps. 9:1–2) or the recollection of God's past deeds (Ps. 44:1–8).

Complaint

In community laments the distress may be military crisis, drought, famine, scourge (cf. 1 Kings 8:33–40); in individual laments the problem may be sickness, threat of enemies, fear of death, or some other "disorienting" experience.[12] In penitential psalms (to be discussed in the next chapter), the distress has been characterized as the experience of guilt (Ps. 38:4, 18). Often the complaint is accompanied by a protestation of innocence (Ps. 17:3–5) or a plea for forgiveness.

Confession of Trust

This is an expression of confidence in God in spite of the problematic situation; often it is introduced by an adversative such as "but" or "nevertheless."

> But I trusted in your steadfast love;
> my heart shall rejoice in your salvation.
> (Ps. 13:5 [cf. 3:3–5], NRSV)

Petition

The psalmist appeals to God to intervene and deliver, sometimes adducing grounds to support the appeal.

> Turn, O LORD, save my life;
> deliver me for the sake of your steadfast love.
> For in death there is no remembrance of you;
> in Sheol who can give you praise?[13]
> (Ps. 6:4–5, NRSV)

Words of Assurance

The suppliant's trust in God finds expression in the certainty that the prayer will be heard. In some laments we deduce that words of assurance (an "oracle of salvation") were actually spoken by a priest or prophet (e.g., Ps. 12:5), thus preparing the way for the concluding vow of praise. Some think that at one point in Psalm 51 the suppliant asks to hear an oracle of salvation that will bring about a shift from the minor key of lament to the major key of rejoicing.

> Let me hear joy and gladness,
> > let the bones that you have crushed rejoice.
> > > > (Ps. 51:8, NRSV)

Vow of Praise and Thanksgiving

In the confidence that God hears and answers, the suppliant vows to call upon the name of God and to testify before the community what Yhwh has done (Ps. 7:17; 13:6). In cases where the lament includes words of assurance, the psalm ends with exclamations of praise (Ps. 6:8–10).

"My God, Why Have You Forsaken Me?"

The structure of a psalm of lament is exhibited in the following translation (BWA) and arrangement of Psalm 22. This prayer, along with Psalm 69 (another lament), is frequently drawn upon in the New Testament for the portrayal of Jesus' passion (see appendix C). Notice the alternating notes of distress and trust, the repetition of key words and motifs, and the movement from lament to praise.

Cry of Distress

> My God, my God, why have you forsaken me
> > and are distant from my cry for help, my groaning words?
> O my God, I call out by day, and you don't answer,
> > by night and find no repose.

Expression of Trust

> But you are holy, enthroned on the praises of Israel.
> > In you our ancestors trusted, they trusted and you rescued
> > > them.
> To you they cried, and they were delivered;
> > in you they trusted and were not disconcerted.

Lament

> But I am a mere worm, not a person, disgraced by human
>   beings, scorned by people.
> All who see me ridicule me, they grimace at me and shake
>   their heads, [saying]
> "He relied on Yhwh: let him deliver him!
> Let him rescue him, since he likes him!"

Prayer of Confidence

> Yet you are the One who drew me out of the womb,
>   who gave me security at my mother's breast.
> Upon you was I cast from birth,
>   from my mother's womb you have been my God.

Petition for Help and Further Description of Distress

> Don't be distant from me, for I'm in trouble.
>   Be near! for there is no one to help.
> Many bulls surround me,
>   mighty bulls of Bashan encircle me.
> Open-mouthed to swallow me
>   are ravenous and roaring lions.
> I am drained away like water,
>   and all my bones are out of joint.
> My heart has become like wax,
>   it melts inside me.
> My palate [?] is dry like earthenware,
>   and my tongue sticks to the roof of my mouth.
> You have brought me to the point of death.
> Indeed, dogs surround me,
>   a company of evildoers encompasses me,
>   they have pierced [?] my hands and feet.
> I count all my bones,
>   they gaze at me and gloat.
> They divide my garments among themselves,
>   and cast lots for my clothes.

Renewed Petition for Help

> But you, O Yhwh, do not be distant!
>   O my Strength, hurry to my aid!

Rescue my life from the sword,
  my solitary self from the power of the dog!
Save me from the mouth of the lion,
  from the horns of the wild ox!
You have answered me!*
  [Transition to next section]

Vow or Praise and Thanksgiving

I will proclaim your name to my comrades,
  in the midst of the community I will praise you:
    [The hymn follows]
"You who fear Yhwh, sing praise!
  All you descendants of Jacob, glorify God!
  All you offspring of Israel, stand in awe!
For God has not spurned or disdained the affliction of an
  afflicted one.
Nor has God's face remained hidden,
but when he cried for help, God heard."

You are the source of my praise in the great community;
  I will fulfill my vows before those who fear him.
Let the poor eat and be satisfied!
  Let those who seek Yhwh sing praise,
  their hearts ever full of vitality.

Renewed Thanksgiving

Let all the ends of the earth remember and turn to Yhwh;
  Let all the families of the nations bow down before God!
For dominion belongs to Yhwh,
  who rules over the nations.[14]

This pattern of the lament, fully elaborated in Psalm 22, is found on
a smaller scale in the beautiful lament in Psalm 13. Notice that the latter poem moves from a fourfold cry, "How long?" (v. 1–2), through a
petition for deliverance from the enemy (v. 3–4), to a concluding expression of trust in God's covenant faithfulness.

---

* This is a literal translation of the Hebrew. The enigmatic words, which are
often emended, may transition to the next section, based on words of assurance
that the petitioner's prayer has been heard. This is the interpretation of H.-J.
Kraus in his commentary on the Psalms (Minneapolis: Augsburg Press, 1988).

The Compassionate God

As can be seen from the overall pattern, these cries out of the depths of distress are motivated by a deep confidence that Yhwh is the compassionate God—the God who hears, who is concerned, and who is involved with the people. The God whom Israel worships is not characterized by apathy, but by *pathos*—by sensitivity to the human condition, as Abraham Heschel observed.[15] The scriptural paradigm for this divine sensitivity was given in the Mosaic tradition, and particularly in the story of the burning bush (Ex. 3:7–8), as we have seen in chapter 2. It is found preeminently in the announcement of the name (identity) of God, an ancient creedal statement echoed in various places in the Old Testament (e.g., Joel 2:13; Ps. 103:8–9). Given this theological orientation, the movement of the lament is from sorrow to rejoicing, from humiliation to exaltation, and thus toward the song of thanksgiving to be considered in the next chapter.

[Note: Some of the psalms of the Psalter are essentially elaborations of a particular motif of a lament. For instance, the protestation of innocence is prominent in some psalms (7; 17; 26), and the cry for vindication in others (69; 109). In still others, as we shall see presently, the laments are deepened into penitential prayers. And the songs of trust (see chapter 7) are basically expansions of the confession of trust, which is an essential part of the lament.]

The Problem of the "Enemies" in the Psalms

One of the thorniest problems in the psalms of lament is the fact that "enemies" have a central place in prayer to God. This issue also appears in other types of psalms, even psalms of trust such as the Shepherd's Psalm (Psalm 23), which expresses the confidence that God (Yhwh) prepares a table "in the presence of my enemies" (Ps. 23:5). Who are these enemies anyway?[16]

In the case of the community laments, the question is not hard to answer. Laments of this type were used on fast days when the community was threatened by military foes, famine, drought, or some pestilence such as a locust plague (cf. the book of Joel). Solomon's prayer in the

Temple gives a clear picture of the kinds of threats that occasioned community laments (1 Kings 8:33–40).

In the individual laments, however, we can never be sure what the trouble is, for the psalmists resort to picturesque language to describe the human condition. We have seen this in Psalm 22, quoted above. The psalmist finds himself encompassed by "mighty bulls of Bashan" (v. 12); he feels "drained away like water" and his heart melts like wax (v. 14); he is brought "to the point of death" (v. 15). In shifting imagery he declares that he is attacked by dogs, lions, wild oxen, the sword (v. 16–21). It is hard to tell from this language whether the suppliant is suffering from sickness, anxiety over death, personal attack by ungodly people, or some other distress.

Thirst for God

In one of the most poignant laments of the Psalter, whose theme is "thirst for God," the problem is clearly ridicule and attack by unidentified enemies. From a literary point of view, Psalms 42 and 43 should be regarded as one poem. As noted in chapter 1, chapter divisions were not found in the original texts but were inserted much later, sometimes arbitrarily. The unity of the poem is evident from the thrice-repeated refrain in which the poet, as in Psalm 103, addresses his or her being or "self" (*nefesh*). It is a kind of "song of myself."

> O my self, why am I so dejected,
> and why am I so troubled within?
> Hope in God,[17] whom I shall again praise,
> my help and my God.
> (Ps. 42:5; 42:11; 43:5, BWA)

The word "soul" is not used in this translation, for it suggests the ancient Greek view, still influential today, of a deathless entity imprisoned in the body. The Hebrew word *nefesh* refers to the self as a psychosomatic (soul-body) unity.

Through the psalm breathes the spirit of a close I-Thou relationship and an intense longing for personal communion with God. It was written in a time of spiritual "dryness" when the poet longed passionately for Yhwh, "the living God"—like a thirsty deer that sniffs for water (Ps. 42:1–2). But this is not a longing for a one-to-one relationship with God in mystic solitude. The poet yearns to be surrounded by the believing and worshiping community: to participate in the worship services of the

Temple and to celebrate with the people the presence of God in their midst. This is not the kind of private piety or spiritual individualism that is often manifest in churches today.

Read, preferably aloud, the three stanzas and their respective refrains.

- In the first strophe (Ps. 42:1–4 1 refrain, v. 5) the poet portrays a time of "the eclipse of God." Some interpreters suggest that the life situation was sickness that made it impossible to go to the Temple to "behold the face of God," though this is not certain from the text. In any case, this person was exposed to doubts by enemies who raised the incessant taunt, "Where is your God?" We see here that the real threat of enemies is that they challenge the faith that God is present in the world. The refrain expresses the confidence of one who waits for the "midnight of the soul" to end and who expects to fulfill a vow of thanksgiving in the Temple.

- The second strophe (Ps. 42:6–10 1 refrain, v. 11) plumbs an even deeper level of distress. The poet is far from the Temple, somewhere in the foothills of Mount Hermon at the source of the Jordan River. But in poetic imagination the tumbling waters of the Jordan fade into the mythical waters of chaos whose "waves" and "billows" pull one downward into the region of death (see Jonah 2:2–9).18 This spiritual crisis occasions an anguished cry in the presence of faceless enemies who expose the poet's faith to ridicule and doubt.

- In the final strophe (Ps. 43:1–4 1 refrain, v. 5) the psalmist's prayer moves to petition for vindication before taunting and oppressing enemies.

> Vindicate me, O God,
>> champion my cause
>> against faithless people;
>> rescue me from the treacherous, dishonest man.
> For You are my God, my stronghold;
>> why have you rejected me?
> Why must I walk in gloom,
>> oppressed by the enemy?
>
> (Ps. 43:1–2, NJPS)

As in other psalms of lament, the poet anticipates being delivered and presenting a vow of thanksgiving. The prayer is that "light" and "truth," personalized as God's escorts, will come to guide the suppliant to the Temple to join with the worshiping community in praising Yhwh in music and song.

Faceless Enemies

Various attempts have been made to identify the enemies in the psalms. It has been suggested, for instance, that the laments presuppose a situation of party strife within the Israelite community, like that which broke out in the Maccabean period between the orthodox Jews and liberals who favored the Greeks.

Another proposal is that some of these laments are "prayers of the accused" offered at the Temple, where fugitives found asylum (sanctuary) from the hasty, arbitrary justice of pursuers. Psalms 7, 26, 35, 57, 59, and perhaps others (139?) suggest this practice of taking refuge in the Temple from enemies (sometimes blood avengers).[19] In the presence of the highest Judge, accused persons raised their cry for help, protested their innocence, threw themselves confidently on the mercy of the divine court, and, when a favorable divine verdict was given, raised their voices in thanksgiving.

Another suggestion is that the "evildoers" were magicians who, by casting a magic spell, inflicted sickness or calamity upon hapless victims. There are still places in the world where people fear the expert in black magic, witchcraft, or sorcery.

> Their mouths are filled with cursing and deceit and
>   oppression;
>   under their tongues are mischief and iniquity.
> They sit in ambush in the villages;
>   in hiding places they murder the innocent.
>   (Ps. 10:7–8, NRSV)

None of these interpretations is completely satisfactory. The plain truth is that we really do not know who the enemies were, for the psalmists express their distress in stylized language that had been employed for centuries in cultic situations. Indeed, it is striking that the Babylonian psalms of lament used the same conventional imagery (engulfing billows of the flood, miring into the waters of a swamp, descent into the pit, attack by wild beasts, etc.) and sometimes even left a blank to be filled in with the name of the worshiper who chose to use the psalm![20] This explains why the enemies in the individual laments are so faceless, and it also helps to account for the fact that these psalms are relevant for many different people in times of trouble. The psalmists do not talk boringly about the details of private life, like the proverbial person who inflicts the story of an operation on friends. Nor do they turn introspectively to their own inner life. Rather, by using conventional language they portray a situation that is typical of every person who struggles with the meaning of life in situations of tension, hostility, and conflict. That is why these psalms have been used through the centuries by suppliants who cry to God out of their particular situation. They leave a blank, as it were, for the insertion of one's own personal name.

Of course, many people in our time have found themselves in hostile social or national situations where their lives have been threatened. Examples come readily to mind, such as the persecution of Christians in India or China, the anti-Semitism manifest in many ways (most horribly in the Holocaust), the oppression of Negro slaves or Native Americans, the persecution of Muslims in Kosovo, to say nothing of abuse of children or the battering of women. The psalms are readily accessible to people in situations of oppression and violence. Even those of us who have been more fortunate, in that we live in more protected and peaceful places, cannot escape the problem of enemies. The point bears repetition that, according to these psalmists, the most insidious and dangerous threat of enemies is their mocking challenge of disbelief in God, which threatens to pull the rug from beneath them:

> O LORD, how many are my foes!
> How many rise up against me!
> Many are saying of me,
> "God will not deliver him."
> (Ps. 3:1–2, NIV)

In a secular culture, many of us have heard these taunting or skeptical voices not only in times of trouble but when things are going well. In the middle of the twentieth century a strange phenomenon appeared in Christian circles, namely, talk about "the death of God," a theme introduced in the writings of Friedrich Nietzsche (1844–1900).

The Cry for Vindication

More problematic is the fact that these psalmists—like the prophet Jeremiah in his laments (see especially Jer. 20:7–13)—cry out to God for vindication and even pray for vengeance against the enemies, whoever they are. A number of these psalms are often called "imprecatory" or "cursing" psalms.[21] Two of them—Psalm 69 and especially Psalm 109—are almost impossible to use in Christian worship. It is often said that the language of these psalms is sub-Christian, that it is out of place in the new age governed by the commandment of the Sermon on the Mount, "Love your enemies and pray for those who persecute you" (Matt. 5:44). For many people the magnificent 139th Psalm is ruined by the hatred expressed in verses 19–22 ("Do I not hate them that hate thee, O Lord? . . . I hate them with perfect hatred.").

A disturbing example of imprecation is the closing passage of Psalm 137, a folk song that cried out for vengeance against the Babylonians who destroyed the nation of Judah in 587 B.C. and the Edomites who assisted them in the sack of Jerusalem (cf. Obadiah 10–14).

> Remember, Jahve, Edom's sons
>   on Jerusalem's day
>   when they shouted,
> "Strip her! Strip her!
> Strip her to the bone!"
> Lady Babylon Violent Destroyer,
> Blessings on the one who returns
>   measure for measure
>   your actions against us.
> Blessings on the one who seizes
>   and shatters your sucking babes
>   against a stone.
>
> (Ps. 137:7–9, SB)

It is surely proper to question whether all 150 psalms should be retained in Christian worship, including these troublesome passages, or whether the Psalter should be censored at those points that seem to be inconsistent with God's revelation in Jesus Christ. Some poet-translators, such as Christopher Smart (1722–1771), thought the imprecation so unchristian that they changed the language of vindication against enemies to prayers for their salvation:

[handwritten margin note: Perhaps not censored in actuality, but taken with a historical understanding]

> But he is greatest and the best,
> Who spares his enemies protest,
> And Christian mildness owns;
> Who gives his captives back their lives,
> Their helpless infants, weeping wives,
> And for his sin atones.[22]

It would be interesting to check the responsive readings included in modern hymnals or books of worship, to see the degree to which the psalms have been edited for Christian worship. Before this question is answered too quickly, however, the voice of contemporary theologians should be heard. Dietrich Bonhoeffer advocated the daily use, especially in our morning and evening devotions, of *all* the psalms. It was his view that we should not "pick and choose," for "otherwise we dishonor God by presuming to know better . . . what we should pray."[23] Similarly Christoph Barth objects to the impropriety of omitting certain passages that offend us (e.g., Ps. 104:35 or Ps. 139:19–22) and insists, "It is impossible to have the Psalter without its reference to the godless enemies."[24]

Other theologians remind us that these psalms give voice to the oppressed and voiceless. To remove these psalms from our liturgy is to conspire with oppressors and silence those whose lives are swallowed up by powerful adversaries.[25]

Admittedly, the laments of the Psalter are raised from the depths of human anxiety, from which the emotions of bitterness and hatred often well up. The Psalter, like the Old Testament as a whole, is very earthy—all the moods and passions of human life find expression here. The psalms do not point to a transhistorical world of pure ideals—the good, the true, and the beautiful—rather, they are concerned with the historical scene of change, struggle, and suffering, where God meets people and lays a claim upon them. Psalm 137, quoted above, comes out of a situation of historical struggle where a small people found itself overwhelmed by the massed might of an empire and was suddenly deprived of everything held precious. The Christian community cannot automatically join in this psalm. Yet we must remind ourselves that Psalm 137 has found many echoes in modern life, especially in situations of protest.[26] The dilemma is whether these human cries of vengeance have a place in our speech to God. Gerald H. Wilson has suggested that in our contemporary North American urban situation where the cycle of poverty continues unabated, these psalms can be prayed against those who act as enemies of shalom, that is, contrary to the well being of the community and individuals. These enemies, whether individuals or institutions, ought to be opposed by those concerned for justice for the weak and marginalized. In the mouths of the oppressed and the friends of the oppressed, the hope that the "enemies" will be called to account for their actions is empowering and hopeful.[27]

We have noticed that the laments use a stylized language that was capable of being reinterpreted in the ever-new situations in which the worshiping community found itself. This language has been described as "dynamic" and "realistic," for it simultaneously expressed the tension between cosmos and chaos, order and disorder. We are, on the one hand, reminded of the precarious nature of our world and, on the other, we are reminded of the sovereignty of God and the goodness of creation. This tension is best expressed through poetic language.[28] In describing the enemies in this traditional language, with its monotonous and exaggerated epithets, the psalmists were not calling for a personal fight; rather, they were concerned about the adversaries of the cause of God (as in Ps. 139:19–22). Indeed, now and then (e.g., Ps. 18:16–19) the enemies are associated with the mythical powers of chaos who stand in opposition to the Creator's purpose.[29] This helps us to understand why the psalmists think of the enemies ("the wicked," "the godless," "the workers of evil") as *God's enemies* who, as such, are to be hated.

The Gospels portray human distress as arising from the threat of demonic powers, organized—according to the apocalyptic view—into an oppressive empire under the rule of Satan. According to this imaginative way of thinking, the human problem is not just the frustration that arises out of one's personal life. Rather, in a time of testing (temptation), individuals experience the threat of evil powers that are external to them, that affect them in the society in which they live, and that may seduce and overwhelm them.[30] Jesus taught his disciples to pray, "Lead us not into temptation, but deliver us from evil," or as the New English Bible translates, "Do not bring us to the test, but save us from the evil one" (Matt. 6:13). We can understand the intention of this language in our time when people, perhaps more than in any other period of human history, find themselves victimized by power structures, by the antagonisms or prejudices embodied in social customs and behavior, by tremendous social forces or "isms" before which the individual feels helpless. In the last century, we are reminded, the laments of Negro spirituals expressed "one continual cry"[31] against oppressive pharaohs.[32] The psalmists' cry for vindication may be closer to our lives than we realize. Oppressed people cry out for justice in the social structures of human society, a justice that would somehow give social expression to love and concern. Justice is not achieved merely by "giving alms" or as we say, giving to charities; it is empowering those who are oppressed so they may participate fully in society.

Therefore the exact identification of the "enemies" can be of limited help to the modern reader, primarily because too much emphasis on explicit identification could have the tendency to make the psalms static and irrelevant. Because psalmic language is "open and metaphorical,"[33] it remains alive in addressing new challenges. Keeping this interpretive principle in mind allows greater freedom in applying the psalms to contemporary situations.

The Vengeance that Belongs to God

In trying to answer the questions raised by the "psalms of vengeance" we must keep several things in mind. First, it is important to consider how biblical language is used, that is, the syntax within which words such as "avenge" and "vengeance" function. It is too bad that these words are translated from the Hebrew by English words which in our thought world have a negative connotation. No one wants to be regarded as vengeful, and therefore it hardly seems right to apply the term to God! However, the Hebrew verb *naqam* ("vindicate") has the basic meaning of "save" in the Old Testament, as it has in other ancient literature, and therefore can be used in exactly the same sense as the verb *yasha'* ("save") from which the noun "salvation" comes. The language presupposes the view that God has entered into covenant relation with the people Israel, and within the terms of that relationship acts as judge or vindicator to defend and uphold justice. Therefore, within the covenant "the people of the Lord" appeal to the Suzerain for help, vindication, "salvation." When considered in this light, it is understandable that "*naqam* [to vindicate] is the sole prerogative of God."[34] And this is precisely what we read in the New Testament:

> Beloved, never avenge yourselves, but leave room for the wrath of God; for it is written, "Vengeance is mine, I will repay, says the Lord." (Rom. 12:19, NRSV)

Here the apostle Paul echoes the note struck in the so-called Song of Moses (Deut. 32:35).

In view of this, it is doubtful whether these psalms should be regarded as imprecatory psalms or as curses in the strict sense. In the ancient world, as in some cultures today, it was believed that the word spoken in curse released a power, or spell, which was automatically effective. Recall the story in Numbers 22–24 about the diviner Balaam, whom Balak, the king of Moab, employed to destroy Israel with the power of the curse. As long as one believed in the power of verbal vengeance, prayer was unnecessary. Claus Westermann explains, "The distinctiveness of the curse lies in the fact that it is aimed directly, without any detour via God, at the one it is meant to hit. A curse is a word of power which the swearer released without recourse to God."[35] The Psalter, it is true, contains traces of ancient curse formulas (e.g., Ps. 58:6–9) that echo traditional language used in cultic ceremonies of covenant renewal, but no longer are they curses in the proper sense. They are prayers to God, who obtains vindication in God's own way and in God's own time.

Another thing to consider is that the psalms wrestle with the problems of human existence within the context of this life—the "threescore years and ten" of Psalm 90:10. Lacking the eschatological horizon of the New Testament, they concentrate on the problems of life *now* with a fierce and passionate intensity. They represent what Zenger calls "realized theodicy: they affirm God by surrendering the last word *to God*."[36] The psalmists are not satisfied with the notion that the imbalances of life will somehow be corrected in another form of existence beyond historical experience. They believe that God's dealings with human beings take place in this earthly sphere. Psalm 73 questions the righteousness of God and the wisdom of faithful living until the psalmist enters the sanctuary of God and "perceives" the end of the wicked. It is only in the context of the here and now that the psalmist finds consolation. For the psalmist, as for many modern people, death is the final limitation; accordingly, as in the case of Job, the answers to the pressing questions of human life must be found now. Like a deer that pines for fresh water, they "thirst for God" (Ps. 42:1) with the whole being, and they seek the satisfaction of that thirst in this life.

In the New Testament the human situation is changed. There the good news rings out that in Jesus Christ, God has conquered the power of death and has thrown open the door into the future. But this victory is only a foretaste of the final consummation when God's action as judge (vindicator) will take place. Thus the parable about the unrighteous judge, to whom a widow came persistently with the plea, "Vindicate me against my adversary," ends with the interpretation:

> And will not God grant justice to his chosen ones who cry
>   to him day and night?
> Will he delay long in helping them? I tell you, he will
>   quickly grant justice to them.
> And yet, when the Son of Man comes, will he find faith on
>   earth? (Luke 18:7–8, NRSV)

The Christian community reads the psalmists' cries for vindication in the larger context of the biblical story that reaches its climax with the gospel of God's triumph over all the powers of sin, death, and darkness. Already, according to the witness of the New Testament, God the Vindicator has responded to people's anxieties, frustrations, and distresses. Jesus, God's Messiah, has experienced the human cry out of the depths, as evidenced in the cry of dereliction from the cross (Mark 15:34, quoting Ps. 22:1). But Jesus' death, crowned with God's vindication in the resurrection, enables people of faith to become "more than conquerors" (Rom. 8:31–39) and thus to move from lament to thanksgiving, from death to life.

5

Psalms of a Broken
and Contrite Heart

In T. S. Eliot's play *The Cocktail Party,* there is a scene in which Celia
Coplestone tries to explain to a counselor her sense of guilt. She hesi-
tates to use the word "sin"—she had always been taught to disbelieve
in that. At least, she said, it was not "sin in the ordinary sense"—
committing immoral acts.

> It's not the feeling of anything I've ever *done,*
> Which I might get away from, or of anything in me
> I could get rid of—but of emptiness, of failure
> Towards someone, or something, outside myself.
> And I feel I must . . . *atone*—is that the word?
> Can you treat a patient for such a state of mind?[1]

In many instances, this is a description of the brokenness of human life
and the inescapable sense of guilt about the human condition. As theologians have been telling us, sin is not so much breaking rules or committing immoral deeds as it is separation—separation from God, from
others, and from one's deepest self. And according to the Bible, there
is a treatment for such a condition: casting oneself penitently upon
God's mercy and receiving the healing gift of divine forgiveness.

It was this same feeling that life was "too much with us" and posed
a threat to our spiritual health that prompted preachers such as Anglican bishop John Fisher (1459–1535) to focus on how the psalms could
heal those who felt weighted down by life. In his view, the psalms were
given to us for three reasons:

1. To create a mindset for learning virtue.
2. To prevent despair in those who have fallen into sin.

3. To use as "letters" of supplication and "spedefull" prayers for remission.[2]

The psalms' value in transforming and aiding Christian growth was to be held in higher regard than their poetic merits.

The Seven Psalms of Penitence

According to a liturgical tradition that reaches back into the Middle Ages, seven psalms are placed under the rubric of penitential psalms. These psalms were originally recited at the deathbed or sickbed of a person for recovery of health or forgiveness in death. Later they were associated with the life of David, which extended their use in the church. The seven psalms appeared together as a collection in prayer books. They were recited after morning prayers in the Liturgy of the Hours on Friday during Lent. In the late Middle Ages and early Renaissance period, some commentators tied the seven psalms to the Seven Deadly Sins, with each psalm serving as a deterrent to one of the vices. In the early Renaissance period, the seven psalms became so popular that poets began to write paraphrases of them, in some cases including a narrative between each psalm for clarity and instructional purposes. At this point, their association with David's sin concerning Bathsheba and Uriah was well established. This association with David is no longer favored, however, since it is evident that at least one of the psalms, Psalm 130, is not a meditation on David's life but belongs to the Songs of Ascent. During the early Renaissance period, the seven penitential psalms evolved from cultic use to private meditation.

During the early Renaissance the popularity of these psalms is attested by the numerous translations and commentaries produced at that time. Most, if not all of these, were considered aids to reflection and piety. The oldest existing English commentary on the penitentials was produced by Dame Eleanor Hull in the fifteenth century.[3] Her work is a translation of a French commentary on the penitentials, the author of which is unknown. The commentary encourages a pietistic and personal reading of the penitentials, with David as the representative of all human struggle.

The classification of penitential psalms is based on content rather than literary form, for one of them is actually an individual song of thanksgiving (Psalm 32), a type to be considered in the next chapter. In these instances the affliction from which suppliants plead for deliverance is interpreted as a deep sense of guilt. In Psalm 6, however, guilt and sin are not mentioned. Here the psalmist seems to be pleading for relief from illness or attack from enemies. Each psalm deserves special attention, but we shall concentrate on four of them: Psalms 32, 51, 102, and 130.[4]

6	"My soul is sorely troubled"
*32	"Thou didst forgive the guilt of my sin" (song of thanksgiving)
38	"There is no health in my bones"
*51	"Create in me a clean heart, O God"
*102	"I mingle tears with my drink"
*130	"Out of the depths I cry to thee"
143	"Enter not into judgment with thy servant"

Sometimes, as in Psalm 143, these psalms refer to "enemies"—external powers that oppress and crush a person. However, these laments are different from others considered previously in that they internalize the problem of evil. The enemy is not just "out there" in society but is also present in the depths of one's own being. Sin is rebellion against God, that is, the will to live on one's own as though God did not matter.

In these psalms, the presence of the Holy God in the midst of the people is experienced as both inescapable judgment (see Psalm 139 to be discussed later) and gracious acceptance. It might be helpful to approach these psalms by reading the account of the prophet Isaiah's experience in the Temple (Isaiah 6). Isaiah's vision of God's holy, transcendent majesty prompted a cry of distress:

> Woe is me! I am shattered!
> For a person of unclean lips am I,
>   and in the midst of a people of unclean lips I am living.
> For my eyes have seen Yhwh the King.
>   (Isa. 6:5, BWA)

According to the account, which echoes in the familiar hymn "Holy, Holy, Holy," the prophet came to realize that divine holiness is manifest, not just in judgment that exposes human sin but in forgiveness that purifies and empowers for a task (cf. Ps. 130:4). Notice that here the "sin" that is "blotted out" by divine forgiveness is not understood individualistically, as we are inclined to do; rather, the self is stained by the society in which one lives—its unjust social structures, economic injustice, violence in various forms.

Psalm 32: Beati Quorum (Confession of Sin)

Psalm 32 provides teaching based on the experiences of sin and for-giveness. As noted, it is not a lament in form, but a song of thanksgiv-ing, but because of its emphasis on the confession of sin, it is included with the penitential laments. This great psalm is said to have been Au-gustine's favorite.

The central part of the psalm, surrounded by a didactic introduction (v. 1–2) and conclusion (v. 8–11), sets forth the movement of the sup-pliant's confession.

Introduction (v. 1–2)

Speaking in the manner of a wisdom teacher, the psalmist announces the theme: "Blessed are those whose transgression is forgiven."

The Way to Spiritual Health (v. 3–6): 3 Steps

1. *Confession of sin* is the first step (v. 3–4). In giving advice to others in trouble, the poet speaks out of personal experience. When he or she kept silent, bottling up or repressing the problem, there were physical effects: "my body wasted away," there was restlessness night and day, "my strength was dried up as by summer heat." In our terms, this was a psychosomatic problem, for "body" and "spirit" are interrelated.

2. *The healing power of divine forgiveness* (v. 5–6). The second step in the healing process, according to this testimony, is to bring hidden, suppressed guilt into the open so that it may be faced in God's merciful presence.

> I made known my sin to you,
>   did not conceal my guilt.
> I said, "I shall confess
>   my offence to Yahweh."
> And you, for your part, took away my guilt,
>   forgave my sin.
>
> (v. 5, NJB)

This is a difficult step because the heart is deceitful (cf. Jer. 17:9); we seek to cover up, and try to deceive ourselves and God. But there is no hiding place from the God who knows us better than we know ourselves (see Psalm 139 again). You will discover, this poet advises, that there is tremendous healing power in God's forgiveness. One is reminded of the story about the healing of the paralytic during Jesus' ministry: "Your sins are forgiven. Rise, take your bed and walk!" (Matt. 9:6).

3. *In the rush of mighty waters* (v. 6). Finally, the healing involves "going public"—making a witness to the community. Speaking out of the experience of sin being forgiven, the suppliant appeals to others to seek God's help: "let all who are faithful offer prayer to you," so that in a time of distress "the rush of mighty waters" will not engulf them in death.

The psalm moves from lament to praise, as the poet tries to plumb the mystery of God's judgment and mercy. Our deepest security is in God who, as another psalmist testifies, is "our refuge and strength" in all the changes and fortunes of life (Ps. 46:1).

> You are a hiding place for me,
> you preserve me from trouble,
> you surround me with glad shouts of deliverance.
>
> (v. 7, NRSV)

Concluding Refrain: (v. 10–11)

The psalm concludes by striking once again and amplifying the note sounded at the beginning. Blessed are those to whom God has demonstrated steadfast love (*hesed*) by hearing their cry out of the depths of distress and performing the re-creating miracle of forgiveness.

Psalm 51: Miserere (Have Mercy on Me)

The well-known penitential Psalm 51 opens with the cry, in Latin, *Miserere* ("Have mercy"), which resounds through the music and liturgy of the Christian church.[5] This is surely one of the pearls of the Psalter. This psalm is found in the so-called Elohistic Psalter, a section in which the personal name of Yhwh was replaced by Elohim (God).[6] Undoubtedly the poet originally used the more intimate, personal form of address, appealing to the abounding *hesed* (covenant faithfulness) of Yhwh as other psalmists do (Ps. 103:6–7; 136; cf. Ex. 34:6–7). In that original form, the poem is a beautiful expression of an I-Thou relationship.

Notice that the structure of this exquisite poem corresponds to that of the lament outlined in the previous chapter:

Address (v. 1–2)

A cry for deliverance from the power of sin, based not on any human merit or achievement but solely on God's "steadfast love" (*hesed*) and "tender mercies."

Complaint (vv. 3–6)

A profound and inescapable awareness of guilt before God. Guilt is not based solely on a personal feeling (a state of mind), but has an objective reference; it is an act against someone outside the self, against the Holy God. No act of self-deception or any cover-up can deal with sin in this radical sense.

> Against you, you alone, have I sinned,
>   and done what is evil in your sight.
>   (v. 4a, NRSV)

Therefore the poet prays for "truth in the inward parts," and for "wisdom in my secret heart"—that is, "the kind of *discernment* that will make a new, responsible life possible."[7]

Petition (vv. 7–12)

In a series of imperatives, the suppliant appeals to God for help (as in the introduction in vv. 1–2): purge me, wash me, blot out my transgression. The most striking imperative is prayer for a new creation, a new being.

> God, create a pure heart for me,
>   and give me a new and steadfast spirit.
> Do not drive me from your presence
>   or take your holy spirit from me.
>   (vv. 10–11, REB)

A couple of matters deserve attention here. First of all the Hebrew word for "heart," here paralleled to "spirit," does not refer to the seat of the emotions as in English (in Hebrew that would be "kidneys" or "bowels"). Rather, "heart" refers to the mind and the will, that is, the center of the self from which action and loyalty spring. "The heart has its reasons," said the French writer Pascal (1623–1662), "of which [abstract] reason does not know."[8]

Second, the creation verb found here (*bara*) is used in the Old Testament only of God's action, the classic example being the Genesis creation story (cf. also Isa. 45:12). Further, the prayer for a "steadfast spirit" (NJPS) is reminiscent of the second story of creation where God is portrayed breathing into clay the divine spirit (*ruach*) which gives vitality to the self (*nefesh*). Here we find the amazing testimony that God's forgiveness may animate the body with new breath, with the "holy spirit" that gives new vitality. A Christian reader will read this passage in the fuller biblical context of God's forgiving grace manifest in Jesus Christ. Paul puts it this way:

> So if anyone is in Christ, there is a new creation: everything old has passed away; see, everything has become new! (2 Cor. 5:17, NRSV)

Vow of Praise (vv. 13–17)

The suppliant concludes by promising to bear witness in the worshiping community to God's recreating grace.

Clearly the person who composed this psalm was not a slavish devotee of the liturgy of the Temple or, as we might say, the forms of organized religion. As a token of gratitude for deliverance from guilt ("the bondage of sin"), we are told, the only appropriate and acceptable sacrifice to God is "a broken and contrite heart." Like the classical prophets of Israel (e.g., Isa. 1:10–17), the psalmist was critical of the Temple services, especially the sacrifices that were presented (see Leviticus 1—7). The psalmist's language, in fact, was so sharply critical that a later revisionist added a qualification at the end of the psalm (vv. 18–19), thereby justifying its use in Temple services. Yet in spite of this criticism, psalmist was profoundly dependent on the forms of worship, as indicated by references to ritual washing (v. 2) and to purification with hyssop (v. 7), an aromatic bush used in rites of cleansing (Lev. 14:4; Num. 19:18). The forms of worship, according to this psalmist, signify nothing unless they are outward expressions of an inward relationship to God. On the other hand, God may use the cultic forms of worship to bring about a new life of health and wholeness (the meaning of "peace," *shalom*).

Sinful from the Day of Birth: Psalm 51:5

There is one statement in Psalm 51 that presents a special theological difficulty:

> Indeed, I was born guilty,
> a sinner when my mother conceived me.
>
> (v. 5, NRSV)

In the past this sentence has been taken to mean that sex is inherently sinful, though necessary for procreation, and that sin is transferred genetically from one generation to another. This dubious understanding of "original sin" finds no support here, though John Calvin argued vigorously that it did.[9] The poet is speaking existentially, not proposing a doctrine that applies to human beings generally. From the standpoint of the existing self, the poet looks back over the story of life to its very beginning in his or her mother's womb and confesses that the whole story of his life stands under Yhwh's scrutinizing judgment. Here again it must be said that "no man is an island unto himself"; everyone is influenced by the brokenness manifest in the family, the nation, the world at large. An egregious example of this is the child abuse and spouse battering that afflicts too many in our society. In any case, in this psalm no attempt is made to exonerate or excuse one's self by laying the blame on heredity or environment. The condition is inescapably personal and can be cured only when a penitent person casts himself or herself on the mercy of God—"just as I am," as we sing in one of our great evangelical songs. Then the forgiving God may perform a new act of creation, giving one a new beginning and putting a new spirit within (cf. Ezek. 11:19; 36:28).

Psalm 102: *Domine Exaudi Orationem Meam* (*Lord, Hear My Prayer*)

This penitential psalm is exceptional because of its vivid imagery describing the experience of the nearness of death. In spite of uncertainties in translation, the beauty and power of the Hebrew poetry come through: "life vanishing like smoke," "bones burning like an oven," "a heart like blighted grass." These are stirring images of the waning hours of life.

The superscription to this psalm is a characteristic description of a lament: "A prayer of one afflicted, when faint and pleading before the LORD." Yet this description only makes the hymnic passage in verses 12–22 stand out as a seeming intrusion. These verses seem to interrupt the plaintive personal cry of lament with hymnic praise for God's universal and eternal rule. The New Jerusalem Bible even sets these verses off typographically, thereby indicating the disjunction.

As with other psalms that display similar discontinuities (e.g., Ps. 89:5–18), we modern readers should endeavor to read the psalm as a whole, from beginning to end. What, then, is the value of pointing out the intrusion of these "fragments?" Several benefits may accrue from considering the problem of continuity in the verses. Careful reading may

- confirm what we may have perceived, that is, that there is an abrupt change of topic;
- enable us to explore new ways of ordering the verses in our liturgy, or experiment with various modes of recitation and performance; and
- enable us to become aware of theological motives oriented more toward the worshiping community and less toward a purely personal reading of the psalm.

Reading the psalm as an integrated whole undoubtedly will enhance its meaning and encourage its liturgical use.

Psalm 102 displays the characteristic structure of a lament, discussed in the previous chapter:

Initial Complaint

In the opening part (vv. 1–11) the petitioner pours out his or her heart in some of the most emotionally charged language of the Psalter. The imagery evokes a deep feeling of existential loneliness.

> I am like a desert-owl in the wastes,
> a screech-owl among ruins,
> I keep vigil and moan
> like a lone bird on a roof.
>
> (vv. 6–7, NJB)

Formerly commentators attempted to identify these birds with various kinds of people, such as a hermit, a penitent person, a righteous one. Beginning with Augustine the psalm was understood to be Christ's dialogue with God; accordingly these images related to the passion of Christ. This christological interpretation was extended to include an elaborate, if far-fetched, identification of the first bird, sometimes translated as "pelican of the wilderness" (KJV), which would kill itself to feed its young (passion of Christ) and in three days (cf. 1 Cor. 15:4) return to life (Resurrection). However, contemporary interpreters generally turn away from attempts to explain these birds by reference to their idiosyncrasies. These metaphors of birds in the wilderness combine to awaken in us a feeling of isolation and abandonment, of "wandering in the wilderness."

In verse 10 the poet gives the reason for having to suffer God's anger:

> Ashes are the food that I eat,
> my drink is mingled with tears,
> because of your fury and anger,
> since you have raised me up only to cast me away.
>
> (vv. 9–10, NJB)

This is a disturbing thought, one that raises question about God's relationship to people. God raises up the petitioner only to cast him or her away. This image of God offends our sensitivities, but the psalmist is not concerned about theological propriety. God must be accountable to the poet's sense of reality, of how things really are.

Comfort and Praise Break In

Then, like a chorus, a different voice—a voice of thanksgiving—erupts from the ashes of deep sorrow and the nearness of death. The chorus extols God as the one whose inscrutable ways are oriented toward the rescue of Jerusalem and its "peace." Language that was once accusatory becomes celebratory.

> Yahweh has leaned down from the heights of his sanctuary,
> has looked down from heaven to earth,
> to listen to the sighing of the captive,
> and set free those condemned to death.
>
> (vv. 19–20, NJB)

The image of Yhwh leaning toward earth to see and hear the desperate cry of the people evokes memories of the exodus, when God "came down" to rescue the people from Egyptian oppression and to give them a future (Ex. 3:8).

Confidence in God

The plaintive voice of the individual returns in verse 23. The suppliant recognizes the transitory nature of life, a familiar theme of wisdom literature, but at the same time appeals to God not to cut the usual term of life in half.

The conclusion of the psalm is a faint echo of the chorus in vv.
12–22:

> Long ago you laid earth's foundations,
> the heavens are the work of your hands.
> They pass away but you remain;
> they all wear out like a garment,
> like outworn clothes you change them;
> but you never alter, and your years never end.
>
> (vv. 25–27, NJB)

Interestingly, it is not Yhwh's *hesed* which is called upon as the motive
for trust, but God's eternal nature. The appeal is to God's sense of justice and a commitment to the proper order of things, a wisdom theme.

Psalm 130: De Profundis (Out of the depths)

Another penitential psalm that deserves special attention is Psalm
130, in liturgical tradition designated by the opening Latin words *De
Profundis* ("Out of the depths"). As part of the penitential tradition it
was prayed for souls in purgatory. Here again we find the main elements of a lament:

Appeal to God in Distress (vv. 1–2)

The psalmist cries out of a situation of deep distress, here poetically
likened to being engulfed by the mythical waters of chaos (as in Ps.
69:2, 14–15). Commentators as early as Chrysostom associated this
perilous situation with despair. Despair was viewed as a severe threat
to salvation because it eliminated hope and trust in God. Preaching on
this psalm, the English bishop John Fisher warned his auditors that the
only way to fight despair is with "strong and steadfast hope in the great
mercy of almighty God."[10]

Trust in God's Saving Power (vv. 3–6)

The distress sensed in the depths of one's being is alienation from
God. This burden could be crushing, but God's forgiveness enables one
to stand erect and to hope for God's renewing word.

Witness of Praise to the Community (vv. 7–8)

Some think that these verses are a postscript, since there is a shift
from a personal confession to the community of Israel. The likelihood

is that here, as in other laments (e.g., Psalm 22), the suppliant, speaking out of experience, teaches the community what this divine grace means in a larger sense.

Since the title of this volume is based on the opening words of this psalm a special word of comment is appropriate. In the poet's speech, the word "depths" (see also Ps. 69:2, 13–15) reverberates with the mythical overtones of the abyss of watery chaos, the realm of the powers of confusion, darkness, and death that are arrayed against the sovereign power of God. The experience of the threat of death is sometimes described as sinking into deep waters, as in Jonah's prayer "out of the depths." (Jonah 2). To be drawn into the realm of chaos (the sphere of darkness and death) is to be separated from the world in which people praise God and find fulfillment in the worshiping community (see the discussion of death in chapter 7). In this instance, however, the poet uses the mythical language to speak about separation from God that results from human freedom (sin). Indeed, the distance between the Holy God and sinful humanity is so infinitely vast that if God were to keep account of iniquities, no one would have a leg to stand on (v. 3). The key sentences of the psalm are found toward the beginning:

> O LORD [Yhwh], if you kept track of sins, LORD, could
>   anyone stand?
> But with you there is forgiveness, so that you may be
>   revered.
>
> (vv. 3–4, BWA)

The psalmist goes on to say that it is this forgiving word for which one waits and hopes, like watchmen who wait through the long night hours for the dawn (v. 6).

But why should God's forgiveness arouse "reverence" (the Hebrew word means "fear")? Some may find this a strange, if not jarring, note in the psalm. The declaration, however, is consistent with the psalmist's sense of the holiness of God, before whose searching judgment no one can stand with an easy conscience. Divine forgiveness is not "cheap grace," as might be inferred from the jest of the dying poet Heinrich Heine, that "it is God's business to forgive." God's forgiveness is not something that comes necessarily or naturally. It is wrong to say that God forgives *because* that is what is expected of God or *because* something in the human situation merits it. Forgiveness is the expression of God's grace, of God's freedom to "be gracious to whom I will be gracious" and to "show mercy upon whom I will show mercy" (Ex. 33:19; see Rom. 9:15). God's forgiveness, then, is a wonderful gift, the appropriate response to which is wonder and praise.

The Paradox of Righteousness

The penitential psalms, taken as a whole, seem to stand out from, and even conflict with, other psalms in the Psalter. They agree on the fact that there is no human ground for *claiming* God's grace. Indeed, in one of the penitential psalms it is said that if God were to enter into judgment with a person, the case would be hopeless from the outset.

> Do not enter into judgment with your servant,
> for no one living is righteous before you!
> (Ps. 143:2, NRSV)

In the presence of God there is human equality because of the democracy of sin. High and low, rich and poor, wise and ignorant come together at the altar. The only ground for human appeal is the "righteousness" and the "faithfulness" of God (Ps. 51:1; 143:1; etc.). If this is true, then the "entrance liturgy" in Psalm 24 poses difficulties. If the requirements were taken absolutely ("clean hands," "pure heart," etc.), then no one would get into God's holy temple!

In some laments, however, the appeal to God is made on the basis of the "righteousness" of the suppliant. How are we to understand these petitions? For instance, one lament contains the appeal:

> Judge [vindicate] me, O LORD, according to my
> righteousness,
> and according to the integrity that is in me.
> (Ps. 7:8; also Ps. 26:1, NRSV)

Moreover, some laments, following traditional literary form, include protestations of innocence, as in the psalm just quoted (vv. 3–5). Indeed, in some instances this element is emphasized (e.g., Ps. 17:3–5; 18:20–24; 26:4–7; 59:3–4). We are reminded of Job, who, before he was overwhelmed by the voice out of the whirlwind, protested that he was innocent and that his record was essentially clean (Job 31). In the end, of course, Job came to realize that his vaunted innocence was no ground for judging God, the Creator whose ways transcend human comprehension.

Admittedly, we are now facing a theological problem that is difficult to resolve, especially in view of the fact that strict consistency cannot be expected in a book of worship that was composed over a long period of time and includes many theological voices. Nevertheless, the question ought to be explored of whether the psalms of "innocence" are in absolute conflict with the psalms of "penitence." As John Godsey concluded in his summary of Bonhoeffer's work on the psalms, "The notion that we can never suffer innocently so long as within us there still hides some kind of defect is a thoroughly unbiblical and demoralizing thought."[11] In facing this question we should divest ourselves of notions of righteousness that we have inherited from our culture, largely under Greek and Roman influence. Normally we assume that a "righteous" person is one who conforms to some legal or moral standard. Such a person is held to be righteous according to the law ("law" here being interpreted in terms of Greek *nomos* or Roman *lex*). Stated in other terms, people measure themselves or others by whether they live up to certain ideals or a particular code of behavior (see the caricatured portrayal of the Pharisee in Luke 18:9–14).

Another view of righteousness is illustrated in the story found in Genesis 15:1–6. In a lament (v. 2) Abraham complained that he (and the people of God) could not possibly have a future when he was without a son and the only legal heir was his household servant. How could God be true to the promise made earlier (Gen. 12:1–3; 13:1–17), when, humanly speaking, there was no possibility of fulfillment? The story goes that Abraham was led outside his tent, where he could view the heavens. With no other evidence than the myriad stars in the sky, Abraham was assured that his descendants would be as numerous as they. Then comes a crucial sentence:

> And [Abram] believed the LORD; and the LORD reckoned it
> to him as righteousness. (Gen. 15:6, NRSV)

This story shows what it means to be righteous in the sight of God (see also Gen. 6:9). Clearly Abraham's righteousness was not the achievement of moral perfection; that can hardly be said in view of the story in Genesis 12:10–20 that tells how his self-interest put his wife in jeopardy! Rather, the righteousness accounted to him was *being in right relationship* with God, as shown by his trust in God's promise even when there was no evidence to support it—none but the myriad stars in the sky! What made Abraham a whole person, a man of integrity, in the judgment of God was his loyal and trusting relationship, not the incidents that demonstrated that he was prone to error and subject to human weakness.

The passage in Genesis 15 asserts that righteousness was "accorded," "reckoned," or "granted" as a divine verdict. The language (the same Hebrew verb is used in Ps. 32:2) seems to reflect a cultic situation in which God deems a person to be "righteous," that is, to be in a loyal, trustful relationship. It may be that the psalms of righteousness also reflect a cultic situation, where this approval was granted to suppliants to enter the Temple. In any case, righteousness in this theological sense is a gift of grace, not a human achievement.

This view of righteousness, as something that one does not assert but is *given,* dominates the New Testament, especially the writings of the apostle Paul. Righteousness (or justification), according to Paul, is not something that a person achieves, but is a free gift that God grants to faithful persons through Jesus Christ. Therefore Paul stands before God "not having a righteousness of my own, based on law, but that which is through faith" (Phil. 3:9). In this view, Christians experience in their own way what members of the Israelite community experienced in worship: the divine recognition of righteousness or the right relationship of trust and dependence upon God, which amounts to salvation. The alternative attitude toward God was expressed by the "wicked," "the fools" who supposed they could live out of their own resources.

The strange thing is that it is "the righteous," "the pious," "the faithful," "the innocent" who pray the so-called penitential psalms. For it is only when people stand in a right relationship with God—that is, having a righteousness they cannot claim as a prerogative but that is graciously granted them in the relationship of the covenant—that they can assert their innocence and plead for God's forgiveness. "It is the righteous who confess their unrighteousness before God," writes Christoph Barth. "Only the godless man refuses to do this, because he regards himself as righteous." We are left, then, with the apparent paradox of "the righteousness of the sinner."[12]

God Who Is Inescapable: Psalm 139

So far we have neglected to find a proper place to treat Psalm 139, surely one of the most magnificent poems in the Psalter. The reason for this neglect is uncertainty about how to classify the psalm. It has elements of petition for help, trust in God's care, hymnic praise, plea of innocence. Tentatively we have listed it with laments (see chapter 4), in agreement with a number of scholars, but this classification may be challenged. Some regard it as a wisdom poem in praise of God (v. 14) who is mysteriously present in one's innermost self and inescapably present in the farthest reaches of the spatial world. Because the poem is the prayer of one who claims innocence and trusts God for vindication (see Psalm 9), it is appropriate to consider it here.

Strophe 1 (vv. 1–6)

The overarching theme, announced in the first strophe of the poem, is the inescapability of God (a theme also treated in Francis Thompson's magnificent poem, "The Hound of Heaven"[13]) In a personal I-Thou relation with God, there is no escape from the most intimate scrutiny. God who knows us in the depths of our being, knows us even better than we know ourselves.

> Lord, you have examined me and you know me.
> You know me at rest and in action;
> you discern my thoughts from afar.
> You trace my journeying and my resting-places,
> And are familiar with all the paths I take.
> For there is not a word that I speak
> but you, Lord, know all about it.
> You keep close guard behind and before me
> and place your hand upon me.
> Knowledge so wonderful is beyond my grasp;
> it is so lofty I cannot reach it.
>
> (vv. 1–6, REB)

There is something of the spirit of wisdom literature in this poetry; affinities with the book of Job are especially close. Job too was overwhelmed by God's inescapability. He complained that God hemmed him in and would not leave him alone long enough to catch his breath.

> What are human beings that you should take them so
> seriously,
> subjecting them to your scrutiny,
> that morning after morning you should examine them
> and at every instant test them?
> Will you never take your eyes off me
> long enough for me to swallow my spittle?
>
> (Job 7:17–19, NJB)

In Psalm 139 the poet also feels that he or she is entrapped by God: "You hem me in, behind and before" (v. 5).

Strophe 2 (vv. 7–12)

With all earthly escape routes cut off, the poet contemplates fleeing into space, perhaps taking "the wings of the dawn"—a beautiful metaphor for traveling as fast as the light of dawn spreads across the sky.

> Where shall I go to escape your spirit?
> Where shall I flee from your presence:
> If I scale the heavens you are there,
> if I lie flat in Sheol, there you are.
>
> If I speed away on the wings of the dawn,
> if I dwell beyond the ocean,
> even there your hand will be guiding me,
> your right hand holding me fast.
>
> (vv. 7–10, NJB)

There is no hiding place from God in heaven above or earth below!

Strophe 3 (vv. 13–18)

In the next strophe the poet reverts to the theme of the opening strophe: the self is known completely by God, who formed the person in the mother's womb. Here we find a rare reflection on the mysterious development of the embryo in the womb into a person enrolled in the covenant community, prompting the poet to break out into praise of God, the creator.

> I praise you, for you fill me with awe;
> wonderful you are, and wonderful your works.
> You know me through and through:
> my body was no mystery to you,
> when I was formed in secret,
> woven in the depths of the earth.*

---

* A reference to the mother's womb, perhaps influenced by the story of God's creation of human beings from the dust (Gen. 2:7).

> Your eyes foresaw my deeds,
> and they were all recorded in your book;†
> my life was fashioned
> before it had come into being.
>
> (vv. 14–16, REB)

Here the omniscience and omnipresence of God are not doctrines about God, as in systematic theology, but express the existential awareness that because God is "my God"—in personal relationship—God sees and knows everything about my (your) life. The language has affinities with Paul's poetic description of the "knowledge" given in a relationship of love: "now I know only in part, then I will know fully, even as I have been fully known" (1 Cor. 13:12).

Strophe 4 (vv. 19–24)

The last strophe begins with a note so jarring that often the offensive verses (vv. 19–22) are omitted in reading. The psalmist fiercely attacks those who display enmity toward God, "those who speak of you maliciously, and lift themselves up against you for evil." His passion against these "wicked" or "bloodthirsty" people knows no bounds.

> How I hate those who hate you, LORD!
> I loathe those who defy you;
> I hate them with undying hatred;
> I reckon them my own enemies.
>
> (vv. 21–22, REB)

This harsh language seems to mar the beauty of the psalm, to say nothing of clashing with the teaching of the Sermon on the Mount about loving one's enemies (Matt. 5:43–44).

Notice, however, that in this case the enemies are not explicitly identified as the poet's persecutors; rather, they are those sinners who are hostile to God and who evoke God's judgment. To be sure, this view of the enemies introduces new problems; many have been burned at the stake or have suffered other forms of punishment because they were adjudged to be enemies of God and hence of the community of faith (i.e.,

---

† God's "book" is the register of the members of the covenant community (Ex. 33; Ps. 69:28; Isa. 4:3).

heretics). But at least the psalmist does not base his prayer to God on a personal grudge.

Moreover, this prayer is an appeal to God, the highest judge who is not limited by human judgments. The psalm seems to reflect the situation of a person who is unjustly accused of a false way of life and who appeals to God for justification, that is, for being put in the right and therefore vindicated. A similar situation is reflected in Psalm 26:

> Vindicate me, O LORD,
>> for I have walked without blame;
>> I have trusted in the LORD;
>> I have not faltered.
> Probe me, O LORD, and try me,
>> test my heart and mind;
>> for my eyes are on Your steadfast love;
>> I have set my course by it.
>> (Ps. 26:1–3, NJPS)

When one cannot get a fair hearing in the law courts or before the bar of public opinion, where else can one turn except to the highest tribunal—to the God who probes and knows each person inwardly? Many people, especially oppressed minorities or the helpless poor, find themselves in this situation today.

This is why the psalmist, at the climax of the prayer, breaks out into passionate hatred of God's enemies who are counted as his or her enemies too. These faceless enemies, apparently, are impugning the person's integrity with false accusations and therefore undercutting the person's place in the community of faith. For this poet the inescapability of God, the God who "hounds" one "down the nights and down the days" (Francis Thompson), is the ground of confidence and trust. To be sure, one must be honest with God, for any cover-up or deceit will be exposed in the light of God's inescapable judgment. Confident of God's fairness, however, the poet submits to the judgment and mercy of God, and—echoing the initial appeal (v. 1)—asks for a favorable sentence.

> Examine me, God, and know my mind;
> test me, and understand my anxious thoughts.
> Watch lest I follow any path that grieves you;
> lead me in the everlasting way.
>> (vv. 23–24, REB)

Probably the last words should be translated "the ancient way" or "ancient paths," as in a passage from the book of Jeremiah:

> These are the words of the Lord: Take your stand and watch at the crossroads; enquire about the ancient paths; ask which is the way that leads to what is good. Take that way, and you will find rest for yourselves. (Jer. 6:16, REB)

Here the psalmist appeals to a faith rooted in Israel's tradition, to the "faith of our ancestors," to recall the well-known hymn, "Faith of Our Fathers."

6

Singing a New Song

Orientation toward the future was characteristic of Israel's faith from the very first. Unlike the Canaanites, whose religion tended to bind people to particular places, the God of Israel led people into the future—like a shepherd who guides the flock into unexpected trails and new pastures, to recall the imagery of the well-known Twenty-third Psalm as well as Psalm 100:3, "we are his, his own people, the flock which he shepherds." In the Old Testament we do not find a nostalgia for the past or a settling down in the present, but a movement toward the future.

This movement from the past through the present to the future is portrayed dynamically in the psalms of lament considered in the last two chapters. In psalms of this type, poets remember the past and the wonderful demonstrations of God's saving power. This retrospective view, however, only heightens the spiritual problem of the present, when in the time of "the eclipse of God" the people find it difficult, if not impossible, to live by the faith of their parents.

Waiting for God

A keynote in psalms of lament is "waiting for God."

> Wait for the LORD;
>> be strong and let your heart take courage;
> wait for the LORD!
>> (Ps. 27:14, NRSV)

This waiting, however, does not have the ambiguity and despair portrayed in Samuel Beckett's play *Waiting for Godot.* The psalmists wait

97

for the God known by the personal name Yhwh, whose presence in history was manifest in the past and whose presence would be revealed again on the horizon of the future. In these contexts, the verb "wait" expresses a straining toward the future, a keen anticipation of what is to come. Hope is waiting with one's whole being for the dawn, when the recreating word of God's forgiveness will be spoken (Ps. 130:5–6); it is waiting eagerly for the Redeemer King to come with saving power (Isa. 40:10–11, 30–31). Thus the psalms of lament move "from hurt to joy, from death to life."[1]

> But those who wait for the LORD shall renew their strength,
>   they shall mount up with wings like eagles,
> they shall run and not be weary,
>   they shall walk and not faint.
>
> (Isa. 40:31, NRSV)

Songs of Thanksgiving

Before we consider the form and content of the type of psalm called a song of thanksgiving, a word should be said about its relationship to the lament, on the one hand, and to the hymn of praise on the other. As we have seen in previous chapters (4 and 5), the lament almost invariably moves from the minor mode of complaint or penitence to the major key of thanksgiving and praise (see chapter 4). In the certainty of being heard by God, the suppliant—whether the community or the individual—looks forward to God's deliverance from a situation of limitation or distress, and, in anticipation of God's gracious action, the lament characteristically ends with a vow of praise (Ps. 7:17; 13:6; 22:22–31; 56:12–13; etc.). Thus the lament in Psalm 57 concludes with a song of thanksgiving:

> I have decided, O God,*
> my decision is firm:
> to you I will sing my praise.
> Awake, my soul, to song!
> Awake, my harp and lyre,
> so I can wake up the dawn!

---

* Here editors have substituted the general name for deity (Elohim) for the personal name of address, Yhwh. The psalm belongs to the Elohistic Psalter (Psalms 42–83).

I will lift my voice in praise,
sing of you, LORD, to all nations.
For your love reaches heaven's edge,
your unfailing love, the skies.
O God,* rise high above the heavens!
Spread your glory across the earth!

(vv. 8–11, ICEL)

This abrupt change of mood in the laments, to which Hermann
Gunkel once called attention, is quite striking. It is doubtful whether it
can be explained solely on the basis of the psalmist's inner certainty.
More likely, the transition from sorrow to rejoicing, from lament to
thanksgiving, was occasioned by something that occurred in the setting
of worship within which these psalms had their final place. There is
reason to believe that at a certain moment in the service, a member of
the Temple personnel, a priest or perhaps a prophet, pronounced an
"oracle of salvation" that assured the suppliant of God's grace and favor. None of these oracles has been preserved, but now and then we
find hints that they were spoken. For instance, at one point in Psalm 85,
it seems that an oracle of salvation, for which a suppliant listens, is
summarized:

Let me hear what God, the LORD, will speak;
He will promise well-being to His people,
His faithful ones;
may they not turn to folly.
His help is very near those who fear Him,
to make His glory dwell in our land.

(vv. 9–10, NJPS)

Other indications of priestly oracles are possibly found in such passages as Psalm 12:5; 55:22; 91:14–16; 121:3–5.

Thus it was the word of God, mediated through the service of worship, that modulated the tone of a suppliant's prayer from lament to rejoicing. We may assume that in Psalm 28, for instance, at the conclusion of the lament (vv. 1–5), a minister delivered words of assurance,
to which the suppliant then responded in grateful praise:

Praise be to the LORD,
for he has heard my cry for mercy.

> The LORD is my strength and my shield;
>   my heart trusts in him, and I am helped.
> My heart leaps for joy
>   and I will give thanks to him in song.
>
> (vv. 6–7, NIV)

This cultic situation reminds one of Christian services of worship in which the liturgical sequence is: confession of sin and need, words of assurance or absolution, and then a doxology or other act of praise.

It can be seen, then, that a very close relationship exists between the lament and the thanksgiving. Indeed, the "song of thanksgiving" is an expanded form of the thanksgiving already present in many of the laments (Psalms 6; 13; 22; 28; 31; 55; 69; 71; 86; etc.). However, it is one thing to praise God in anticipation of deliverance or on the basis of an assurance given in worship; it is another thing to praise God *in response* to an event of deliverance already experienced. It is the latter accent that characterizes the songs of thanksgiving. These songs are sung by people who, after a time of patient waiting (see Ps. 27:13–14: a lament), have experienced the goodness of God in the everyday world.

> Taste and see that Yahweh is good.
> How blessed are those who take refuge in him.
>
> (Ps. 34:8, NJB)

Looking in another direction, we see that the songs of thanksgiving are also closely related to hymns of praise (see chapter 7). The English reader is apt to think that all psalms that begin with an invocation to "give thanks" to God must be thanksgivings. But this is not necessarily so, for the Hebrew verb *hodah* cannot be limited to the meaning of our word "to thank"; it has the wider connotation of "acknowledge," "confess," "proclaim," and therefore is often used in parallel with verbs meaning "praise," as in the hymn:

> Come within his gates giving thanks [*todah*],
> to his courts singing praise [*tehilah*],
> give thanks [*hodu*] to him and bless [*barak*] his name!
> For Yahweh is good,
> his faithful love [*hesed*] is everlasting,
> his constancy from age to age.
>
> (Ps. 100:4–5, NJB)

Therefore we are really dealing with two ways of praising God, which can be distinguished from each other only by the form and content of the psalm. In one case, the psalmist praises God in general terms, extolling the God whose name is majestic in heaven and earth, whose sovereign might rules human history (e.g., Psalms 8; 33). This is the hymn. In the other case, the psalmist praises God for particular action in a concrete situation of limitation and distress. This specific praise is what we mean by the song of thanksgiving. It must be admitted, however, that sometimes the line between the hymn and the song of thanksgiving cannot be drawn sharply. For instance, the beautiful prayer found in Psalm 103 (to be considered later) is sometimes regarded as a song of thanksgiving and sometimes as a hymn. And Psalm 100, a hymn, is labeled "A psalm for the thank offering [*todah*]" in the superscription.

Psalms of Thanksgiving

The songs of thanksgiving, like the laments, may be divided into songs of the community and songs of the individual. Sometimes, however, this division is uncertain, since the first person pronoun "I" may be used in both.

Community Songs of Thanksgiving

The community songs of thanksgiving are relatively few in number, and even these come close to being hymns. Perhaps the reason for this is that in corporate praise, which transcends the situation of individuals, the community tends to use the form of the hymn that extols God's saving power in broader terms, such as the mighty acts of God in history or the display of God's providential care in creation. In any case, the community songs of thanksgiving were used in the major festivals at the Temple, such as the great fall harvest festival of ingathering (see chapter 8). This type of psalm is found in the following places.

Community Songs of Thanksgiving

65	"Thou crownest the year with thy bounty" (this may be regarded as a hymn)
67	"The earth has yielded its increase" (this may be regarded as a hymn)
75	"We recount thy wondrous deeds" (classification uncertain; possibly a liturgy)

*107	"Let them tell of his deeds in songs of joy!"
*124	"The snare is broken and we have escaped!"
136	"His steadfast love endures forever!" (this litany
	may be regarded as a hymn)

Other songs of thanksgiving are found outside the Psalter, notably the Song of Hannah in 1 Samuel 2:1–10.

Individual Songs of Thanksgiving

The individual songs of thanksgiving were composed for recitation at the Temple as an expression of a person's praise to God for deliverance from a situation of distress, such as illness. In that situation the individual "acknowledges" or "testifies" (the meaning of the Hebrew verb *hodah*) that God has acted in a particular situation in life. Since the noun usually translated "thanksgiving" (*todah*) is the same word used for "thank offering" (Jonah 2:9; Ps. 50:14, 23), it is clear that these psalms were appropriately used in a cultic setting, that is, at a festival or other worship service at the Temple. On such an occasion the individual, in the presence of the worshiping congregation (Ps. 22:22; 26:12b), testified personally to God's saving deeds to the accompaniment of a ritual act (a thank offering). This is the picture given in a passage in Jeremiah, which announces that in the time of restoration the voices of mirth and gladness will be heard once again, including "the voices of those who sing, as they bring thank offerings [*todah*] to the house of Yhwh":

> Give thanks [testify] to the LORD [Yhwh] of hosts,
>   for the LORD [Yhwh] is good,
> God's faithfulness endures forever!
>   (Jer. 33:11, BWA)

In this manner the individual confesses out of personal experience the faith of the whole believing community, whose shared history is a witness to the saving deeds of the Lord.

Individual Songs of Thanksgiving

18	"With the loyal thou dost show thyself loyal"
	(a royal thanksgiving)
21	"In thy strength the king rejoices" (a royal

	thanksgiving, paired with Psalm 20: prayer for the king's victory)
30	"Thou hast turned my mourning into dancing"
*32	"Thou dost encompass me with deliverance" (one of the penitential psalms)
*34	"Look to God, and be radiant!" (this alphabetic acrostic is possibly a wisdom psalm)
40:1–11	"He put a new song in my mouth" (the second part of the psalm is a lament)
66:13–20	"I will tell what God has done for me" (the first part of the psalm is a hymn)
*92	"At the work of thy hands I sing for joy"
*103	"Forget not all God's benefits" (probably to be classified as a hymn, discussed below)
108	"Awake, O harp and lyre!" (a mixed type, composed of Ps. 57:7–11 [thanksgiving] and Ps. 60:5–12 [lament])
*116	"I will lift up the cup of salvation"
*118	"This is the day which the Lord has made" (a liturgy of royal thanksgiving)
*138	"On the day I called, thou didst answer me"

Individual songs of thanksgiving are also found in Isaiah 38:9–20 and Jonah 2:2–9.

Notice that in this list, three of the psalms are designated as royal thanksgivings. In these the reigning monarch ("the anointed one" in Hebrew, the word equivalent to "messiah") speaks not just as an individual but as the representative of the people. This is the case in Psalm 118 (Luther's favorite psalm) which is often quoted in the New Testament (see appendix C). The king's song of thanksgiving in vv. 5–21 is offered in a cultic situation, as evidenced by the request for admission through the Temple gates so that he may give thanks (v. 19), the choral blessing from the Temple (v. 26), and the solemn festal procession to the altar (v. 27). Thus the worshiping community takes part in the thanksgiving and identifies itself with the king's testimony to the saving power of God.

It is not surprising that this royal psalm that belonged so deeply to Israel's worship was eventually taken to refer to "the one who is to come," *the* Anointed One (Messiah), as happens in the New Testament. In the larger context of the Christian Bible the central image of Psalm

118—the stone, rejected by the builders, that has become the chief cornerstone (vv. 22–25)—is identified with Jesus Christ, the "King," whom God has exalted from rejection and humiliation to a lofty place of honor in the divine administration (Matt. 21:42; Acts 4:11;1 Peter 2:7). And since in every Christian worship service the community celebrates God's triumph in Christ with praise and thanks, it is appropriate for the liturgist to say on "the Lord's Day" (Sunday, the day of resurrection):

> This is the day that the LORD has made;
>   let us rejoice and be glad in it!
>   (Ps. 118:24, NRSV)

The Structure of the Song of Thanksgiving

The song of thanksgiving is cast in a form that, allowing for variations, may be traced quite clearly in the songs of the individual.

Introduction

Some indication is given of the worshiper's intention to give thanks to God. The opening invocation, which may be short or omitted altogether, is usually made to Yhwh in the second person, as in Psalm 30, for example.

> I will exalt you, O LORD,
>   for you lifted me out of the depths
>   and did not let my enemies gloat over me.
> O LORD my God, I called to you for help
>   and you healed me.
>   (vv. 1–2, NIV)

The poet lingers on this note of praise, recalling a personal experience of being delivered from distress.

> O you faithful of the LORD, sing to Him,
>   and praise His holy name.
> For He is angry but a moment,
>   and when He is pleased there is life.
> One may lie down weeping at nightfall;
>   but at dawn there are shouts of joy.
>   (vv. 5–6, NJPS)

Main Section: Narration of the Psalmist's Experience

1. Portrayal of the distress that the suppliant once experienced. In Psalm 30 a past sickness unto death is only mentioned briefly (vv. 4, 9); in other psalms the distress is described at length.

2. The suppliant's cry for help is expressed in powerful language in Psalm 30:8–10. He remembers how he cried out passionately:

> Hear, O LORD, and have mercy on me;
> O LORD, be my help!
> (vv. 10 [11], NJPS)

3. The deliverance from trouble.

> You turned my lament into dancing,
> you undid my sackcloth and girded me with joy,
> that [my] whole being might sing hymns to You
> endlessly;
> O LORD my God, I will praise You forever.
> (vv. 11–12 [12–13], NJPS)

Conclusion

Striking the same note as heard in the beginning, the worshiper offers praise out of experience for God's restoring and renewing grace (Ps. 30:12). Some psalms end with a prayer for future help, a confession that the Lord is gracious, or some other expression of gratitude.

Jonah's Psalm

A good example to guide us in the study of the psalms marked with an asterisk in the above list is the psalm of thanksgiving that has been inserted into the story of Jonah. We say "inserted" because the psalm is obviously out of place in its present context. In the belly of a "fish" a cry for help (i.e., a lament) would be appropriate, but not a thanksgiving for deliverance already experienced!

Introduction: A Summary of the Testimony of the Psalmist (Jonah 2:2)

The worshiper remembers a time of distress:

> In my trouble I called to the LORD,
> And He answered me;

> From the belly of Sheol* I cried out,
> And You heard my voice.

Main Section

1. Portrayal of Affliction (Jonah 2:3–6a). Using mythical language the poet describes the experience of dying as sinking down, down into the subterranean waters of chaos, to the realm of death.[2]

> You cast me into the depths,
> Into the heart of the sea,
> The floods engulfed me;
> All Your breakers and billows
> Swept over me.

Death, to this poet, means separation from God, whose presence is known in the Temple where people gather for worship.

> I thought I was driven away
> Out of Your sight:
> Would I ever gaze again
> Upon Your holy Temple?
> The waters closed in over me,
> The deep engulfed me.
> Weeds twined around my head.
> I sank to the base of the mountains;
> The bars of the earth closed upon me forever.

2. Cry for Help and Answer (Jonah 2:6b–7). The poet recalls God's saving activity in response to his distress.

> Yet You brought my life up from the pit,
> O Lord my God!
> When my life was ebbing away,
> I called the Lord to mind;
> And my prayer came before You,
> Into Your holy Temple.

3. Deliverance from Trouble. This motif is found at the preface to the petition: "Yet you brought my life up from the pit."

---

* The mythical region of darkness and death.

Conclusion: Acknowledgment of God's Gracious Act and Promise to Present a Thank Offering (Jonah 2:8–9)

> They who cling to empty folly [idols]
> Forsake their own welfare,
> But I, with loud thanksgiving [*todah*],
> Will sacrifice to You;
> What I have vowed I will perform.
> Deliverance is the LORD's!
>
> (NJPS)

The example from the book of Jonah shows that a song of thanksgiving looks back to a former time when a suppliant, in a situation of distress, cried to Yhwh for help. That situation, however, no longer prevails. The interim of God's absence, reflected in psalms of lament, has ended. In response to a cry out of the depths, Yhwh has graciously acted. Once again God has "shown his face" (presence) and this new situation in life calls for the singing of "a new song."

> I waited and waited for God.
> At long last God bent down
> to hear my complaint,
> and pulled me from the grave
> out of the swamp,
> and gave me a steady stride
> on rock-solid ground.
> God taught me a new song,
> a hymn of praise.
> Seeing all this,
> many will be moved
> to trust in the LORD.
>
> (Ps. 40:1–3, ICEL)

Eucharistic Praise

It is noteworthy that these songs of thanksgiving retained their basic form even after they were detached from their cultic setting and became "spiritual songs." This is evidenced in the songs of thanksgiving found among the Dead Sea scriptures, to which we referred in chapter 1. These songs characteristically begin with the testimony "I thank thee." Then follows an address to the Deity; this in turn is followed by a clause, introduced by the motive word *ki* (usually translated "for" or "that"), that gives the specific reason for offering thanks to God.[3] This thanksgiving genre, which was current in the Judaism out of which Christianity emerged, came to be prominent in the New Testament eucharistic tradition. ("Eucharist" comes from a Greek verb meaning "to thank.") The epistle to the Ephesians contains this advice to the Christian community:

> Instead, be filled with the Spirit. Speak to one another with psalms, hymns and spiritual songs. Sing and make music in your heart to the Lord, always giving thanks to God the Father for everything, in the name of our Lord Jesus Christ. (Eph. 5:18b–20, NIV)

Lifting the Cup of Salvation

Psalm 116 is an excellent example of the eucharistic poem called the "song of thanksgiving." In view of its significance in Christian tradition, it deserves special attention.

Introduction (Ps. 116:1–2)

The psalmist begins by ascribing praise to the Lord and giving the motive for praise.

Retrospect (Ps. 116:3–9)

1. The poet then recalls the past experience of being in deep trouble and his cry for help. In a time of distress, when the power of death almost prevailed, the suppliant appealed to God for help and received an answer (v. 3–4).

2. At this point, the poet declares his trust in God (vv. 5–7).

3. Divine Answer. This section concludes with a testimony to the wonderful grace that restored the suppliant's being:

> He has rescued me from death, my eyes from tears,
>   and my feet from stumbling.
> I shall pass my life in the presence of Yahweh,
>   in the land of the living.
>
> (vv. 8–9, NJB)

Conclusion: Vow of Praise (Ps. 116:10–19)

Finally, in gratitude for God's gracious action the suppliant lifts a libation in the presence of the worshiping community as testimony to the divine grace that supports all the people:

> What shall I give back to Yhwh
> for all God's bounty to me?
> The cup of salvation I'll lift,
> and call on the name of Yhwh.
> My vows to God I will complete
> here in the presence of all God's people.
>   (vv. 12–14, BWA)

A votive offering in the form of lifting "the cup of salvation" may be only a metaphor in this psalm, but at one time it was a cultic act, on which archaeology has shed some light. (See illustration on p. 110) Otto Eissfeldt draws our attention to a Phoenician votive stele (upright stone) from the fifth century B.C. that belonged to Yehawmilk, king of Byblos. The text is addressed to the goddess Ba'alat, the female counterpart of the great storm god Baal:

> Yehawmilk, king of Byblos, to my Lady, Ba'alat of Byblos. For when I cried to my lady, Ba'alat of Byblos, then she heard me and showed me favor.

Interestingly, there is a picture above the inscription that shows the king standing before the goddess, who is seated on her throne. In his hand he holds a libation cup, which he lifts up to her. Thus the acknowledgment of thanks and the thank offering are combined in this votive stele, precisely as they are combined in the psalms.[4] Here again we have evidence that Israelite worship was influenced by ancient forms of worship, though these forms were transformed to express Israel's distinctive faith. Indeed, this thanksgiving rite of "lifting the cup" has survived in both Jewish and Christian liturgy. Paul, for instance, refers to "the cup of blessing" in a discussion of the Lord's Supper (1 Cor. 10:16).

Deliverance from the Power of Death

One passage in Psalm 116 deserves special attention. This passage provided the motif for Bach's chorale, "Christ lag in Todesbänden"

A king presenting a libation cup before a goddess

*From a Phoenician votive stele, fifth century B.C. See J. B. Pritchard, The Ancient Near East in Pictures Relating to the Old Testament (No. 377). Illustration after the original: Joan Anderson. *

("Christ lay in the bonds of death"). Here an affirmative view of life is linked with a realistic view of death.

> The cords of death bound me,
> Sheol held me in its grip.
> Anguish and torment held me fast;
> then I invoked the Lord by name,
> "Lord, deliver me, I pray."
> (vv. 3–4, REB)

The view of life and death presupposed in the psalms is quite different from modern conceptions. Most people think of a death as a biological event that occurs when the heart stops beating and consciousness goes out like a light. Death, according to this generally accepted notion, comes *at the end of life*. This terminus is often recognized with a mixture of melancholy and sentimentality in the ritual of the funeral service, especially funerals that are taken out of the context of the worshiping congregation and handed over to the funeral home.

The psalms are suffused with an awareness of the brevity and frailty of human life (e.g., Ps. 90:3–10; 103:14–16). But what strikes us most is the psalmists' view that death works its power in us *now,* during our historical experience. According to the Israelite view, death brings about "a decrease in the vitality of the individual."[5] Death's power is felt in the midst of life to the degree that one experiences any weakening of personal vitality through illness, handicap, imprisonment, attack from enemies, or advancing old age. Any threat to a person's welfare (Hebrew, *shalom*), that is, one's freedom to be and to participate in the covenant community, is understood as an invasion of the empire of death into the historical arena.

This reference to death's imperialism, its territorial ambition to encroach into "the land of the living," calls for further consideration. The psalmists' portrayals of the threat of death are couched in a pictorial, mythical language expressive of a way of thinking that, at first glance, seems alien to our experience. Israel inherited a picture of the universe that depicted the world as surrounded on every hand by "the waters of chaos" which, at the time of creation, the Creator subdued and pushed back in order to give creatures space in which to live and to perform their God-given tasks. The earth is portrayed as a kind of island, suspended over the waters of the "deep," within which is located Sheol, the kingdom of death. Beyond the great blue dome overhead are the waters of the heavenly ocean which, unless held back by the protective barrier of the firmament, would flood the world with chaos (as almost happened, according to the Flood story in Genesis 6–9). It is wrong to convert this pictorial view into a prescientific three-storied conception of the universe, as has happened in some modern discussions of the Bible. In the psalms this language is used religiously or poetically to express the awareness that on all sides the historical world is threatened by powers of chaos that, were they not held back by the Creator, would engulf the earth and reduce existence to meaningless confusion. The earth is not self-sustaining, but is contingent, dependent upon God. As John Calvin put it, "If God should but withdraw His hand a little, all things would immediately perish and dissolve into nothing."[6]

This helps us to understand the many references in the Psalter to coming into deep waters, to the engulfing waves and billows, or to the "descent into hell" (Sheol, the Pit, Abaddon ["the place of destruction"]). In the psalm of Jonah, as we have noticed, the suppliant cries

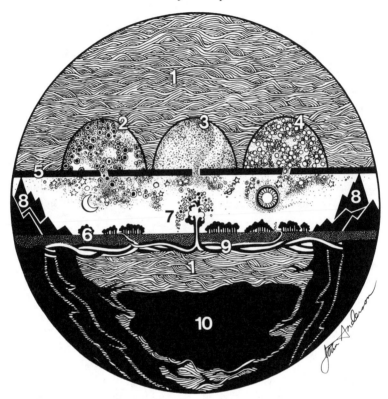

The Ancient Pictorial View of the Universe

1. The waters above and below the earth
2, 3, 4. Chambers of hail, rain, snow
5. The firmament with its "sluices"
6. Surface of the earth
7. The navel of the earth: "fountain of the Great Deep"
8. The mountain–pillars supporting the firmament
9. Sweet waters (rivers, lakes) on which the earth floats
10. Sheol, the realm of Death (the "Pit")

to Yhwh "out of the depths." Using poetic imagery he says that he has been "cast into the deep," that the waves and billows have gone over him, and that he has plunged, like a drowning man, down to the very roots of the mountains. The same imagery is found in the royal thanksgiving, Psalm 18 (see v. 4–6). In the latter psalm, however, the divine rescue is vividly described in terms of mythical language appropriated from the Canaanites. Yhwh is portrayed as the Divine Warrior who, in an awe-inspiring theophany of thunderstorm (vv. 7–15; cf. Ps. 29:3–9), comes to battle with the waters of chaos (the mythical sea) and drives them back to their place.

> He reached down from on high, snatched me up,
> pulled me from the watery depths,
> rescued me from my mighty foe,
> from my enemies who were stronger than I.
>
> They assailed me on my day of disaster
> but Yahweh was there to support me;
> he freed me, set me at large,
> he rescued me because he loves me.
> (Ps. 18:16–19, NJB)

Here we see how the historical enemies of the king, especially in Davidic society, are associated with the powers of chaos that threaten God's creation (see also Ps. 144:1–11).[7] Deliverance from social chaos and divisive conflict, especially when it means overcoming oppression and social injustice, is understood to be God's creative, redemptive work.

Death as a Hostile Power

In the Canaanite mythology that has profoundly influenced these portrayals, Death (Mot) was regarded as a god in his own right—the powerful king of the underworld. According to Ugaritic mythological literature from about 1400 B.C., Mot seeks to extend his kingdom over the earth and thereby challenges the authority of El, the father of the gods. However, the youthful storm-god, known as Aleyn Baal, takes up the challenge and wins a great victory over Mot, whereupon Baal is acclaimed king. The conquest of death is not decisive, however; it has to be repeated every year as the cycle of the seasons moves from the barrenness of winter to the renewal of fertility in the spring, from death to resurrection.

When confronting the Baal religion that dominated Canaan, Israelite spokepersons challenged the view that the meaning of human existence is given in the rhythms of nature. Characteristically, Israelite poets and storytellers proclaimed God's historical actions in decisive, nonrecurring events (chiefly the exodus) that called the people Israel into being and guided them in their historical journey. However, Israelites appropriated the old mythical language and reinterpreted it to express, on the one hand, experiences of God's blessings manifest in the seasonal cycles of nature and, on the other, the threat of forces of chaos that call into question the goodness of life.

In the psalms, death is a power (though no longer a deity) that reaches out greedily to lay hold of the living, a deposed king whose shadowy kingdom encroaches upon the historical world, an enemy that stands in opposition to the purpose of God. The psalmists testify that it is only God who can save one from the power of Death—in the language of Paul, "the last enemy to be destroyed."[8]

In the psalms this struggle against the encroachment of death into the historical world is never resolved by a clear and unambiguous expression of belief in a future life. Indeed, when we read in English translation the affirmation, "Thou hast delivered my soul from death" (Ps. 116:8), we must guard against reading into the word "soul" the notion of an element within the body that by nature is deathless and indestructible. The Greek doctrine of the immortality or deathlessness of the soul is not attested in the Old Testament or, for that matter, even in the New Testament.[9] Only God is essentially immortal (1 Tim. 6:16); *'adam* ("human being") is a mortal who, as the story in Genesis 2 puts it, is made "from the ground" and "returns to the ground." The word translated "soul" (Hebrew, *nefesh*) means "self" or "person" as a psychosomatic unity. If the self has a future, as indeed the New Testament emphatically proclaims, God will—in a marvelous way, past our comprehension—raise it and give it a new "body," a new form of existence. The "resurrection of the body" (i.e., the self) is attested in Paul's great discussion in 1 Corinthians 15, and of course is basic to the church's creedal affirmation: "I believe in the resurrection of the body [not "flesh"] and the life everlasting." This Christian view, however, is not found in the Psalter, though there may be intimations of a future life here and there.[10]

"You Restore My Soul [Self]"

What, then, is the concern of the psalmists when they give thanks to God for delivering them from the power of death, as in Psalm 23: "you restore my soul [self]"? Certainly they are not just glad to regain physical health, or to add more years to their life, or to enhance the life they now enjoy with greater comfort or security. That is a modern conception of life, the emptiness of which is inevitably disclosed. According to Israel's way of thinking, life is missed when people do not *choose* it (see Deut. 30:15–20 with its alternative: "See, I have set before you life and death. . . . Therefore choose life!"). Moreover, the life of "the righteous" is eroded in vitality when death works its power. As Christoph Barth observes, what the psalmists pray for in laments, or thank God for in thanksgiving is "the restoration of life that they have lost" or "its radical *renewal* through true life"—that is, the life that is given through relationship to God in the covenant community.[11] For the psalmists, the tragedy of death is that it transposes people into another, nonhistorical realm where they can no longer praise God and experience God's presence in the temple.

> Who among the dead celebrates
> > Your miracles? Do shadows rise
> > > to praise You?
> Do those in the Grave speak
> > of Your kindness? Is Your love proclaimed
> > > in Ruin?
> Are Your wonders declared in Darkness?
> > Is Your justice announced in the Land
> > > of Forget?
> > > > (Ps. 88:10–12, SB; also Ps. 6:5)

When a person is separated from a community of people who remember and celebrate the goodness of God, life ebbs to the vanishing point. But when a person is restored to a meaningful place in the believing and worshiping community, when one's relationship to God and fellow human beings is renewed, then it is possible for life to begin again and for the person to join in the singing of praises with the whole being (*nefesh*). The Germans have a nice way of expressing what it means for the individual to be restored to life in community: *Leben ist loben* ("To live is to praise").*

---

* See my chapter in *Contours of Old Testament Theology*, "Life, Death, and Resurrection."

Crowned with Love and Mercy

The theological perspective on life in relationship to God may be seen by turning to Psalm 103, "one of the finest blossoms on the tree of biblical faith" (Artur Weiser). As pointed out previously, there is uncertainty about the classification of this psalm. Often it is regarded as a "thanksgiving for recovery from sickness" (as in *The New Oxford Annotated Bible*).[12] On the other hand, one could argue that the psalm is a hymn because of its lack of reference to a concrete life situation and its general expression of praise. Probably we have here a song that wells up from an individual's thanksgiving for healing and expands into hymnic praise.[13] In any case, the psalm provides an excellent transition from the songs of thanksgiving considered in this chapter to the hymns of praise to be considered in the next.

The psalm falls into three parts, on the scheme of concentric circles—dealing with the self, the community, and the cosmos, respectively. The starting point (the inner circle) is the life story of an individual, and from this point the poet's thought expands to the farthest reaches of the cosmos. In this first part (Ps. 103:3–5), the poem exuberantly discloses that the poet's life story is the sphere of God's saving activity. Indeed, the *nefesh* (self, being) is addressed as "you" and is summoned to thank God, who "forgives all *your* iniquities," who "heals all *your* diseases," who "redeems *your* life from the Pit [Sheol]," who "crowns *you* with *hesed* and mercy," who revitalizes *you* with vigor like that of the proverbial eagle. This personal language seems to suggest that the psalmist's praise arises out of thanksgiving.

In the second part (vv. 6–18), the psalmist's thought expands outward to the community with which the psalmist is identified, as evidenced by the grammatical shift from singular pronouns to plural ("us," "our"). The same amazing grace (*hesed*) has been evident in Israel's history, right back to the beginning when Yhwh "made known his ways to Moses, his acts to the people of Israel" (Ex. 33:12–33; 34:8), by taking the side of the oppressed.

In the third part (vv. 19–22), the psalmist's praise ascends above individual and social experience to the cosmos, over which God is enthroned in transcendent majesty. Every creature in heaven and earth is summoned to join in the anthem, which originates in the life of a solitary person. With literary artistry, the psalm is rounded off at the end by returning to the note sounded in the beginning: "Bless [praise] Yhwh, my whole being."

Psalm 103 is like a jewel that glistens from various angles. Notice how, in this case, the self is related to the drama of Israel's history.

Standing within the community whose tradition reaches back to Moses, an individual testifies out of personal experience to the same divine grace that has supported the people as a whole. In this sense, the psalm is related to the storytelling psalms considered in chapter 3.

God's Pity for Human Weakness

One of the striking aspects of Psalm 103 is that the poet reflects on the motive behind the divine grace that constitutes a covenant people. In the exodus story, to which the poet refers (v. 7), God's grace is unmotivated. God's *hesed* is an expression of divine freedom (Ex. 33:19: "I will be gracious unto whom I will be gracious"). Divine freedom is manifested in God's decision to go with and to be with the people in spite of their fickle, sinful ways. In this psalm, however, a motive for God's display of grace is suggested, namely, God's pity.

> As a father has compassion for his children,
>   so the Lord has compassion for those who fear him.
> For He knows how we are formed;
>   He is mindful that we are dust.
>   (vv. 13–14, NJPS)

God knows our mortality, the weakness of the flesh. Because of our human frailty, according to the psalmist, God shows compassion—like a father who pities his children or, one may add, like a mother who consoles her young (Isa. 66:13).

> As for mortals, their days are like grass;
>   they flourish like a flower of the field;
> for the wind passes over it, and it is gone,
>   and its place knows it no more.
> But the steadfast love [*hesed*] of the LORD is from
>   everlasting to everlasting
>   on those who fear him,
>   and his righteousness to children's children,
> to those who keep his covenant
>   and remember to do his commandments.
>   (vv. 15–18, NRSV)

The heart of Israel's faith pulses in the poetry of this psalm. It is God's faithfulness that endows the individual's life, the history of the people, and the whole cosmos with ultimate meaning.

That is why we do not believe that God can come directly to us

The Old Testament Love of Life

A robust this-worldliness characterizes the faith of Israel. The notion that this world is only a preparation for the next, or that earthly experience is lower and therefore inferior to some higher realm of reality, is completely alien to the Old Testament. This view, which still prevails in much Christian thinking, originated under the influence of Hellenistic philosophies that drew a sharp distinction between the eternal realm of unchanging reality and the temporal realm of change, flux, and contingency where eternal truth is, at best, only intimated in a shadowy form. The psalms, however, bear witness to the fundamental goodness of life as God has given it to us. All the senses—sight, hearing, taste, touch, and smell—are to be employed in the enjoyment of life to the full, in whatever time is given. To be sure, this love of life is not a shallow sense of happiness such as modern people try to find in the midst of sensual pleasures and technological benefits. There is, as we have noticed repeatedly, a minor strain of grief, anxiety, and even God-forsakenness that runs through life's experiences. But even the sufferings and perplexities of everyday life are transmuted into praise by people of faith who expect to "see the goodness of Yhwh in the land of the living" (Ps. 27:13). This hope is not postponed indefinitely or transferred to an otherworldly existence. The songs of thanksgiving joyfully announce that the saving presence of God is experienced again and again in the everydayness of human life. People of faith celebrate with joy and thanksgiving, knowing that "God's Yes is spoken in the midst of life" (Claus Westermann).

It is therefore highly appropriate that the Christian church, which has heard God's Yes pronounced decisively in Jesus Christ, should find its faith nourished by the psalms of the Old Testament. Dietrich Bonhoeffer, the martyred Christian whose life and thought have profoundly influenced Christian theology in our time, came to appreciate the life-affirming, this-worldly faith of the Old Testament more and more during his career. In an Advent meditation, composed in prison before his death, he wrote:

> My thoughts and feelings seem to be getting more and more like the Old Testament, and no wonder, I have been reading it much more than the New for the last few months. It is only when one knows the ineffability of the Name of God that one can utter the name of Jesus Christ. It is only when one loves life and the world so much that without

them everything would be gone, that one can believe in the resurrection and a new world. It is only when one submits to the law that one can speak of grace, and only when one sees the anger and wrath of God hanging like grim realities over the head of one's enemies that one can know something of what it means to love and forgive them. I don't think it is Christian to want to get to the New Testament too soon and too directly.[14]

There is much truth in this. Those who bypass the psalms, with their taste for the goodness of life, are apt to miss the fullness of the New Testament gospel which announces that Jesus Christ came that people might have life and have it abundantly (John 10:10).

7

The Wonder of God's Creation

As we have seen, Israel's praises, were evoked in the first instance not by a general religious awareness of God's wisdom and power manifest in the broad expanse of creation or in the long sweep of human history, but rather by a particular experience of God's saving power and purpose in the life situation of a people. Divine intervention into the historical plight of a band of slaves—victims of the mightiest emperor of the time—had the wonderful effect of creating a people "out of nothing" and opening a way into the future from a no-exit situation. Hence Israel's earliest songs, as in the case of the Song of Miriam (Ex. 15:21) or the Song of the Sea (Ex. 15:1–18), were jubilant cries of praise in response to the God who had acted with saving power.

Since Israel turned primarily to its own historical experience to find the musical themes of praise, it is appropriate that we have considered initially psalms that express prayer to God out of concrete distress (laments) and praise to God for a particular act of deliverance just experienced (songs of thanksgiving). However, these songs "out of the depths" lead in the direction of *hymns,* which praise God in general terms for God's greatness and faithfulness as creator of the cosmos and ruler of history. The lament found in Psalm 102, for instance, contains hymnic elements (vv. 12–22, 25–28). And Psalm 107, a thanksgiving on behalf of various groups (those who had traveled safely in the desert, those delivered from prison, those healed from sickness, and those who voyaged safely on storm-tossed ships), appropriately concludes with a hymn of praise for God's providential care (vv. 33–43).

Psalm 98 is an excellent illustration of how situation-specific praise of God, the "Vindicator" of Israel, leads to the singing of "a new song" in which all the inhabitants of the earth and even the vast realms of nature are summoned to worship.

> Sing a new song to Yahweh,
> for he has performed wonders,
> his saving power is in his right hand
> and his holy arm.
>
> Yahweh has made known his saving power,
> revealed his saving justice for the nations to see,
> mindful of his faithful love and his constancy
> to the House of Israel.
>
> The whole wide world has seen
> the saving power of our God.
> Acclaim Yahweh, all the earth,
> burst into shouts of joy!
>
> (Ps. 98:1–4, NJB)

In this hymn Israel's horizon expands from the praise of "our God"—the God dynamically present in Israel's historical experience—to general praise of the God who is Creator and Lord of the whole earth.

The Form and Setting of the Hymn

The hymn (Hebrew, *tehillah*) is concisely defined as "the song which extols the glory and greatness of Yhwh as it is revealed in nature and history, and particularly in Israel's history."[1] This definition rightly indicates that Israelite hymns placed particular stress upon Yhwh's active involvement in the life story of Israel. In the so-called storytelling psalms (chapter 2) the "mighty deeds of the Lord" were retold didactically "so that the next generation might know them" (Ps. 78:1–8). Indeed, some suggest that during the great festivals God's actions were reenacted in a ritual drama so that worshipers might "see" what God had done for Israel and thereby experience directly the power and meaning of the drama of Israel's history (cf. Ps. 66:5, 6; 46:8).[2] It is equally true, however, that the hymns of Israel have a universal and cosmic dimension. In the temple of Jerusalem, worshipers confessed that the "glory" or splendor of Yhwh which filled the sanctuary also suffused the whole universe. This is evident from the account of Isaiah's call (Isa. 6) where, in the prophet's vision, the Jerusalem temple seems to be a miniature of the heavenly temple in which Yhwh is enthroned as *the* king par excellence. The hymn that the prophet hears in the heavenly temple undoubtedly echoes one that was sung in the earthly sanctuary in Jerusalem, even as it resounds in modern services of worship.

> Holy, holy, holy is the LORD of hosts;
> the whole earth is full of his glory.
>
> (Isa. 6:3, RSV)

The structure of the hymn is found in its simplest form in the Song of Miriam (Ex. 15:21; see chapter 2), which begins with an imperative summons to praise and continues with an announcement of the motive for praise introduced by the motive word "for" (*ki*). This form is found also in the shortest psalm of the Psalter, Psalm 117:

> Praise Yhwh, all nations!
> Extol him, all peoples!
> For [*ki*] great is his faithfulness toward us,
> and the fidelity of Yhwh is unending.
> Praise Yhwh!
>
> (BWA)

[Note: The concluding hallelujah ("Praise Yhwh") is sometimes regarded as the beginning of Psalm 118, as in the Greek translation of the Old Testament. But such a conclusion is found at the end of Psalms 104, 105, 106, 113, 115, 116. In this case too it is probably a formal part of the psalm. The first verse of the psalm is quoted in Romans 15:11.]

This psalm is purposefully short and simple, as Luther once remarked, so that anyone can grasp its meaning. The simplicity of the content is matched by the clarity of its form.

Elements of a Hymn

Introduction: Call to Worship

This is usually an imperative, in the second person plural. It can be a "bidding" formula such as "O come, let us sing" (Ps. 95:1–2) or a summons addressed to the psalmist's *self,* such as "Bless [praise] Yhwh, O my being" (Ps. 104:1). The note struck in the introduction may be repeated in the psalm (e.g., 95:6) or even expanded to great length (as in Psalm 148).

Main Section: The Motive for Praise

In many cases the transition to the motive for praise is introduced by "for" (Hebrew, *ki*), as in Psalm 33:4 or 95:3, 7. This is sometimes varied by using "who" clauses, as in Psalm 104:2ff, to be discussed presently, or by introducing long passages that portray God's majesty as displayed in history or creation (e.g., Ps. 33:4–19).

Recapitulation

Often the psalm concludes with a renewed summons to praise, thus echoing the note struck at the beginning.

In the genre of the hymn the most important element is the main section, which gives the ground or motive for praise. A typical example is this hymnic outburst in the poetry of so-called Second Isaiah:

> Break into singing together, you ruins of Jerusalem!
> For [*ki*] Yhwh has comforted his people,
> has redeemed Jerusalem.
>
> > (Isa. 52:9, BWA)

Or again:

> Shout with joy, O heavens,
> for [*ki*] Yhwh has acted.
> Raise a shout, you depths of the earth!
> Break into singing, O mountains, you forests with all your
>   trees!
> For [*ki*] Yhwh has redeemed Jacob, has displayed his glory
>   in Israel.
>
> > (Isa. 44:23, BWA)

Hymns with this form were undoubtedly used on a variety of worship occasions in the Temple, much as general hymns of praise in modern hymnbooks are used in regular services of worship. Other hymns seem to have been used for special festal occasions, corresponding to special music used in churches today at Christmas, Thanksgiving, or Easter. A number of hymns, the so-called psalms of God's enthronement, were probably used in connection with the great festival held in Jerusalem in the autumn (the New Year festival). These "enthronement psalms," along with psalms celebrating the Davidic kingship and the choice of Zion, will be considered in chapter 8.

In the following outline, the hymns of praise are grouped according to three general thematic categories: God's creation (redemption) of Israel, God's creation of the world, and God's sovereignty over history. Admittedly, the assignment of a hymn to a particular theme is somewhat arbitrary, but the arrangement provides a helpful sequence for study. As usual, an asterisk indicates those psalms that deserve special attention.

I. Hymns to God, Who Created (Redeemed) Israel

66: 1–12	"Come and see what God has done!" (the second part of the psalm is an individual song of thanksgiving)
*100	"The Lord, who made us, is God"
111	"God sent redemption to his people" (an acrostic psalm)
*114	"When Israel went forth from Egypt"
149	"Let Israel be glad in his Maker"

Other hymns outside the Psalter:
> *The Song of the Sea (Ex. 15:1–18)
> The Song of Moses (Deut. 32:1–43)
> The prayer of Habakkuk (Hab. 3:2–19)
> Good tidings of peace (Isa. 52:7–10)

II. Hymns to God, Who Created the World

*8	"When I look at thy heavens"
*19: 1–6	"The heavens are telling the glory of God" (the second part of the psalm is a meditation on the Torah)
95: 1–7a	"In his hand are the depths of the earth" (note that vv. 6–7 strike the note heard in psalms listed above: the creation of Israel)
*104	"In wisdom hast thou made them all"
*148	"He commanded and they were created"

Other hymnic passages:
> God the Creator and King (Ps. 74:12–17; interlude in a lament)
> The incomparable God (Ps. 89:5–18; included in a psalm of the Davidic covenant)

III. Hymns to the Creator and the Ruler of History

*33	"He spoke and it came to be"
*103	"Your youth is renewed like the eagle's"

113	"He raises the poor from the dust"
117	"Extol him, all peoples!"
*145	"The eyes of all look to thee" (an acrostic psalm)
*146	"I will sing praises to my God while I have being"
*147	"He sends forth his command to the earth"

(See also the hymns to Yhwh the King [Psalms 47; 93; 95–99], considered in the next chapter.)

Psalm 150 is not included in the above outline because it is a doxology that rounds off the whole Psalter. Nevertheless, it is particularly interesting because it calls upon a whole orchestra of instruments, including trumpet, lute, harp, timbrel, strings, pipe, and cymbals, to join in praising God. This psalm clearly indicates that Israel's praise was not a quiet meditation but rather the making of a "joyful noise" to the Lord "with timbrel and dance" (v. 4; cf. Ps. 33:2–3; 149:3). Such a psalm is reminiscent of the earliest days when Miriam and her companions praised Yhwh to the accompaniment of timbrels and dancing (Ex. 15:20–21). Here again we notice that worship, as the response of the whole being to God's overture, may take the form of bodily movement, set to the rhythms of music and dance. This does not necessarily suggest the frenzied excitement of prophetic groups who used music, drugs, and dancing to stimulate religious ecstasy (cf. 1 Sam. 10:5–6, 9–13). It is perhaps more like the Greek dramas in which the chorus, through singing and dancing, expressed the people's involvement in the drama.

Calling upon the Name of God

The hymn was not unique with Israel. Thanks to archaeological research we now have at our disposal a large treasury of hymns from Israel's neighbors: hymns to Amon-Re, to Ishtar, to Marduk, and to other gods and goddesses worshiped by Egyptians, Sumerians, Babylonians, Hittites, and Canaanites.[3] What is unique about Israel's hymns is that they are praises of *Yhwh, the God of Israel*. This praise found expression in a new kind of speech to God. In some respects this new speech carried over idioms of the past: for instance, the expression "a great King above all gods" (Ps. 95:3) is traditional language, based on the ancient picture of the King who presides over the heavenly council, "the assembly of the holy ones" (Ps. 89:5–6; cf. 1 Kings 22:19; Job 1:6). More importantly, Israel praised God by pouring *new content* into the ancient form of the hymn. Israel's hymn is appropriately called "a new song" (Ps. 96:1; 98:1).

Back in chapter 1, when introductory matters pertaining to the Psalter were under consideration, we noticed that one collection of psalms stands apart because of its use of the general term for deity, Elohim (God), in preference to the special name Yhwh (Adonai, the Lord). This Elohistic Psalter (Psalms 42–83) was compiled in a circle that was reticent to use the sacred name, the so-called Tetragrammaton ("four letters"). This reverence in regard to the name is so striking that it focuses attention sharply on the fact that the Psalter as a whole ascribes praise to Yhwh: "Know that the LORD [Yhwh] is God!" (Ps. 100:3); "Bless the LORD, O my soul; and all that is within me, bless God's holy name!" (Ps. 103:1). Since Israelite faith was not a tolerant polytheism, the stress upon the divine name deserves attention. Usually Christian worshipers skip lightly over this matter when reciting the words of the Lord's Prayer: "Hallowed be thy name."[4]

In the ancient Israelite world, as in some societies today, the question of the name was a supremely important issue—one that could not have been challenged, as it was in Shakespeare's tragedy, with the innocent query, "What's in a name?" (*Romeo and Juliet,* act 2, scene 2). Among the Israelites the name was understood to express the nature or identity of a person.[5] Although in our society names have tended to become labels, we can still appreciate the Israelite view, at least imaginatively. Nothing is more tragic than a person who, because of amnesia or mental disease, cannot remember his or her own name. And almost nothing is more shocking than the report that prisoners in concentration camps were divested of their personal names and given numbers. A person's name designates the self that has a particular history, a unique life story. To be introduced to a person by name, if the introduction leads into a relationship of any depth, is to perceive and, to some degree, to enter into the life story of the person who bears the name.

This helps us to understand the Israelite concern to know the name of God. God's personal name symbolizes God's identity, who God is. As in personal relationships, the "whoness" of God (God's self-revelation) is given in the context of a story, a history. Therefore the God whom Israel worships is identified in "who" clauses, which may include a narrative reduced to a single sentence, as in the prologue to the Decalogue: "I am the LORD, your God, who brought you out of the land of Egypt, out of the house of bondage" (Ex. 20:2). Psalm 136, which has been referred to previously in connection with our discussion of storytelling psalms (chapter 3), is a long chain of who-clauses, punctuated with the antiphonal refrain: "For the *hesed* [faithfulness] of Yhwh is unending!" Who-clauses, which identify who God is, are characteristic of hymns.

Living as we do in an increasingly cosmopolitan world, we may think that this Israelite zeal to know and honor God's name sometimes seems narrow-minded, if not anachronistic. There is considerable interest today in the mystical religions of the East, which declare that the divine is unnameable. The name of God, it is said, is a limitation that reduces God to the human realm of experience, to cultural relativity; therefore all divine names (Allah, Yhwh, Brahma, Christ, etc.) point beyond to a higher order of divine reality, to "God beyond the gods" of this world. How, then, are we to understand the announcement, found at the heart of the Torah, that the Holy God—the One who transcends our human world and is therefore beyond our naming—chooses to be known and worshiped as the One who has a personal name? This momentous announcement is reported in the third chapter of Exodus in the story of the burning bush.

In Israelite worship it was not a simple either-or: either the God known in a particular historical experience or the God whose sway is universal. On the one hand, the name of God signifies the Holy God who turns personally to the people who, in response, may "call upon the name of the Lord" in lament or thanksgiving (e.g. Ps. 116:13). This people knows Yhwh as the God of the exodus, the God who liberates.

> I am Yhwh your God from the land of Egypt,
> You know no God besides me,
> and there is no liberator except me.
>   (Hosea 13:4, BWA)

There is something very special about the name of God. As one psalmist says, "Those who know your name put their trust in you" (Ps. 9:10, NRSV).

On the other hand, the liberating God whom Israel "knows" is actually the sole and universal God, the ruler of human history and the creator of the cosmos. Thus hymnic invocations to praise Yhwh are addressed, not just to Israel, but to all peoples and to "the ends of the earth."

> Sing a new song to Yahweh!
> Let his praise be sung from remotest parts of the earth
> by those who sail the sea and by everything in it,
> by the coasts and islands and those who inhabit them.

Let the desert and its cities raise their voices,
the encampments where Kedar lives.
Let the inhabitants of the Rock [*Sela*] cry aloud for joy
and shout from the mountain tops.
Let them give glory to Yahweh
and, in the coasts and islands, let them voice his praise.

                              (Isa. 42:10–12, NJB)

Even the most remote and isolated places, Kedar (Jer. 49:28–29) and
Sela (2 Kings. 14:7), are embraced within the purpose and power of the
God revealed to Israel.

The name of God, then, signifies the Holy God who turns personally to the people, whose self (or identity) is disclosed in the people's
historical experience. It is significant, then, that an ancient formula for
the act of worship is "to call upon the name of Yhwh." We have en-
countered this idiom in our previous study of psalms of lament and
thanksgiving (e.g., Ps. 116:13). Indeed, the faith of the psalmists cannot be understood apart from the belief that the identity (the "whoness") of God has been disclosed in the shared history of Israel and that
the people may address God personally, by name.

The Heavens Are Telling the Glory of God

One of the creation psalms, Psalm 19, testifies that the God whose
name is known in Israel is the God whose glory is displayed in the
cosmos.

This psalm is composed of two distinct pieces: the first (vv. 1–6) is
an old hymn that praises God, the creator, whose "glory" (radiance,
splendor) is displayed in the heavens. The second part (vv. 7–14) is a
meditation on the Torah (Law) in which the will of Yhwh, the God
known in Israel's history, is revealed. Let us consider how these two
parts belong together.

In the first part of the psalm (designated Psalm 19A), the special
name of God, Yhwh, is not employed. Psalm 19A seems to be an old
song that praises El (translated "God" in v. 1), the ancient Semitic title
for the "Father of the Gods." The psalmist affirms that the phenomena
of the heavens, especially the sun, are constantly proclaiming the glory
of El in a great anthem of praise, inaudible to human ears.

The heavens are telling the glory of God [El];
    and the firmament proclaims his handiwork.

Day to day pours forth speech,
and night to night declares knowledge.
(vv. 1–2, RSV)

Night and day, like antiphonal choirs, take up the ceaseless strains of
the anthem of praise. Yet while this anthem is sung in the universal language of nature, it is a *silent* testimony that is not clearly understandable to any human being. This seems to be emphasized in the next lines:

There is no speech, nor are there words;
their voice is not heard;
yet their voice goes out through all the earth,
and their words to the end of the world.
(vv. 3–4b, RSV)

The psalmist then draws upon the ancient myth of the sun-god, who at
night has his abode in the mythical "sea," where he rests in the arms of
his beloved, and at dawn emerges from his bridal chamber with youthful vigor and radiant splendor.

In them [i.e., the heavens] he has set a tent for the sun,
which comes forth like a bridegroom leaving his chamber,
and like a strong man runs its course with joy.
Its rising is from the end of the heavens,
and its circuit to the end of them;
and there is nothing hid from its heat.
(vv. 4c–6, RSV)

In these verses a deep human response to the wonder of being and of
the majestic order of the cosmos, as expressed in the mythopoeic language of the ancient world, is reinterpreted to express faith in the God
who is not a power of nature (such as the deified sun) but is the creator
who transcends the cosmos. The light that suffuses the universe is more
than the radiance of the sun; it is the "glory" of deity, the shining light
that hides God's being (cf. Isa. 6:1–3; Ezek. 1–3).

It is questionable whether the psalmist affirms that the heavens *re-
veal* God. The celestial phenomena display God's *glory* and praise the
Creator by functioning in the ordered whole, but they do not disclose
who God is or God's purpose. There is a kind of knowledge of God
available to human beings through contemplating the works of creation—knowledge of God's "eternal power and deity," as Paul ob-

serves in Romans 1:19–20—but it is not the saving knowledge of God's will and relationship that answers the psalmist's question, "What are human beings that you remember them?" (Ps. 8:4).

The second part of the psalm (Ps. 19B), as we have noted, is an independent literary piece. Probably it was composed much later than the first part. Yet the editorial combination of the psalms was hardly accidental. The Old Testament theologian Gerhard von Rad maintains that the second part was meant to be a supplement to and correction of the old hymn that draws upon mythical ideas found in the religions of the ancient world. Psalm 19B, he says, expresses "a certain doubt" that we can know God on the basis of the works of the creation. The combination of the two songs—one on the creation and the other on the Torah—is a theological testimony that "Israel's praise is directed to Yhwh's historical self-revelation given peculiarly to herself."[6] In other words, the psalm in its combined form is not concerned merely with El (deity); rather, it is based on the conviction that God has broken through the silences of nature, disclosing the divine self (name) and speaking and acting in the historical experiences of the people Israel.

This understanding of Psalm 19 is expressed in the lines of a well-known hymn by Isaac Watts (1674–1748):

> The heavens declare thy glory, Lord;
> In every star thy wisdom shines;
> But when our eyes behold thy Word,
> We read thy name in fairer lines.

For persons of faith, nature does bear impressive witness to the glory of God, but only because, first of all, in the history remembered and actualized by the believing community, "we read thy name in fairer lines." Contrast the view expressed in the hymn by Joseph Addison (1672–1719), where the language reflects the faith of the Enlightenment:

> What though in solemn silence all
> Move round the dark terrestrial ball?
> What though no real voice nor sound
> Amidst their radiant orbs be found?
> In reason's ear they all rejoice,
> And utter forth a glorious voice;
> Forever singing, as they shine,
> "The hand that made us is divine."

[Note: Addison's hymn, "The Spacious Firmament on High," is usually set to the music of a chorale from Franz Joseph Haydn's oratorio, *Creation.* The hymn, which at one point declares that "in reason's ear" the anthem of nature is heard, reflects the rationalism of the Enlightenment. Blaise Pascal (1623–1662) spoke more authentically for the modern mind when he confessed that he was torn between evidences of the Creator in nature and evidences from nature that negated his faith.[7] However, just because this hymn echoes the faith of the Enlightenment does not warrant removing it from modern hymnbooks (as was done with the United Methodist Hymnal [1989]); after all, hymns expressing other philosophical viewpoints are retained.]

God Who Created a People

Our study of the relationship between the two parts of Psalm 19 provides an avenue of approach to other psalms in which God, addressed by the personal name Yhwh, is extolled as creator. To understand Israel's creation faith sympathetically, it is best to start with psalms that praise Yhwh as the God who created a people out of the historical nothingness of slavery and gave them a future and a vocation. This view of creation as the formation of a community is deeply rooted in Israelite tradition. It is found in ancient Israelite poetry, for instance, in the Song of the Sea (Ex. 15:1–18), which was discussed in chapter 2. In this poem the event of the deliverance at the Reed Sea is portrayed in imagery that reflects the old myth of the Creator's conflict with the powers of chaos. Addressing Yhwh, the singer speaks of "the people whom you have redeemed" (Ex. 15:13) and "the people whom you have created"[8] (Ex. 15:16).

It is striking that here redemption and creation are blended together. Creation is not understood as a cosmic event—the creation of heaven and earth—but as a historical event of liberation.

This view of creation is expressed in the various hymns listed above under the heading, "Hymns to God, Who Created (Redeemed) Israel," such as Psalm 114 ("When Israel went forth from Egypt"), or the familiar psalm often called "Old Hundredth."

> Know that it is Yhwh who is God!
> He made us and to him we belong;
> We are his people, the flock of his pasture.
> (Ps. 100:2, BWA)

The affirmation that Yhwh is our creator has its counterpart in the confession that "we are his" (probably the correct reading of the Hebrew at this point) and therefore are dependent, like a flock, upon the shepherd.

Victory over Leviathan

A beautiful example of this view of creation is found in Psalm 74, a lament in which a hymnic passage (vv. 12–17) is included as an expression of confidence in a time of distress. Since the psalm is found in the Elohistic Psalter (Psalms 42–83), we may assume that originally the hymn was addressed not to "God" in general but to the God known personally by the name Yhwh.

> God, my King from of old,
> whose saving acts are wrought on earth,
> by your power you cleft the sea monster in two
> and broke the sea serpent's heads in the waters;
> your crushed the heads of Leviathan
> and threw him to the sharks for food.
> (vv. 74:12–14, REB)

In the ensuing lines the poet moves to the subject of creation in a cosmic sense: the creation of day and night, the heavenly bodies, brooks and springs, summer and winter. Notice, however, that initially the poet effectively employs the old creation myth of the Divine Warrior's victory over the multiheaded dragon, Leviathan (cf. Isa. 27:1), to portray the crucial event at the Reed Sea when a people was redeemed from powers of chaos. God's saving deed at the sea was also an act of creation.

Outside the Psalter the prophet known as Second Isaiah (Isaiah 40—55) resorts to hymnic poetry to proclaim that Yhwh, the God whom Israel worships, is both Creator and Redeemer. This poet also understands creation, in one sense, as the creation of a people, for Yhwh is identified as the one

> . . . who created you, O Jacob,
> he who formed you, O Israel.
> (Isa. 43:1; also v. 7, RSV)

The New Exodus

Accordingly, in a lyrical poem in which the poet gives an apostrophe to the powerful "arm of Yhwh," the event of the exodus at the Reed Sea is portrayed in mythopoeic language as the time when the Divine Warrior created (redeemed) a people. And this event in poetic imagination typifies the new exodus of salvation or new creation that is about to occur.

> Awake, awake! Clothe yourself in strength,
> arm of Yahweh.
> Awake, as in the olden days,
> generations long ago!
> Was it not you who split Rahab in half,
> who pierced the Dragon through?
> Was it not you who dried up the sea,
> the waters of the great Abyss;
> who made the sea-bed into a road
> for the redeemed to go across?
>
> (Isa. 51:9–10, NJB)

In the prophet's view, Yhwh is the Creator/Redeemer of Israel who creates "the new thing" in history (Isa. 43:19) because, in a larger sense, this God is the Creator of the cosmos (Isa. 40:2–23, 25–26; 45:9–13). The Creator whom Israel worships transcends the whole sweep of time and, being "the first" and "the last" (Isa. 48:12), grasps the drama of history in its totality, from beginning to end.

The Majestic Name (Psalm 8)

In the foregoing discussion we have seen that Israel's praise is not directed to deity in a general sense but to the God whose identity or "name" is known in the shared history of the people. This discussion has prepared us to consider a number of hymns in which the people praise Yhwh as the creator of the cosmos and the ruler of history.

The exquisite Psalm 8 is a hymn of praise to the Creator. Notice the hymnic pattern:

Invocation

The psalm begins with an exclamation of praise to "Yhwh, our Sovereign," whose name is great throughout the whole earth. The initial address to Yhwh is expanded by a who-clause (vv. 1b–2) that portrays the divine majesty in the heavens. The details are not clear, but apparently the poet depicts the splendid "bulwark" or celestial palace (temple) above the firmament, from which Yhwh comes to subdue foes that threaten the divine rule.

Motive for Praise

The motive for praise is introduced in verse 3 with the transitional particle *ki,* here translated "when." The poet reflects on what it means to "know" God personally, by name. Looking up at the star-studded night sky, the psalmist is overwhelmed with a sense of the relatively ephemeral and frail character of human beings and wonders why the Creator pays any attention to such infinitesimally tiny creatures.

> When I survey your heavens, your fingerworks,
> the moon and the stars that you have established,
> what are human beings that you consider them,
> mortals that you care for them?
>
> (BWA)

The psalmist's question does not stand by itself but is followed by a contrasting statement, introduced by an adversative "yet." Such an insignificant creature, yet one who is elevated to a high role in the Creator's cosmic administration!

> Yet you have placed them slightly below heavenly beings,
> and with honor and majesty have crowned them.
> You have given them dominion over your handiwork,
> everything you have put in subjection to them:
> sheep and oxen altogether,
> wild beasts also, birds of the air and fish of the sea,
> everything that courses through the waterways.
>
> (vv. 3–6, BWA)

Refrain

In the typical style of the hymn, the poem is rounded off by sounding the note struck at the beginning:

> Yhwh, our Sovereign,
> how majestic is your name throughout the earth!
>
> (BWA)

Psalm 8 deals with two inseparably related questions: who God is and what the role of humankind is. The psalm is closely related to the creation story in Genesis 1. The psalmist's affirmation that Yhwh has created human beings so that they fall short "just a little" from the divine status of Elohim ("God" or, more likely in this case, "heavenly beings") is parallel to the statement made in the Genesis creation story that God made human beings "in the image of God" (Gen. 1:26–27). In both cases the writers affirm that human beings are made for *relationship* with God, a relationship that elevates them above the natural world and enables them to have dominion over "nature." Contrast the psalmist's question of amazement about the human role in God's creation with the same question in Psalm 144:3–4 (cf. Job 7:17–18), where the emphasis is on human transience.

> [Note: The word Elohim in Psalm 8:5 may refer to "the sons of God" or heavenly beings who, according to the ancient pictorial way of thinking, surround God in the heavenly court. This view may be presupposed in Gen. 1:26, where the plural forms ("Let us . . . in our image") suggest that God is addressing the heavenly council (cf. 1 Kings 22:19). The Greek translation of the Old Testament (Septuagint) reads "angels" at Psalm 8:5, and this interpretation is adopted in the epistle to the Hebrews (2:6–8) where the psalm is quoted.]

This view of human dominion over nature is revolutionary when measured against ancient religions that portrayed the gods as forces within the cosmos and that regarded human life as embraced within the order of creation, with its rhythmic cycles of the seasons and its mysterious power of life (fertility) and death. The God whom Israel worships is not a power within the cosmos. Rather, as Creator, Yhwh transcends the cosmos and hence is "Ruler of all nature," to use an expression from the Crusader's hymn, "Fairest Lord Jesus." In a lesser sense, human beings, though related to their natural environment (as shown by the creation stories at the beginning of the Bible), stand over against nature in freedom as creatures who are given the high calling to have dominion over the works of God's creation. They are to "image" or represent the rule (kingdom) of God on earth.

Let us pause to reflect on the implications of this biblical theology of creation. The biblical view, which emptied "nature" of divinity, opened the way for a "scientific" approach to nature as a realm that human beings can study and explore and whose resources can be used in

God-given stewardship ("to till and keep" the garden, Gen. 2:15). It is hardly accidental that the scientific movement, which brought about revolutionary developments in the twentieth century on earth and in space, has been nourished in the soil of the biblical tradition. The tremendous achievements of science in the fields of medicine, transportation, communication, and space exploration (to mention only a few) may be regarded as a partial fulfillment of the task that the Creator has given human beings in crowning them to have dominion over the earthly realm of creation. What we have to do is achieve a proper balance between the centrality of human dominance and the boundaries set by the sovereignty of God. To think only in terms of the centrality of *homo sapiens* is to invite environmental disaster. Through the misguided application of our autonomy we have jeopardized the physical condition of the world and misappropriated our status as "keepers of the earth."[9]

The other side of this picture, of course, is the biblical portrayal of the risk that God has taken in elevating human beings to a high role of responsibility in the creation. This risk is portrayed in the story of paradise lost (Genesis 2–3), which is included as a supplement to the creation story in the final canonical edition of the Torah (Pentateuch). The biblical narrative shows that the position of dominion over the natural world may tempt human beings to assert their independence vis-à-vis God and to use their God-given freedom in such a manner that the earth becomes a scene of exploitation, warfare, and chaos. The biblical narrators give us no simple assurance that human beings, who fall just short of divine status, will use their honored position to execute God's purpose on the earth and to order social life in accordance with God's will. This is the fundamental problem to which the opening chapters of the Bible are addressed: human grandeur and human misery, the high calling and the lost opportunity.

In our own time we can sense this human problem clearly as we see how science, which could be the form of imaging God's rule on earth, holds the terrifying possibility of nuclear destruction of the earth and of carrying military adventures into space. Moreover, we have been made painfully aware of the fact that human exploitation of the earth's resources may upset the balance of nature, with the result that the earth will no longer be a habitable place for human and animal life. The question is whether human beings—as scientists, industrialists, or technologists—can fulfill the high calling that was given to humanity by the Creator.[10]

In Wisdom God Made Them All (Psalm 104)

An exquisite expression of Israel's creation faith is found in Psalm 104, a hymn that also has many affinities with the Genesis creation story. In Psalm 104, as in Psalm 8, the poet's praise is directed to the Lord ("O Yhwh, my God"), whose name is great in the earth. In composing this poem, the poet has drawn upon mythopoeic motifs known outside Israel. Indeed, at points this psalm displays striking resemblance in style and content to the "Hymn to the Aton," composed by Akhenaton, the reforming Egyptian king of the fourteenth century B.C. who introduced a kind of monotheism based on the worship of the benevolent divine power symbolized by the sun disc.[11] Moreover, the poet has made use of the myth of the Creator's subduing the powers of chaos, which was known in Mesopotamia and particularly in the Canaanite (Ugaritic) literature from the fourteenth century B.C.[12]

Invocation

Psalm 104 is prayer expressed in beautiful poetry. In the style of a hymn, Psalm 104 begins with an invocation addressed to the poet's *nefesh* (self or being): "Praise God, O my being!" All the powers of one's being in their psychosomatic unity are invited to join in praising God. In this respect Psalm 104 is like Psalm 103, which opens on the same note.

Motive for Praise

The invocation to praise God leads into the main body of the psalm (vv. 2–30), which provides the motive for praise. The elaboration of the grounds for praise is developed in seven strophes, which follow the sequence of the Genesis creation story, as can be seen from chart 1. The poet ascribes praise in a series of who-clauses: Yhwh is the one who "stretched out the heavens like a tent," "who set the earth on its foundations," etc.

Creation versus Chaos (Psalm 104:2b–7)

It is evident, then, that there are striking affinities with the Genesis creation story, but there are important differences. For one thing, in the creation story God is spoken of in the third person: "In the beginning God," "God created humanity in God's image," etc. In carefully wrought prose the narrator describes the emergence of an ordered whole (cosmos), in which everything in heaven and on earth has its as-

Strophe 1 Ps. 104:2–4 Gen. 1:6–8	In pictorial language the poet speaks of God's "stretching out" the heavens and laying the foundations of the heavenly palace on the cosmic ocean above the firmament.
Strophe 2 Ps. 104:5–9 Gen. 1:9–10	God has firmly established the earth by putting the rebellious waters of chaos to flight and establishing bounds for them so that chaos would not engulf the earth.
Strophe 3 Ps. 104:10–13 Implied in Gen. 1:6–10	The chaotic waters, having been tamed, were converted to beneficial use. The waters gush up from underground springs and pour down in rain from the sky.
Strophe 4 Ps. 104:14–18 Gen. 1:11–12	As a result, vegetation flourishes, which makes life possible for birds, beasts, and human beings.
Strophe 5 Ps. 104:19–23 Gen. 1:14–18	God created the moon and the sun to mark the rhythm of seasons and of day and night, so that beasts may seek food during the darkness and human beings may perform their work in daylight.
Strophe 6 Ps. 104:24–26 Gen. 1:20–22	The poet reflects upon the remnant of watery chaos: the sea, which teems with creatures great and small. Leviathan is no longer the dreaded monster of chaos, but is God's "plaything" (cf. Job 41:5).
Strophe 7 Ps. 104:27–30 Gen. 1:24–30	The dependence of human beings and animals upon God, their Creator, for life.

Chart 1.   The "Order" of Creation

signed place and function. The statements are weighty, reflective, expressive of the wisdom of priests and sages. But they are statements *about* God; they are *theos-logos,* (theology). As such, they have been the object of intense scrutiny and controversy, especially in the science versus religion debates of the twentieth century.

What a different world is presented in Psalm 104! Here we do not find statements *about* God, but statements *to* God. We do not find theology based on reflection but prayer based on our experience of the goodness and wonder of God's creation. It would make a big difference

if we started with Psalm 104, that is, with prayer in an I-Thou relationship, and then went to the Genesis creation story with its profound theological statements.

In this part of the psalm the poet uses mythical language much
more freely than it is used in the creation story. In the Genesis story
one hears mythical overtones, such as the pushing back of the waters
of chaos to make room for a habitable earth, but by and large the
story has been "demythologized." In Psalm 104, however, the poet
gives free rein to poetic imagination, describing first of all God's majestic enthronement in a heavenly palace whose beams are sunk
deeply into the mythical waters of chaos (vv. 1–4). Then the poet describes the establishment of the earth upon the waters of the deep (as
in Ps. 24:1). Interestingly, these waters of chaos are described as un-
ruly, insurgent powers that have to be subdued, echoing the ancient
myth of the conflict between the Creator and the powers of chaos,
symbolized by the raging sea, the turbulent floods, the threatening
monster of chaos sometimes called Rahab or Leviathan (Ps.
74:13–14; 89:10; Job 9:18; 26:12).

> You fixed the earth on its foundation so that it will never be
>   moved.
> The deep covered it like a cloak,
> and the waters stood above the mountains.
> At your rebuke they fled,
> at the sound of your thunder they rushed away,
> flowing over the hills,
> pouring down into the valleys to the place appointed for
>   them.
> You fixed a boundary which they were not to pass;
> they were never to cover the earth again.
>
>   (vv. 5–9, REB)

In the Genesis creation story, at least in its present form, the waters are not regarded as hostile. But in Psalm 104 they are adversar-
ial; God rebukes them and they flee (v. 7). God sets a boundary so
that they are held back. As a result, the world is ordered and secure.
Later in this poem we hear that "the sea, great and vast" is not threatening, for it teems with marine life, ships ply their course through it,
and the mythical monster of chaos (think of Moby Dick!) is only a
zoological creature that God has formed to sport around in the water
(vv. 25–26).

Waters of Life (Psalm 104:10–13)

At the beginning of the next strophe, however, something wonderful happens. The chaotic waters are transformed, so that they are no longer hostile but benevolent. Note that the waters of chaos are not eliminated, they are only assigned their place in the wonderful order of creation. They gush forth from springs that flow into the valleys, giving drink to wild animals. Birds make their nests and sing in the trees beside streams of living water. From the mountains clouds form to bring rain that waters the earth. Here the poet highlights a fundamental aspect of life on this planet: water that makes life possible for both human and nonhuman forms of life. If we were to portray an ecological crisis in hydrographic terms, it would include not just too much water (as in floods) but not enough water to nourish life (as in severe droughts). We know well the indispensability of water on the planet, and on others too, if life flourishes there.

Wonderful Diversity (Psalm 104:14–23)

The conversion of the disorderly waters to beneficial waters prompts the poet, in the ensuing strophe, to meditate on the wonderful diversity of God's creation: the grass that grows for cattle, the plants for people so that food may be produced from the earth, even "wine to gladden the human heart" (v. 15). The list continues: the trees for birds, the high mountains for wild goats, the moon to mark the seasons, and the sun to run its daily course. These heavenly bodies mark the times of our lives, both for animals and humans. When the sun sets, the animals come forth and the lions follow their predatory instincts "seeking their food from God." And when the sun rises, the animals withdraw and human beings go out to labor until eventide. In this view, work is not a curse but part of the goodness of God's creation. Here we are given a beautiful view of a "peaceable kingdom" in which animals and humans take their place in an ordered whole. There is plenty of room in God's "house" for all God's creatures, humans and animals, to live together, sharing the hospitality of God's table.

The Wisdom of the Creator (Psalm 104:24–26)

We are coming toward the climax of this great poem. Having contemplated the rich diversity of God's creation, the poet breaks out into an exclamation:

Countless are the things you have made, Lord;
by your wisdom you have made them all;

(v. 24 BWA)

Here we have evidence that this is a wisdom psalm, which would
help to explain the influence of Egyptian wisdom (especially the beautiful hymn to the sun disc mentioned above), as well as the lack of
specifically Israelite themes such as the exodus and the Sinai Covenant.
Wisdom has an ecumenical, universal outreach, appealing to experiences that are shared by all human beings: the beauty of the natural
world, the transcience of human life, human dependence upon powers
greater than ourselves, and the inescapable moral law that actions have
consequences.

Continuing Creation (Psalm 104:27–30)

The high point of Psalm 104 is reached in a passage that comes just
before the concluding refrain. Psalm 8, it will be recalled, follows the
Genesis creation story by stressing the supremacy of human beings in
God's earthly creation. This note is lacking in Psalm 104. Instead the
poet stresses the equality of human beings and animals, who together
depend upon the Creator. In this "peaceable kingdom" there is no su-
periority: all creatures belong to God's good and glorious creation and
are equally dependent upon their Creator for vitality.

This theme of the parity between humans and animals does not make
Psalm 104 preferable to the Genesis creation story, which has been
blamed—mistakenly—for precipitating the ecological crisis because it
elevates human beings to dominion over "nature." Both creation texts,
when read side by side, are theologically important. We should not surrender the motif of "the image of God," especially in this so-called
postmodern age when some philosophers are saying that we are imprisoned in the "language worlds" that we create and have no access to
"outside reality." In this view, truth, spelled with a small *t,* is relative to
one's language world, but Truth, spelled with a capital *T,* is inaccessi-
ble.[13] However, the image of God implies that there is some sort of correspondence between humans and God, enabling us to explore God's
creation and to have dominion over the earthly creation as representatives of God.

Human beings, however, not only transcend the natural environment, they are inescapably involved in it, along with animals and other

forms of life. This is evident in the inclusive "all of them" at the beginning of the climactic strophe, an expression that stylistically echoes the "all of them" of the previous strophe: "In wisdom you have made all of them" (v. 24). In this way the poet situates us among all of God's wonderful creatures, animal and human.

> All of them [animals and humans] look to you
> to give them their food in its season.
> When you give to them, they gather up;
> when you open your hand, they are satisfied to the full.
> When you hide your face, they are disturbed,
> when you take away their breath, they expire and return to
>   their dust.
> When you send forth your spirit, they are [re]created,
> and you renew the surface of the soil.
>
> (vv. 27–30, BWA)

It is difficult for English readers to sense the full force of this passage because of a problem of translation. In the Hebrew text, the verbs refer to continuing actions. They are frequentative verbs, describing actions that take place not just once but again and again. The only way we can render this into English is to use verbs of the present tense: "When you give to them (not once but again and again), they gather it up (not one time but frequently)." Notice what this means in the final line of the strophe, which uses the special verb for God's creation (*bará*). In Genesis 1, the same verb is used, but there it refers to a past event, a one-time happening. Also, in its opening strophe Psalm 104, using mythopoeic language, speaks of creation as a past event (when God "stretched out the heavens"). Here, however, at the climax of Psalm 104, we find a revolutionary idea. Creation is not just an event that occurred in the beginning, as in the Genesis creation story, but is God's continuing activity of sustaining creatures and holding everything in being. The cosmos is not a self-existing whole, perpetuated through its own internally operating dynamic. On the contrary, the whole order of being is radically dependent on God, the Creator. If for an instant God were to "hide his face" or to "withdraw his *ruah*" ("breath," "wind," "spirit"), to use the psalmist's poetic language, then every being would languish and fall back into primeval chaos.

Of course, this is the language of religious poetry, not of science. Yet this poetic language expresses in a profound way the universal

human experience that existence is contingent—suspended, as it
were—over the abyss. Modern poets, novelists, and philosophers have
also portrayed the depth dimension of existence and

> The desperate catabasis
> Into the snarl of the abyss
> That always lies just underneath
> Our jolly picnic on the heath
> Of the agreeable
>   W. H. Auden[14]

The Goodness of God's Creation (Psalm 104:31–35)

In Psalm 104, then, we are given a picture of the marvelous order
and design of God's creation: a carefully wrought whole in which all
creatures, including human beings, have their proper place and times.
There is even an element of esthetic enjoyment in this poem, a feeling for the beauty of God's creation. This experience of beauty, however, is not based merely on human perception. The psalm is a commentary on God's approving judgment that the creation as a whole
and in all its parts is "very good" (Gen. 1:31). This is God's world,
marred only by human wickedness, a melancholy note struck briefly
in the concluding refrain of the poem (vv. 31–35, especially v. 35).
Human enjoyment may be full because God "rejoices" in the works
of creation.

In good hymnic style the psalm concludes by striking the note of invocation sounded at the beginning, thus rounding off the whole.

> [Note: The concluding "Hallelujah" ("Praise Yhwh") actually
> belongs with the following psalm. This transposition means that
> both Psalms 105 and 106 are hallelujah psalms (see Pss.
> 111–118), each beginning and usually ending with the liturgical
> exclamation.]

Praise to God from the Ends of the Earth

The use of mythopoeic imagery that expresses the depth dimension
of human existence shows that there is a universal perspective in Israel's worship of God. The psalmists' praise does not lead to a theological confinement within Israel's history but, rather, to a spacious

view that embraces all peoples and the whole cosmos. For the God whose name (identity) is disclosed in Israel's historical experience is the God upon whom all human beings, and all forms of creaturely existence, are dependent.

It is therefore significant that some of Israel's hymns move without a break from the praise of God the Creator to the praise of God as the Lord of history. We have already found this to be the case in a story-telling psalm such as Psalm 136, which departs from the outline of Israel's credo by prefixing to the sacred history the rehearsal of God's great deeds of creation (Ps. 136:4–9). This kind of ecumenical praise finds even more magnificent expression in Psalm 33, which announces that Yhwh is enthroned as celestial King (Ps. 33:14) and therefore is Creator and Lord of the earth.

Creation by the Word (Psalm 33)

Psalm 33, which accents creation by the power of God's Word (as in the Genesis creation story), also displays the characteristic form of a hymn:

Invocation

The psalm begins by summoning the community to praise Yhwh and to sing "a new song" to the accompaniment of musical instruments (vv. 1–3).

Motive for Praise

The main section (vv. 4–19), introduced by "for" (*ki*), announces the motive for praise.

> For the word of Yhwh is just,
> and all his work is done faithfully.
> He loves righteousness and justice,
> the faithfulness [*hesed*] of Yhwh fills the earth.
>   (vv. 4–5, BWA)

The psalmist expands this theme by saying, first, that it was by the "word of Yhwh" that the heavens and the earth were made (vv. 6–9), and second, by declaring that "the counsel of Yhwh" is the determining power in human history (vv. 10–18). The psalmist refers to the special relationship between Yhwh and Israel, "the people whom he has chosen as his heritage" (v. 12), but concentrates on God's sovereignty over all nations (vv. 13–15). In this poet's view, to be a nation "under God" means abandoning trust in military arms (vv. 16–17).

Recapitulation

Psalm 33 concludes with an expression of trust in Yhwh, Creator and Redeemer (vv. 20–22), thereby resounding the note struck at the beginning.

In this psalm we perceive once again that, as in the case of other psalms, God's historical self-disclosure to Israel provides the basis for the universal horizons of thought. The revelation (word) of Yhwh is not only the inner meaning of the events of Israel's history; it is also the meaning of every individual's experience (see especially Psalms 103 and 113), the meaning of human history, and the meaning of the whole cosmos.

> By the word of Yahweh the heavens were made,
> by the breath of his mouth all their array.
> He collects the waters of the sea like a dam,
> he stores away the abyss in his treasure-house.
>
> Let the whole earth fear Yahweh,
> let all who dwell in the world revere him;
> for, the moment he spoke, it was so,
> no sooner had he commanded, than there it stood!
> (vv. 6–9, NJB)

Creation by the word is expressed also in the hymn Psalm 148 (see vv. 5–6) and, of course, in the liturgical prose of the Genesis creation story. From this point it is not a far cry to the announcement made at the opening of the Gospel of John. Echoing the "in the beginning" of Genesis 1:1, this Gospel affirms that God's revelation in Christ was the Word by whom all things were created and in whom all things are sustained. And this Word is not confined to a corner of history: it is "the true light that enlightens every human being" (John 1:9).

8

Zion, the City of God

One of the intriguing problems in the study of the Psalms is the identity of the "I" and the "we" in psalms that employ these first person pronouns. Often the "I," the individual, is consciously involved in the worshiping community, as in the invocation, "O come, let us worship and bow down, let us kneel before the LORD our Maker" (Psalm 100). Sometimes, however, the individuality of the speaker is stressed, as in the poet's address to the self: "Praise the LORD, O my being" (Ps. 103:1), although in the same poem there is a shift to plural ("us," "our," vv. 10–14). How do we understand the "I" of the Psalms?

In the past many interpreters, believing that the Psalms were used at great temple celebrations, have been prone to say that with few exceptions the literary types considered in the previous chapters—the laments, thanksgivings, and hymns—are "cultic songs." Supposedly these songs were designed for use in a setting of worship in which the cultic community responded to the overtures of God toward the people in their ongoing history.[1] But this view needs considerable qualification. Admittedly the psalms, as arranged in the final form of the Psalter, seem to have been used by the choirs of the Second Temple (see chapter 10). Originally, however, many psalms seem to reflect a noncultic situation, that is, a situation outside the temple. Some were intended for the circle of the home or tribal gathering, some were for the purpose of teaching, some were composed as private meditations or reflections on the ups and downs of daily experience. The voice of the "I," although an anonymous individual, sounds out loud and clear.

The Face of God

Nevertheless, this is not individualism, at least in the modern sense, for many of the "I-psalms" have a community horizon. This is evident in the very first lament of the Psalter (Psalm 3), which reflects a private moment at bedtime, when one thinks of the day that is past and looks toward tomorrow ("I lie down and sleep, I wake again, . . ." vs. 5). It is striking that in this setting of personal privacy, far away from the temple, an individual prays in the direction of Zion, hoping for an answer from God's "holy hill" (v. 4). This orientation toward the temple is analogous to a modern Jew who faces toward the Western Wall of the former temple or a Muslim who prays toward Mecca.

> But I, through the abundance of your steadfast love,
>   will enter your house,
> I will bow down toward your holy temple
>   in awe of you.
>
> (Ps. 5:7, NRSV)

Another notable example of this is the psalm found in the book of Jonah, in which a poet imagines himself to be sinking into the subterranean waters of the deep (that is, on the verge of death). "Out of the depths" the suppliant cries out to God whose presence in the midst of the worshiping people is symbolized by the temple on Mount Zion.

> As my life was ebbing away,
>   I remembered the LORD,
> and my prayer came to you,
>   into your holy temple.
> (Jonah 2:7, NRSV)

Many psalms express longing to "behold the face of God," that is, to ascend the "holy hill" and visit the temple where Yhwh is "enthroned on the praises of Israel," to cite the striking NRSV translation of Psalm 22:3. This yearning to be present in the worshiping community is expressed passionately in one of the laments:

> As a deer yearns
>   for running streams,

> so I yearn
>> for you, my God.*
> I thirst for God,
>> the living God;
> when shall I go to see
>> the face of God?
>>> (Ps. 42:1–2, NJB)

The psalmist's consuming desire is to "dwell" (inhabit, remain, live) in "the house of the Lord" (Ps. 23:6), that is, to be ensconced in the Temple environment.

> One thing I ask of Yhwh, that I seek:
> To dwell in the house of Yhwh all the days of my life,
> to contemplate the favor of Yhwh,
> and to inquire in his temple.
>> (Ps. 27:4, BWA)

The verbs of seeing used in these poetic contexts ("see" and "contemplate") are intriguing, for Israel's poets characteristically use verbs of hearing (e.g., Ps. 81:5b–10). Outside of Israel language like this would refer to something very concrete: beholding the god's statue in the temple or in a ceremonial procession. However, since Israelite religion from the time of Moses prohibited making images of God (Ex. 20:4; Deut. 5:8–10), this visual interpretation is excluded. Some have suggested that expressions like "seeing God's power and glory" (Ps. 63:2) may refer to a cultic drama or "liturgical mime" in which God's deeds were enacted.[2] Of course, the visual language, at least in many cases, is merely a metaphorical expression for the nearness of God experienced in the Temple services. In any case, the Temple is the particular place where God's glory "dwells" (Ps. 26:8). Therefore a psalmist prays:

> Send forth your light and your truth, let them guide me,
> let them escort me to your holy hill, to your tabernacle.
> Then I will come to the altar of God,
>> to God my delightful joy,
> and praise you on the harp,
> O Yhwh my God.
>> (Ps. 43:3–4, BWA)

---

* This psalm stands at the beginning of the Elohistic Psalter (Psalms 42–83); we would expect to read the personal name Yhwh here (as in an ancient version).

[Note: The last line translated is redundant in Hebrew, "O God, my God." This psalm, however, is the opening psalm in the so-called Elohistic Psalter, which prefers to substitute the general term "God" for the personal name Yhwh. Following the Greek translation (Septuagint), we should read here "Yhwh, my God."]

The psalms, then, lend no support to the notion that a person's relationship with God is a private affair and that God is accessible outside the liturgical forms and sacraments of the worshiping community. On the contrary, the individual is related to God as a member of the covenant community. To be sure, God is not bound by the limitations of the community but can deal with people freely and graciously (see Ex. 33:19). Yet if persons would have access to God in worship, then they must come, or even make a pilgrimage, to the established meeting place with others and engage in a corporate form of worship. In the Psalter, therefore, the individual praises God in concert with the worshiping community.

> O praise the Lord with me,
> and let us exalt God's name together!
> (Ps. 34:3, BWA)

Liturgies of the Tribal Federation

The practice of making pilgrimages to "the house of God" has had a long history. Even in the period before the formation of the state under David, when Israel was loosely bound together as a tribal confederacy (ca. 1200–1000 B.C.), it was customary for people to gather from all the tribes of Israel to the central sanctuary, located first at Shechem (Josh. 24) and subsequently at Shiloh (1 Sam. 1). Israel's ancient covenant law specifically enjoined three annual pilgrimages, at which times the representatives of the people "must appear before the Suzerain [*'Adon*] Yhwh" (Ex. 23:14–17; 34:18, 22–23). These pilgrimage festivals, originally adopted from the Canaanite sacred calendar, coincided with the major agricultural seasons. The first, the festival of Unleavened Bread (later associated with the Passover), was held in March-April at the time of the barley harvest; the second, the festival of Firstfruits (also called Weeks or Pentecost), occurred in May-June at the time of the wheat harvest; and the third, the festival of Ingathering (also called Tabernacles), took place in September-October at the time of the grape and olive harvest.

Of these three festivals, the most important was the autumn vintage festival. This wine festival, held at the turn of the year according to the old agricultural calendar (and later connected with New Year's Day, Rosh Hashana), was celebrated with dancing and merrymaking (Judg. 21:19–23). It was a time of drinking new wine, to judge from Eli's suspicion that Hannah was drunk (1 Sam. 1:14–15). However, what had originated as a Canaanite seasonal festival was radically transformed by being reinterpreted in terms of Israel's historical experiences. The custom—which has continued to the present day—of making huts or booths out of tree branches and erecting them in the vineyards while the grapes were being harvested was reinterpreted as a commemoration of the time in the wilderness when Israel lived in huts or shelters (Lev. 23:43). (The Latin Vulgate translated the Hebrew word *sukkoth,* "huts" or "booths," as *tabernacula,* from which comes our word "tabernacles.")

In the early period, even before the time of David, the Israelites seem to have celebrated this festival as a time for renewing the covenant with Yhwh. In the service of worship the saving deeds of Yhwh in Israel's history were proclaimed, and the people were called upon to reaffirm their allegiance to the God of Israel. Perhaps the service held at Shechem under the leadership of Joshua (Joshua 24), when Israel's history in Canaan began, provided the precedent and prototype for periodic services of covenant renewal.[3] It is difficult to specify which psalms actually belonged to the covenant renewal festival. In his commentary on the Psalms, Artur Weiser assigns a great number to this festival, but he surely goes too far.[4] Many of the psalms so classified belong to the Zion festival (to be considered presently), which emphasized God's "everlasting covenant" with David and the choice of Zion as the central sanctuary. Two psalms, however, seem to reflect liturgies of covenant renewal.

Covenant Renewal Liturgies

50	"Gather to me my faithful ones, who made a covenant with me"
*81	"Honey from the Rock"

Let us concentrate on Psalm 81, which closely parallels the liturgy of covenant renewal found in Joshua 24:

The call to assembly (Josh. 24:1)
Recital of God's deeds of deliverance (vv. 2–13)
Call to reaffirm covenant loyalty (vv. 14–22)
Putting away of foreign gods (vv. 23–24)
Renewal of the covenant and hearing the covenant law (vv. 25–26)
Dismissal (vv. 28)

The psalm begins with an invocation to praise "the God of Jacob" at the sanctuary "on our feast day," presumably a reference to the fall festival (Ps. 81:1–5a). Then comes a recitation, perhaps given by a cultic priest or prophet, of what Yhwh has done for the people, including the deliverance from Egyptian bondage, the revelation at Sinai ("the secret place of thunder"), and the sojourn in the wilderness (v. 5b–10). The psalm reaches a climax with an appeal to the people to repent and reaffirm their loyalty to Yhwh, and to walk in Yhwh's ways (vv. 11–16), that is, to accept anew the obligations of the covenant law. The theological assumption of Psalm 81 is that of the Mosaic covenant: "If you will obey my voice and keep my covenant, you shall be my own possession among all peoples" (Ex. 19:5).[5] This conditional covenant, when broken, may be renewed in the grace of God, so that the people would be satisfied with "honey from the rock," a motif picked up in old gospel songs. Some of the elements of this covenant renewal service are present in contemporary worship services. It would be interesting to compare the form of this service with the Covenant Renewal Service of John Wesley, designed primarily for use at the turn of the year.[6]

This liturgical tradition persisted even after the unity of the Davidic kingdom was broken and the people were politically divided into the Northern Kingdom (Israel or Ephraim) and the Southern Kingdom (Judah). According to 1 Kings 12:32–33, Jeroboam I (931–910 B.C.), the first king of the Northern Kingdom, instituted an autumn festival "like the feast that was in Judah"—a reference to the harvest or New Year festival (Tabernacles), which was celebrated in the South. For political reasons he wanted to deter his people from making pilgrimages to the Temple in Jerusalem, so he revived the old covenant renewal festival that had been celebrated during the days of the tribal confederacy (the time of the Judges). Subsequently, Bethel became one of the major cultic centers in the North, a fact recognized by the prophet Amos more than a century later when he traveled from his home in the South to Bethel, where "a temple of the kingdom" was located (Amos 7:13). Amos's contemporary, Hosea, seems to have referred to the fall festi-

val in the North (Hos. 9:5, "the day of the feast of Yhwh"). Undoubtedly some of the psalms now found in the Psalter were used in the
Bethel cult. A good example of a North Israelite psalm is the community lament of Psalm 80, which begins with an address to Yhwh, "Shepherd of Israel," and then, shifting metaphors, speaks of the people as
Yhwh's vineyard:

> You brought a vine from Egypt;
> you drove out nations and planted it;
> you cleared the ground for it,
> so that it struck root and filled the land.
> The mountains were covered with its shade,
> and its branches were like those of mighty cedars.
> It put out boughs all the way to the sea,
> its shoots as far as the [Euphrates] river.
>
> (Ps. 80:8–11, REB)

Psalms like these may go back to covenant renewal services held in
the time of the tribal confederacy and kept alive in North Israel
(Ephraim). It may be surmised that after the fall of the Northern Kingdom under Assyrian aggression (722 B.C.), these psalms were taken
over in the Southern Kingdom, where they were adapted for use in the
worship of the Jerusalem temple. That would account for the fact that
in the covenant-renewal Psalm 50, Yhwh is portrayed as coming not
from Sinai (Ps. 68:7–8; cf. Judg. 5:4–5), but from Zion.

> From Zion, perfect in beauty,
> God shines forth.
> Our God comes and will not be silent;
> a fire devours before him,
> and around him a tempest rages.
>
> (Ps. 50:2–3, NIV)

In any case, ancient covenant renewal psalms of this kind were taken
over in the Southern Kingdom, where they were adapted for use in the
festivals of Zion.

Pilgrimage Psalms

Some psalms express an intense longing to make a pilgrimage to the
temple of Jerusalem. This longing, as we have noticed at the beginning

of this chapter, could be expressed in the lament of a person who could not join the procession (Psalms 42–43), but it could also be expressed in joyful anticipation by pilgrims on their way to Jerusalem.

The Psalter now includes one collection of psalms known as "psalms of ascents" (Psalms 120–134). In at least two of these psalms, Psalms 120 and 121, this title refers to festival caravans that enabled pilgrims to go up to "the hill of Yhwh." Foot travel was difficult in those days, but pilgrims took confidence in the protecting care of Yhwh, "your shade on your right hand" (Ps. 121:5). After many experiences along the way, people rejoiced to be standing at last within the gates of Jerusalem and were glad that they had responded positively to the invitation to join the pilgrimage.

> I rejoiced that they said to me,
> "Let us go to the house of Yahweh."
> At last our feet are standing
> at your gates, Jerusalem!
> (Ps. 122:1–2, NJB)

We should not suppose the psalmists thought of God being present in the Temple in the sense that it was literally the divine dwelling. In various ways the interpreters of Israel's faith have sought to do justice to the paradox that the Holy God, who is not part of our human world, becomes present to the people in worship. In Solomon's prayer, associated with the dedication of the Jerusalem temple, the speaker exclaims: "Heaven and the highest heaven cannot contain thee [God]; how much less this house" built by human hands (1 Kings 8:27)! The problem of the "transcendence" and "immanence" of God, to use philosophical language, was dealt with by saying that Yhwh, the Holy God, causes the divine name to be in the sanctuary. The Name, according to the view that prevails in the book of Deuteronomy and material edited from a Deuteronomic point of view, is Yhwh's alter ego, or "other self." The name of God can be invoked in the sanctuary without God becoming localized there.

One of the most beautiful songs of Zion (to be considered presently) is Psalm 84, a pilgrimage psalm in which a poet envies the birds that find security in the Temple structure and exclaims that even one day spent in the Temple courts is better than a thousand spent elsewhere.

> How lovely is your tabernacle,
> O Yhwh of hosts!
> My whole being longs and yearns for Yhwh's [temple]
> courts.

My heart and my flesh sing for joy to the living God.

Even the sparrow finds a home, and the swallow a nest
in which she lays her young, right at your altars,
O Lord of hosts, my King and my God.

(Ps. 84:1–3, BWA)

Here we seem to have a distinctive view of God's real presence in the midst of the people. The central sanctuary is described as the "dwelling place" or, as rendered in some translations, the "tabernacle" (*mishkan-oth*, the Hebrew word is in plural). This may reflect the ancient tradition that Yhwh "tents" or "goes about" among the people (cf. Lev. 26:11–13).[7] In this view, the Temple is not Yhwh's "home," as though Yhwh dwelt or resided there, but the place of divine visitation from time to time.

In this sense, the psalmist—probably on a pilgrimage to Jerusalem—anticipates the "tabernacling presence" of God in the Temple as the people invoke the name of Yhwh and engage in the drama of worship. Strikingly, the psalmist says that "the God of gods will be seen in Zion" (Ps. 84:7), perhaps a reference to dramatic ceremonies such as the ark procession. Both auditory and visual elements, hearing and seeing, song and sacramental rite, combine in the service of worship in which God chooses to become present, enthroned on the praises of the people.

The Festival of Zion

The theme of the kingdom (dominion) of God, which was the burden of Jesus' preaching according to early gospel tradition (Mark 1:14–15), is deeply rooted in Israel's history of worship, going back to a time long before Israel had an earthly king. The ancient hymn found in Ex. 15:1–18, the Song of the Sea, concludes with the exclamation: "Let Yhwh be King forever and ever!" (Ex. 15:18b)

In the period of the tribal confederacy the confession that Yhwh is King was maintained tenaciously, especially in conservative circles that resisted the introduction of monarchy "like the nations" (Judg. 8:22–23; 1 Sam. 8:4–22). Even after the monarchy was founded under the leadership of Saul and especially David, this ancient confession persisted and received great prominence in the Jerusalem temple services. According to the report of Isaiah's call, it was in the Temple that the prophet caught a vision of Yhwh, *the* King par excellence enthroned upon a celestial throne, whose glory fills the whole earth (Isa. 6:1–5).

In the southern kingdom of Judah, which was ruled by Davidic monarchs from beginning to end, a special festival was held, during which worshipers celebrated the enthronement of Yhwh as King over Israel, the nations, and the cosmos. The theme of God's kingship is central in a cluster of psalms that seem to reflect this great religious festival celebrated in "Zion," a term that referred originally to the fortified ridge captured by David but soon came to include the adjacent Temple area and eventually the whole city of Jerusalem. All the psalms belonging to this category are hymns. A prominent feature is the cultic exclamation *Yhwh malak,* usually translated "the Lord reigns" or "the Lord is King."

Enthronement Psalms

29	"Enthroned as king for ever"
*47	"God is the king of all the earth"
93	"Thy throne is established from of old"
*95	"A great King above all gods"
*96	"Declare his glory among the nations!"
97	"Thou art exalted far above all gods"
*98	"The ends of the earth have seen the victory of our God"
*99	"Mighty King, lover of justice"
	(See also Psalm 24, an entrance liturgy.)

These hymns presuppose the centrality of Zion, where Yhwh is magnified in the praises of the people (see, e.g., Pss. 96:6; 97:8; 99:2, 9).[8] It is clear, however, that the divine rule is not confined to Zion. The whole earth, indeed the entire realm of creation, is full of the King's glory. In these psalms the particularities of Israel's historical experience as the people of Yhwh are noticeably sublimated, if not ignored, except for a few pale allusions (e.g., Ps. 99:6–8). In Zion the God of Israel is extolled as the king of the nations and of the universe. According to one ecumenical text, it seems that the peoples of the earth, represented by their princes, attend the festival as members of the people of God.

> God is king over the nations;
>> God sits on his holy throne.
> The princes of the peoples gather
>> as the people of the God of Abraham.

For the shields of the earth belong to God;
he is highly exalted.

(Ps. 47:8–9, NRSV)

(Again it should be noted that at this point we are in the Elohistic Psalter and that originally this psalm celebrated the kingship of Yhwh, not "God" in general.)

Throne-Ascension Psalms

In the festival of Zion the kingship of Yhwh was not just announced, it was celebrated in a ritual enactment of enthronement. A passage in Psalm 47 announces that Yhwh has "gone up" (ascended the throne) amid shouts of acclamation and with the sound of the trumpet (*shofar*):

God has gone up with a shout [of acclamation],
Yhwh, to the sound of the *shofar!*
Sing praises to our God, sing praises;
sing praises to our King, sing praises.
For King of the whole earth is God,
sing hymns of praise.
God reigns over the nations,
God sits on his holy throne.

(vv. 5–8, BWA)

This passage seems to refer to the bearing of the ark of the covenant in procession to the Temple (Ps. 24:7–10) where Yhwh "sits enthroned upon the cherubim" (Ps. 99:1), the winged figures that flanked the ark. Since, however, the earthly temple was regarded as a microcosmic copy of the heavenly one, as in Isaiah's vision, the drama symbolized God's entrance into the heavenly palace (temple) and the ascension to the celestial throne. Thus Yhwh, "the great King" (Ps. 47:2), not only reigns in Israel, where earthly praises are sung, but over the whole cosmos.

The psalms of Yhwh's enthronement may reflect a festival held in the fall, at the turn of the year, when worshipers made a pilgrimage to Jerusalem to celebrate Yhwh's kingly triumph over all powers hostile to the divine rule. This view has been championed effectively by the Scandinavian scholar Sigmund Mowinckel, who, with excessive enthusiasm, assigns some twenty psalms to this category (Psalms 8; 15; 24; 29; 33; 46; 48; 50; 66A; 75; 76; 81; 82; 84; 95; 100; 114; 118;

132; 149). In his view the fall festival celebrated in Jerusalem was patterned after festivals of divine kingship known among Israel's neighbors.[9]

The chief example is the Babylonian New Year festival, the *akitu,* at which the Babylonian creation myth was recited and reenacted. The myth depicts the violent struggle between the youthful god Marduk and the goddess Tiamat, the dragon of chaos, and her chaotic allies. Victorious in the conflict, the divine warrior was acclaimed king in the council of the gods and the hymnic cry was raised: "Marduk has become king." The myth portrays human involvement in the processes of nature which, moving in a circle, ever return to the beginning when the god must win a new victory over the powers of darkness and chaos.

Since Israel's worship was profoundly influenced by the surrounding culture, it is tempting to interpret these enthronement psalms in the light of cultic practice in Mesopotamia and Canaan. Some scholars argue that the cultic exclamation *Yhwh malak* should be translated, "Yhwh has become King," in which case the Jerusalem cult would have celebrated Yhwh's accession to the throne as king. To be sure, Hebrew grammar permits this translation. But it is exceedingly doubtful whether the Israelite faith, even in the cosmopolitan atmosphere of Jerusalem, adopted wholesale the ancient mythical views. The notion that Yhwh is involved in the cycles of the cosmos and must fight to win kingship anew at the turn of the year is completely alien to Israel's faith. "The gods of the peoples are idols," that is, natural powers within the cosmos, if not figments of human imagination, "but Yhwh made the heavens" (Ps. 96:5) and therefore transcends the whole cosmos. These psalms are explicit in saying that Yhwh's throne is established "from of old" (immeasurable past time), that God's kingdom is "from everlasting" (Ps. 93:2). Yhwh is the King who was, who is, and who is to come—to judge the earth with righteousness (Ps. 96:13). God who established the divine kingdom of old, and who will come in power to realize the divine rule with finality, is *now* enthroned on the praises of the people. The dimensions of time, expressed in the tenses of human experience—past, present, and future—are expanded to their limit in the acclamation, "Yhwh is King!"[10]

The Sacramental Power of the Psalms

Nevertheless, it must be said that the kingship hymns celebrate an event, not a general truth; they effect transformation in the present, not just give hope for the future. The translation of the cultic shout as "Yhwh reigns" is too mild to do justice to the spirit of the Zion festival. The proclamation has a dynamic, eventful ring, something like the Easter hymn, "Christ the Lord is risen today, Alleluia!" These psalms, in the view of contemporary scholars, are sacramental in nature, for when enacted in worship they have the power to effect a change.

Scandinavian Sigmund Mowinckel forcefully called attention to this dimension of the Psalms in *The Psalms in Israel's Worship.*[11] Usually people concentrate on the first theme, his view that a New Year's festival was celebrated in the Jerusalem temple that was analogous to cultic celebrations elsewhere in the ancient world (discussed above). But even more significant is his view of the eschatology (or the realization of God's kingdom) implicit in the exclamation, "Yhwh reigns." He proposed that such language functions as a sacrament, which has the power to bring about a new reality that did not exist before. When used in the cult the words of the psalms are active forces that do something, that effect a transformation.

Centuries ago a sacramental view of the Psalms was advocated by St. Athanasius (ca. 297–373) who held that "the distinctive nature of the psalms lies in their ability to 'affect' and 'mold' a person."[12] In our time various scholars, more directly influenced by Mowinckel, have emphasized the transformatory power of the language of the psalms. In the liturgy, they affirm, the reality of God's rule is brought into the present and dramatically actualized. Commenting on the "liturgical enactment" of God's throne-ascension, Walter Brueggemann observes:

> This psalm [Ps. 96] marks the beginning of a new reign. Liturgy is not play acting, but it is the evocation of an alternative reality that comes into play in the very moment of the liturgy. So this moment is when God's rule is visible and effective.

"Liturgical use of the psalm," he adds, "is more than hope," the hope for the coming of God's kingdom. "It is making the future momentarily present now through word, gesture, practice."[13] Similarly James Luther Mays maintains that the Psalms present a "language world" that, when we enter it by praying the poetic words, becomes a "means of grace" that shapes us as new persons with a new sense of the reality of God's dominion.[14]

Enthroned over the Powers of Chaos

These psalms show how Israel appropriated the mythical imagery of the ancient world and converted it to the praise of Yhwh, the King of Israel and of the cosmos. The ancient myth of the Creator's victory over the powers of chaos, symbolized by "the deep," "the floods," "the sea," is used poetically to express the faith that no powers—whether historical enemies, evil, death, or anything else in creation—can subvert God's rule. In an ancient Israelite hymn, which displays the influence of Canaanite poetry, it is said:

> Yhwh is enthroned above the flood,
> Yhwh is enthroned as king forever.
> (Ps. 29:10, BWA)

This language also occurs in one of the hymns of Yhwh's kingship, where the poet portrays "the floods," "many waters," and "the sea" lifting up their stormy waves, as though seeking to challenge the sovereignty of Yhwh. But the tumult is in vain, for Yhwh is enthroned transcendently.

> The floods lift up, Yhwh,
> the floods lift up their sound,
> the floods lift up their pounding.
> More majestic than the thunders of many waters,
> more majestic than the breakers of the sea,
> on high Yhwh is majestic!
> (Ps. 93:3–4, BWA)

As we have already seen in other psalms (e.g., Ps. 104), it is impossible to translate this poetic language into flat prose. The biblical poets express a human experience that is not confined to ancient Israel. There is disorder in the world that, from a human point of view, seems to challenge the sovereignty of God. The experience of the threat of chaos may be occasioned by the imminence of an invasion of a foe from the North, as in the case of Jeremiah's moving vision of the return of chaos (Jer. 4:23–26), or, in our own time, the ominous possibility of ecological catastrophe. In the faith of the psalmists, however, God is enthroned triumphantly over the powers that threaten to plunge human history into meaningless disorder and chaos. As Creator, God stands beyond history, above the cosmos. Therefore Yhwh's kingship, celebrated in Zion, demonstrates firm divine control over the powers of chaos that threaten human existence. Notice that the poet extends a special invitation to "the sea," "the floods"—the remnant of chaos that potentially threatens the ordered world of creation—to join with nature and human beings in an anthem of praise:

> Let the sea thunder, and all that it holds,
> the world and all who live in it.
> Let the rivers clap their hands,
> and the mountains shout for joy together,
>
> at Yahweh's approach, for he is coming
> to judge the earth;
> he will judge the world with saving justice
> and the nations with fairness.
>   (Ps. 98:7–9, NJB; see also Ps. 96:10–13)

Here the verb "judge" means much more than the English word suggests. It refers to the power to obtain and maintain justice and proper order—power that human rulers should have ("Give us a king to judge us," 1 Sam. 8:6) but that, in the biblical view, is vested supremely and ultimately in God.

The psalm just quoted shows that an important dimension of psalms of this type is their eschatological outlook. In hymnic tones they express the expectation that the King is coming on the stage of history to consummate the divine rule. In the prophecy of Second Isaiah, this announcement was transposed into the key of the "good news" that later was heard in Jesus' preaching (Mark 1:15).

> How beautiful upon the mountains
>   are the feet of the messenger who announces peace,
> who brings good news,
>   who announces salvation,
>   who says to Zion, "Your God reigns."
>   (Isa. 52:7, NRSV)

Today the exclamation "The Lord is King" is raised hymnically in services of Christian worship. Indeed, in some Christian circles a feast has been celebrated in the autumn known as "the feast of Christ the King." The Christian church reads the enthronement psalms in the context of the gospel that, through Jesus Christ, God has inaugurated the divine kingdom by striking a decisive blow against all powers of oppression, darkness, chaos, and death. Those who celebrate Christ's kingship in the festivals of his enthronement are summoned to new action and responsibility in the world, whatever the odds may be, knowing that the decisive victory has already been won. We still live in a world where the weak are oppressed by the mighty, where the powers of chaos threaten to break over humanity, and where death imposes the final threat to the goodness and meaningfulness of life. Yet the Christian community, which celebrates God's triumph in Jesus Christ, also lives toward the final establishing of God's dominion when, in accordance with the intention of the original creation, all human beings will become fully human and the nonhuman creation as well will participate in the consummation of God's creative and redemptive purpose (Rom. 8:19–23)—"a new heaven and a new earth." In the time between the advent of the King and the final establishment of the kingdom, Christians also pray the enthronement psalms in the spirit of the Lord's Prayer:

> Thy kingdom come, thy will be done,
> on earth as it is in heaven.
>
> (Matt. 6:10, KJV)

The Promises of Grace to David

We turn now from the theme of God's kingship to the related theme of the earthly king as the viceregent of God, or, to use the more familiar language, God's "messiah." The Hebrew word for messiah (*mashiah;* Greek, *christos*) literally means "anointed one," and in the period of early Israel was used of the reigning king. A good illustration is found in the story of David's flight from King Saul, in which at one point we are told that, when the opportunity presented itself, he declined to kill "Yhwh's anointed" (1 Sam. 24:1–7; cf. 26:6–10). Eventually the term "messiah" came to be used of "the one who is to come" (Matt. 11:3; Luke 7:19–20). As we have seen in chapter 1, the book of Psalms was finally edited and issued in the name of David, the royal prototype of the future messiah.

The rise of David as king and the selection of Jerusalem as the place of the central sanctuary had a far-reaching influence upon Israel's worship, and specifically upon the covenant festival celebrated in the Jerusalem temple. Jerusalem theologians wanted to say that the rule of David was the climax of the sacred history that began with the migration of Abraham from Mesopotamia (Gen. 12:1–9) and that issued in the exodus from Egypt and the covenant at Sinai (Exodus 1—24). It was their conviction that, in raising up David to be king and in choosing Zion as the central sanctuary, Yhwh had led Israel into a new era which required a new theological understanding. This is the theme of Psalm 78, a storytelling psalm that we considered briefly in chapter 3.

To understand this new kind of covenant theology that centered in David and Zion, it is necessary to turn to the portion of the David story found in two important chapters: 2 Samuel 6 and 7. The first of these chapters relates that David, desiring to unify his kingdom on the basis of the religious loyalty of the tribal confederacy, brought the Ark of the Covenant—the portable "throne" on which Yhwh was thought to be invisibly enthroned in the midst of the people during their wars and wanderings—into his new capital of Jerusalem with the intention of housing it in a temple. Jerusalem was not to be just the city of David but "Zion, city of our God," the locus of Yhwh's real presence in the midst of the people. The last part of Psalm 24 is an ancient liturgy, possibly as old as the time of Solomon, which undoubtedly was used in reenacting the processional bearing of the Ark into the Jerusalem temple where Yhwh was acclaimed as King. As the procession reaches the gates of Zion, voices sing antiphonally:

> O gates, lift up your heads!
> Up high, you everlasting doors,
>   so the King of glory may come in!
> Who is the King of glory?—
>   the Lord, mighty and valiant,
>   the Lord, valiant in battle.
> (Ps. 24:7–8, NJPS)

In the following verses the ritual is repeated, and once again the Divine Warrior, Yhwh, enthroned invisibly on the ark, is acclaimed as the glorious King.

God's Choice of David and His Line

Let us return for a moment to the story in 2 Samuel 6 and 7. David wanted to build Yhwh a "house" (temple), comparable in magnificence to his own palace. The prophet Nathan, however, opposed this plan and delivered to the king an oracle in which Yhwh promised to build *David* a "house" (dynasty), which would stand in perpetuity.

> Yhwh announces to you that Yhwh will make a "house" for
>   you:
> When your days are completed and you rest with your
>   ancestors,
> I will raise up after you your offspring, who will issue from
>   your body,
> and I will stabilize his kingdom.
> He shall build a "house" for my name,
> and I will establish his royal throne in perpetuity.
> I will be Father to him, and he will be Son to me.
> When he does wrong, I will chasten him with the rod of
>   human punishment,
> and with the stripes of human beings,
> but my loyalty [*hesed*] I will not withdraw from him,
> as I did in the case of Saul, whom I removed before you.
> Before me your house and your kingdom will stand secure
>   perpetually,
> your throne will be established in perpetuity.
>
> (2 Sam. 7:11b–16, BWA)

This passage has been called "the magna carta of Old Testament
messianism" (Roland Murphy). Notice that the Davidic covenant, unlike the Mosaic covenant, is not couched in conditional terms: "If you
will obey my voice . . ." (Ex. 19:5–6). To be sure, it contains a conditional element in that wrong actions will have consequences that not
even a king can escape. But God's relationship with the people, mediated through the reigning Davidic king, the "anointed one," is based
solely on divine grace. Under no circumstance will Yhwh withdraw
the covenant promise of loyalty [*hesed*] to David that is the basis of
the stability of the kingdom and its indefinite duration. Fundamentally
the covenant is unconditional—grounded on God's faithful promises,
not upon the fallible actions of human beings or the contingencies of
history. This is an important theological line that leads into the New
Testament, where the proclamation is made that God's relationship
with people, mediated through Jesus, the Anointed One (Greek, *christos,* "Christ"), is grounded unconditionally in divine grace and that
through Christ, God has ratified the promises of grace to Israel (Rom.
15:8).

The fall festival in Jerusalem, then, acquired a special character
owing to the celebration of the simultaneous founding of the
Jerusalem sanctuary and the Davidic dynasty. According to this

covenant theology, Yhwh is *the King* par excellence, as Isaiah perceived in his inaugural vision.

> I saw Yhwh sitting upon a throne, high and lifted up;
> and his train filled the temple.
>
> (Isa. 6:1, BWA)

The King, whose throne is in heaven (Ps. 11:4), has chosen Zion as the center of the divine rule on earth and has chosen the Davidic king as the representative of the kingship of God in Israel.

Psalms of the Davidic Covenant

Several psalms express this theological understanding of God's relationship to the people.

*78	A recitation of Yhwh's great deeds
*132	A liturgy commemorating Yhwh's choice of David and of Zion
*89	A hymn and a lament based on Yhwh's covenant with David

Psalm 78 (see chapter 3) contains a long summary of Yhwh's historical deeds, beginning with the exodus (vv. 1–66). According to the psalmist, the old sacred history has come to an end, owing to the unfaithfulness of North Israel ("the tent of Joseph"). Yhwh has made a new beginning in history by raising up David to be king and by selecting Zion as the central sanctuary (vv. 67–72).

In Psalm 132 the story in 2 Samuel 7 is clearly in mind. The psalm begins by recalling David's intention to build a sanctuary for Yhwh (vv. 1–5). It continues with a ritual that was undoubtedly used during the processional bearing of the Ark into the Jerusalem temple (vv. 6–10). Recalling the ancient Song of the Ark (Num. 10:35–36), worshipers affirm that Yhwh has found a new dwelling place in Zion.

> Arise, Yhwh, and go to your resting place,
> You and the ark of your power!
> Let your priests be vested in righteousness,
> and let your devotees sing for joy!
>
> (Ps. 132:8–9, BWA)

The psalm concludes (vv. 11–18) with a reaffirmation of Yhwh's covenant with David and Yhwh's choice of Zion as the earthly center of the divine presence.

Promises of Grace to David

Psalm 89 is a very important psalm theologically. The first part (vv. 1–37) is a hymn that praises Yhwh for the faithfulness (*hesed*) manifested in the covenant with David. The hymn echoes the covenant theology of 2 Samuel 7 and, in addition, strikes the note that Yhwh's power as Creator upholds the stability and continuity of the Davidic throne. The second part of the psalm is a lament (vv. 38–51) in which the psalmist complains that Yhwh apparently has forsaken the covenant with David, as evidenced by the defeat of the king in battle. The psalmist appeals to God to remove the calamity and thus to reaffirm the covenant loyalty once sworn to David.

> [Note: See also 2 Samuel 23:1–7, an old poem often called "the last words of David." Here the theme is the "covenant in perpetuity" (*berith 'olam*) that Yhwh has made with David and the resulting security and welfare of the Davidic rule. In this hymnic passage David is called, according to some translations, "the sweet psalmist of Israel" (RSV), though the meaning may be that David is "the favorite of the songs of Israel" (RSV margin). The NJPS translates "The favorite of the songs of Israel" with marginal notes suggesting either "The favorite of the Mighty One of Israel" or "The sweet singer of Israel."]

The Anointed One

This Davidic covenant theology, with its twofold emphasis upon the choosing of David and the choosing of Zion, casts light on two groups of psalms in the Psalter: the royal psalms and the psalms of Zion.

The first group consists of those psalms in which the king is the central figure.

Royal Psalms

*2	"You are my son, today I have begotten you" (coronation psalm)
*18	"With the loyal thou dost show thyself loyal" (thanksgiving for the king's victory)

20	"May we shout for joy over your victory!" (prayer for the king's victory)
21	"In thy strength the king rejoices" (coronation psalm)
45	"Your divine throne endures for ever" (ode for a royal wedding)
72	"Give the king thy justice, O God" (coronation psalm)
101	"I will sing of loyalty and of justice" (coronation psalm)
*110	"The order of Melchizedek" (coronation psalm)
144: 1–11	"Rescue me from the many waters" (royal lament)

Israel lived in an environment in which the king's authority was based upon a mythology that made him the representative and mediator of the divine order of the cosmos. An ancient Sumerian text traces kingship to a divine origin in primeval times, "when kingship was lowered from heaven."[15] The king, by virtue of his royal office, was elevated to a lofty status in society and, indeed, in God's cosmic administration. In ancient Babylonia the king was regarded as divinely commissioned; in Egypt, the pharaoh was considered to be the divine Son of God. *Ex officio* the king was the channel of cosmic blessing to the social order. He was the representative of his subjects before God, and the representative of God (or gods) to human beings.

In the royal psalms of the Psalter the king is extolled in the extravagant "court style" of the ancient Near East. He is called "the fairest of human beings" (Ps. 45:2); his rule is the source of divine blessing in society (Ps. 72:17); he is victorious over the powers of chaos symbolized by "the sea" and "the rivers" (Ps. 89:25); he is exalted to Yhwh's throne, where he sits at "the right hand of God" (Ps. 110:1). According to some translations of the royal wedding ode, Psalm 45, he is addressed as "God": "Your throne, O God, endures forever and ever." (v. 7, NRSV)

> [Note: This translation is also given in the New Jerusalem Bible and in the New American Bible. In this sense the passage is quoted from the Greek translation (Septuagint) in the New Testament at one place: Hebrews 1:8. Some modern translations gloss over the problem by translating "your divine throne" (e.g.,

RSV). Even if the more difficult reading of the Hebrew is adopted, this isolated text provides no basis for the notion that in ancient Israel the king was regarded as divine.]

Israel, however, did not adopt the mythical view of the king without modification. According to Israelite tradition, kingship emerged not in mythical times but out of the harsh realities of secular politics, particularly the crisis caused by the Philistine attempt to build an empire in Palestine. Above all, the institution of kingship in Israel was connected with Israel's sacred history, that is, the formation of Israel as the people of God. The raising up of David was a decisive act of Yhwh in Israel's historical pilgrimage. Therefore, the royal psalms, despite their dependence upon the court poetry of the ancient world, do not confer divinity upon the king. The king is God's "son" by adoption, as we read clearly in Psalm 2:7 (quoted in Acts 13:33).

This view, of course, reflects the theology of Nathan's oracle to David, discussed above. A special relationship exists between God and king ("I will be his father, and he shall be my son," 2 Sam. 7:14), a relationship based on divine choice or adoption. This view is elaborated in Psalm 89, for instance, in these lines:

> He will cry to me, "You are my father,
> my God, the rock of my salvation!"
> So I shall make him my first-born,
> the highest of earthly kings.
> (Ps. 89:26–27, NJB)

In short, the king's authority is not absolute: it is derived from Yhwh, who is *the* King. The Davidic king is *chosen* to perform a task: to rule as Yhwh's representative in the kingdom on earth. In this royal capacity, his role is to obtain justice for the weak and the oppressed and to mediate divine blessing to the social order (see Psalm 72). Above all, the king rules under the judgment of God (cf. Deut. 17:14–20). But let us focus our attention on a couple of royal psalms that portray the king as being elevated to a high position in God's cosmic administration.

The Son of God

In Psalm 2, quoted several times in the New Testament (see appendix C), the king is designated "son of God." The psalm was originally composed to celebrate the coronation of an Israelite king, at which time his divine "election," or adoption, was announced.

In the judgment of some scholars, the psalm reflects a ritual of coronation known in the ancient world, particularly in Egypt.[16] The king was crowned in the sanctuary, where he received the decree from God that made his rule legitimate. After the coronation, he ascended the throne and issued an ultimatum to his enemies. Couriers then ran to the surrounding districts, announcing that "so and so has become king!" At this the people rejoiced, for his reign was regarded as the beginning of a new era of blessing for society and even for the natural realm (see Ps. 72:15–17).

Notice how the structure of Psalm 2 seems to accord with such a coronation ceremony.

Preparation (Ps. 2:1–3)

The psalm begins with a portrayal of the rebellion of the nations against Yhwh's "anointed" (messiah, or reigning king). In antiquity a change of throne was the signal for revolutionary forces to break loose.

Installation (Ps. 2:4–6)

Next the announcement is made of Yhwh's installation of the king in the sanctuary, the "holy hill" of Zion.

Legitimation (Ps. 2:7–9)

Then "the decree" of Yhwh—the protocol that endows the king with authority—is announced: the king is declared to be Yhwh's son, "begotten this day" (the day of coronation) and elected to universal rule.

Ultimatum (Ps. 2:10–11)

Finally, the king issues his ultimatum: rebellious rulers and territories are warned to recognize his authority.

At the Right Hand of God

Psalm 110 also seems to reflect a coronation ceremony. The Hebrew text has suffered in transmission, which may indicate that the psalm is very old, reaching back into the period of the early monarchy. At one point the poet makes use of the ancient tradition about Melchizedek, a Canaanite priest-king of the pre-Israelite city–state of Salem (Jerusalem). According to the tradition found in an unusual chapter in the book of Genesis, Melchizedek blessed Abraham in the name of the Canaanite god, 'El 'Elyon, "God Most High," who is acclaimed as "maker of heaven and earth" (Gen. 14:17–20).

Building on this curious tradition, the psalm begins with an oracle (Ps. 110:1), presumably given in the sanctuary, in which the officiating priest addresses the king as "my lord," a royal title. According to the oracle, Yhwh invites the king to sit on the heavenly throne—at Yhwh's right hand! This is an astounding idea—that a king should, as it were, sit beside God, sharing the throne of God.

> [Note: Once the psalm was taken out of a coronation setting, the language concerning Yhwh (Adonai, translated "the Lord") and "my lord" (the king) was taken in a new way. In the postexilic period, when there were no kings on the throne of Judah and when David was regarded as the author of the psalm, it was construed, somewhat freely, to mean that David addressed the coming messiah as "my lord." In this sense ("The Lord said to my Lord") the verse is interpreted messianically in the New Testament (e.g., Mark 12:36). See appendix C.]

The remainder of the psalm portrays the exaltation of the king to the highest position of honor. Speaking in the name of Yhwh, the priest first announces that from Zion the power of the king will extend throughout the nation and beyond (Ps. 110:2–3). Then he sets forth the divine oath by which the king is legitimated as priest-king in the succession of Melchizedek, who had both political and religious authority (v. 4). Finally (vv. 5–7), he gives the assurance that the Lord (Yhwh) will be at the king's right hand (here the idiom differs from "the right hand" in v. 1). This means that Yhwh will ever be near the king to help in overthrowing hostile powers.

In using this hyperbolic language, found in both coronation psalms (Psalms 2 and 110), Israelite court poets have glorified the office of the king far beyond the political realities of the modest Davidic monarchy. At no time did Davidic kings achieve the universal sway promised in the coronation ritual. The portrayal of the king does not conform to any specific king of the house of David, not even David himself. Rather, it depicts the *type* of the true king who perfectly combines power and goodness—historically a rare, if not impossible, combination! Since the type was not perfectly embodied in any of the Davidic kings, it is understandable that in the course of time, especially after the collapse of the Davidic monarchy in 587 B.C., these psalms were interpreted to refer to *the* Anointed One (Messiah) of the future, who would come in the fullness of time to rule over God's kingdom on earth.

Thus the extravagant language of the royal psalms, which was once court flattery, came to be understood as pointing to *the* king, *the* messiah, of the future. The distinguished Old Testament theologian Gerhard von Rad once observed that we really do not know whether those who paid homage to the king in this extravagant manner were filled with doubt about him and were asking in their hearts, as did John the Baptist later, "Are you he who is to come, or shall we look for another?" (Matt. 11:3).[17] In any case, the royal psalms were retained and used in worship long after kingship had become a thing of the past. It is significant that in the postmonarchic period, when the final revision of the Psalter was issued, the songs (psalms) of Israel were attributed to David. The people regarded David as the type of the true king, who represented them before God and who mediated God's kingly rule on earth. They prayed the psalms "in David," so to speak. The New Testament shows that early Christians prayed the psalms "in Christ," the Anointed One (*christos*) who belongs in David's lineage but who far exceeds the Davidic type.

The City of the Great King

Several psalms are often grouped under the rubric of "songs of Zion," for they express the view that Yhwh has chosen Zion as the earthly center of the divine rule. The title itself is taken from Psalm 137, which voices the despondency of people uprooted from their homeland and taken into Babylonian exile. Their captors taunted them, doubtless saying, "Where is your God?" (Lam. 2:15; Ps. 79:10; cf. Ps. 42:3, 10), and demanded that they sing "one of the songs of Zion."

> How can we sing Jahve's song
> upon a foreign soil?
>
> Jerusalem, if I forget you
>   let my hand forget
>   let my tongue stick fast in my mouth
> if I do not remember
> if I do not lift you, Jerusalem
> to my highest joy.
>   (Ps. 137:4–6, SB)

The title "songs of Zion," although actually drawn from a lament, is quite appropriate for the psalms we are about to consider, whose mood of exultation stands out all the more sharply by contrast with that of exiles who wept over the destruction of the Temple.

Songs of Zion

The songs of Zion presuppose a major tenet of Davidic covenant theology: Yhwh has chosen Zion as the place of the divine presence (see Ps. 132:13–18). Just as Israel's poets spoke of the Davidic king in extravagant court language, so Zion was glorified in poetic language that has mythical overtones. The holy mountain, "beautiful in elevation" and "the joy of all the earth" (Ps. 48:2), was identified with Mount Casius (Mount Zaphon) in Syria, the Olympus of the north, which Canaanites regarded as the dwelling place of the gods. According to poetic vision, the Temple was situated at the "navel," or center, of the universe, where heaven and earth meet; and from a source beneath the Temple a life-giving stream sprang up ("the river of God," Ps. 46:4) and flowed from the city to the Dead Sea, transforming the wilderness into a fertile region and converting the Dead Sea into a freshwater lake (Ezek. 47:1–12; cf. Rev. 22:1–2). In a priestly passage of the Pentateuch there is a suggestion that the sanctuary in Jerusalem was constructed according to a heavenly model (Ex. 25:9), just as Babylonian temples were regarded as miniature replicas of a heavenly prototype.[18]

This mythical language is used, of course, for poetic adornment. The mythical view of the temples of the ancient Near East has been modified. In the Israelite view, Zion was not a holy hill from primeval times; rather, at a particular point in history, in the time of David, it became sacred, the place where Yhwh chose to be present in the midst of the people. Hence, it came to be the sanctuary to which the people made their pilgrimages.

In our age of universalism this emphasis upon the centrality of Zion is hard to understand. It sounds a bit nationalistic and theologically offensive. Surely if God is present at all in the midst of the people, the divine presence could be celebrated in one place as well as in another. Why should Zion receive theological priority over sanctuaries in Rome, Canterbury, New York, or elsewhere? The answer is that Zion has come to be a symbol whose meaning transcends the politics of David or the geography of Palestine. The Zion psalms express an ecumenicity that arises out of historical rootedness and particularity. To the psalmists, Zion was the center of historical meaning that God had disclosed to Israel and, through Israel, to the whole world. The meaning unveiled in Israel's history is not confined to Israel; it is the meaning of all human existence with its history of wars, animosities, and misunderstandings—the history portrayed in the story of the tower of Babel (Gen. 11:1–9). In a passage about the "last days"—the consummation of history—it is announced that ultimately all nations and peoples will make a pilgrimage to Zion (Isa. 2:2–4).

The Christian faith, with its spacious universalism, does not surrender the centrality of Zion. The whole drama of God's dealings with the people leads up to the appearance of the Messiah in Jerusalem, and to his death and victory there—the crucial event which is reenacted in Christian worship. Zion is the historical center around which is gathered the people of God, whose membership is determined by God's choosing, not by human standards. It is theologically appropriate, then, that Psalm 87:3 became the text of Augustine's monumental work *The City of God*. Centuries later, the same text inspired this hymn by John Newton (1725–1807):

> Glorious things of thee are spoken,
> Zion, city of our God;
> God, whose word cannot be broken,
> formed thee for his own abode.
> On the Rock of Ages founded,
> what can shake thy sure repose?
> With salvation's walls surrounded,
> thou mayst smile at all thy foes.

Our Refuge and Strength

In the songs of Zion and in many other psalms in the Psalter the temple of Jerusalem is regarded as a bulwark of security precisely because it is the place where God is present in the midst of the people. In popular theology, the confidence in the Temple as a sanctuary of protection led to a false sense of security and to the notion that people can worship God and "get away with murder" and exploitation of the poor. In his "Temple sermon" (Jer. 7:1–15; see also 26:1–19), Jeremiah issued a strong condemnation of this popular "Temple theology."

> Listen to the word of Yahweh, all you of Judah who come
> in by these gates to worship Yahweh. Yahweh Sabaoth, the

God of Israel, says this: Amend your behaviour and your
actions and I will let you stay in this place. Do not put your
faith in delusive words, such as: This is Yahweh's
sanctuary, Yahweh's sanctuary, Yahweh's sanctuary! But
if you really amend your behaviour and your actions, if you
really treat one another fairly, if you do not exploit the
stranger, the orphan and the widow, if you do not shed
innocent blood in this place and if you do not follow other
gods, to your own ruin, then I shall let you stay in this
place, in the country I gave for ever to your ancestors of
old. (Jer. 7:2b–7, NJB)

The "ifs" in this sermon indicate that Jeremiah, who stood in the tradition of Mosaic covenant theology with its conditional emphasis, was
attacking the false confidence in the Temple engendered by Davidic
theology.

> [Note: The translation of verses 3 and 7 of the Temple sermon, "I
> (Yhwh) will dwell with you in this place" (RSV; cf NAB), reflects
> the premise of Davidic theology that Yhwh elected Zion as the
> divine dwelling place; therefore, the Temple was a sanctuary of
> safety in the presence of God. Jeremiah attacks this view with the
> kind of theological emphasis reflected in Psalm 81 (see the
> discussion on pages 151–2)].

However, the Temple theology associated with Zion cannot be dis-
missed on the basis of its popular misunderstanding or its misuse to jus-
tify a particular lifestyle. To appreciate Zion theology, one should turn
to its best interpreters. In the prophetic tradition, one should turn to Isaiah of Jerusalem, who preceded Jeremiah by about a century. Standing
firmly in the tradition of Davidic theology, with its twin convictions of
Yhwh's election of the Davidic king and the election of Zion, this
prophet announced that the presence of the Holy God in the midst of the
people (Immanuel, "God with us") means a divine judgment that purifies Zion so that it may truly be the City of God (Isa. 1:21–26) and the
raising up of a faithful king to sit upon the throne of David (Isa. 7:1–17;
9:2–7).[19]

Be Still and Know

In the Psalter the theme of Yhwh's dwelling in Zion receives its profoundest treatment in Psalm 46, one of the best-known psalms, thanks in
part to Martin Luther, who found in the psalm the keynote for his hymn

of the Reformation, "A Mighty Fortress Is Our God." In the spirit of Isaiah of Jerusalem, the psalmist glorifies Zion for the purpose of announcing that human confidence is grounded in the transcendent sovereignty of God, whose cosmic rule is known and celebrated in Zion. The theme of confidence in the transcendent God, whose sovereignty over the cosmos and history is centered in Zion, is developed in three strophes. Each strophe is punctuated with the choral refrain:

> The Lord [Yhwh] of hosts is with us,
> the God of Jacob is our bulwark.
>
> (BWA)

[Note: This is, of course, the theme of Immanuel, "God with us," which was prominent in the message of Isaiah of Jerusalem (e.g., Isa. 7:14; 8:8) and indeed in Israelite worship in general (cf. Amos 5:14). The Immanuel ("God is with us") antiphonal refrain is heard in verses 7 and 11 of the psalm in its present arrangement. However, from a stylistic point of view, it should also resound at the end of verse 3 at the point marked by *Selah,* possibly a term referring to a musical interlude. The threefold choral response is proposed in some modern translations (e.g., NEB and JB).]

In the first strophe (vv. 1–3 + refrain), the poet draws on mythical language to describe the shaking of the foundations of earthly existence. Even if the earth should be shaken with cosmic tumult and the waters of chaos were to threaten to overwhelm, God is the transcendent source for the meaning of human existence and the whole cosmos.

> Therefore we will not fear, though the earth should change,
> though the mountains shake in the heart of the sea;
> though its waters roar and foam,
> though the mountains tremble with its tumult.
>
> (vv. 2–3, NRSV)

In the second strophe (vv. 4–6 + refrain), the poet also draws on mythical language to portray the transcendent meaning of Zion, "the city of God." Zion is portrayed as an Olympus (cf. Ps. 48:1), through which runs a marvelous river of God, welling up from the subterranean abyss. The life-giving river, which erupts at the center of the earth, signifies that God is "in the midst" of Zion. God is present "with us." Therefore, the people may trust that, even when they are threatened by conflict and catastrophe, divine help will come with the break of dawn.

The climactic third strophe (vv. 8–10 + refrain) opens with an invitation to worshipers to contemplate the awesome deeds of God in the earth (cf. Ps. 66:5). The "raging of the nations," referred to in the previous strophe, is now portrayed as feverish military preparations, perhaps for an assault on the citadel of Zion (as in Ps. 2:1–3).

> Come, consider the wonders of Yahweh,
> the astounding deeds he has done on the earth;
> he puts an end to wars over the whole wide world,
> he breaks the bow, he snaps the spear,
> shields he burns in the fire.
>
> (vv. 8–9, NJB)

Seen under the aspect of God's eternal sovereignty, the military activities of nations, who foolishly suppose that their power is decisive, are in vain. Above the tumult and shouting of history the community of faith hears the sovereign command of the God whose deity must finally be recognized.

The divine oracle ("Be still and know . . .") with which the strophe concludes has often been misunderstood as a summons to quiet meditation or a spiritual pause. However, the Hebrew imperative carries the strong meaning of "Desist!" (NAB, NJPS), "Give in!" (Moffatt), "Let be!" (NEB), "An end to your fighting!" (ICEL)—as in an authoritative command to contentious persons to "Shut up!" or "Stop it!"

> Yield, and acknowledge that I am God!
> I am exalted among the nations, exalted in the earth!
>
> (v. 10, BWA)

Powers that oppose God's will for *shalom* (peace, welfare) are summoned with a stentorian command to cease and desist, and to admit that God is in ultimate control of the affairs of human history.

Martin Luther's Reformation hymn, alluded to earlier, has given the tones of Psalm 46 a new resonance. The hymn affirms that God is a bulwark against the prevailing "flood" of mortal ills, that we would be lost in the battle with dark and demonic forces if we trusted in our own resources, and that through Jesus Christ, God speaks the divine word "above all earthly powers."

9

Like a Tree Planted by Waters

As we have seen in the previous chapter, sometimes the psalms reflect a situation in which the people are gathered for worship on holy days or high holy days of religious festivals, such as the Day of Atonement or the New Year. But we have also seen—and this point bears repeating—that the psalms cannot be confined to a cultic function or setting. Many of the psalms are simply "spiritual songs," to use a New Testament expression (Eph. 5:19), such as affirmations of trust in God, "wisdom" meditations upon the problems of life, and expressions of delight in God's teaching (Torah).

Spiritual Songs

Previously we have noticed that the type of psalm called a lament moves quickly from a cry out of distress toward an expression of trust in God. Frequently this note of confidence is introduced by a conjunction (in Hebrew) translated by an adversative: "but," "yet," "nevertheless." *In spite of* affliction, the psalmist affirms faith in God.

> But I put my trust in you, Yhwh,
> I say, "You are my God."
> My times are in your hand.
> (Ps. 31:14–15a, BWA)

Affirmations of Trust

There are a number of psalms, however, in which the motif of trust is developed as a self-contained song. These "songs of trust" have been plausibly explained as an independent development of the confession of trust which is a characteristic feature of the lament.

Songs of Trust

11	"If the foundations are destroyed"
16	"In thy presence there is fullness of joy"
*23	"My cup overflows"
*27:1–6	"He will set me high upon a rock" (the second part of the psalm is a lament)
62	"For God alone my soul waits in silence"
*63	"Thy steadfast love is better than life"
*91	"My refuge and my fortress"
*121	"I lift up my eyes to the hills" (also classified as a pilgrimage psalm)
125	"Like Mount Zion, which cannot be moved"
131	"Like a child that is quieted is my soul"

The line between the lament and the song of trust often cannot be drawn sharply. In the above list, Psalm 63 may be regarded as an individual lament, and Psalm 125 may be considered a community lament. Moreover, the exquisite Psalm 139, which we tentatively classified as a lament (see chapter 4 and discussion at the end of chapter 5), sounds like a psalm of trust in the inescapable God who knows us better than we know ourselves and from whom there is no escape, whether in the depths of Sheol or the farthest reaches of the universe (Ps. 139:1–6, 7–12).

In these psalms of trust we find various references to cultic actions such as the offering of sacrifices (Ps. 4:5), singing and dancing before Yhwh (Ps. 150:4), or sojourning (dwelling) in Yhwh's "tent" (Ps. 27:4–6). In these cases, however, traditional language, once associated with worship services, came to be "spiritually interpreted." The primary concern of the psalmists is the sense of the nearness and saving power of God, which the people once experienced—or longed to experience—in the Temple cult. In a different situation, however, when the Temple had lost its centrality for many people, "the concrete experience of the nearness of God in the Temple" as Artur Weiser observes, was "expanded and deepened"[1] and thus the old language was interpreted metaphorically. This emancipation of the language of the psalms from the sphere of worship in the Jerusalem temple took place, as we shall see more clearly in the next chapter, during the postexilic period when the synagogue began to occupy an important place in the life of the people. This development, in turn, paved the way for the time when Jesus proclaimed that God is not to be worshiped exclusively in any geographical sphere, whether in Shechem (as the Samaritans advocated) or in Jerusalem (as the Jews claimed); rather, "the true worshipers will worship the Father in spirit and truth" (John 4:23–24).

A Mother's Psalm

An appropriate place to begin our study of psalms of trust is with the little gem, Psalm 131, which expresses an attitude of humble trust in God. The poet begins by saying that she is not proud or arrogant, and that she is not occupied with "things too great and marvelous" for her.

> But I have calmed and quieted my soul [self],
> like a weaned child with its mother,
> my soul is like the weaned child that is with me.
>
> (Ps. 131:2, NRSV)

The language of this psalm, as translated, pictures a woman coming into the Temple precincts with her child. The child is described with a word whose root ("weaned") means "to deal with bountifully, fully or adequately"; thus the child is satisfied. Such a child has given up the need to suckle because it has been "dealt with" in a bountiful manner, rather than being forced to give up nursing for some arbitrary reason. The feeling of contentment derived from God's bountiful provision is the overriding feeling of the psalmist when approaching the Temple.[2]

These poetic words should not be construed to bolster the former stereotype of women, who do not aspire for great things in the political or economic realm but modestly retire into the background. Rather she is like Baruch, the scribe of the prophet Jeremiah, who was enjoined not to seek "great things" for himself, but to keep his eye fixed on the horizon, on God's purpose for Israel and the nations (Jer. 45:5).

Some think that the concluding line, which turns from the "I" of the psalmist to the community Israel, is a later addition. But individual and community belong together here as elsewhere (Psalm 130 also ends with an appeal to Israel). Because of the "marvelous things" done by God, before whom this individual stands in humble trust, Israel may "hope in the Lord" (v. 3), who leads the people into "green pastures" and through "the valley of the shadow of death."

The Shepherd's Psalm

This leads us to a study of the well-known Twenty-third Psalm. By virtue of its profound simplicity and matchless beauty this psalm has touched the hearts of countless people down through the centuries. Here is a poem that children have learned by heart, that has sustained the mature in the perplexities of life, and that has been a peaceful benediction on the lips of the dying. No single psalm has expressed more powerfully many people's prayer of confidence "out of the depths" to the God whose purpose alone gives meaning to the span of life, from womb to tomb. Since the Twenty-third Psalm is so familiar, especially in the classical King James Version, it may be well to read it in a fresh translation.

> Yhwh is my Shepherd, nothing do I lack.
> In grassy meadows you make me repose,
> By restful waters* you lead me.
> You revive my whole being!
> You guide me into the right paths for your name's sake.
> Even when I go through the valley of deep darkness,
> I fear nothing sinister; for you are at my side!
> Your rod and staff reassure me.
> You spread out before me a table,
> in sight of those who threaten me.
> You pour upon my head festive oil.
> My cup is brimming over!
> Certainly, divine goodness and grace attend me throughout
>   all my days,
> and I shall be a guest in Yhwh's house as long as I live.
>
> (Psalm 23, BWA)

[Note: After the thematic sentence found in verse 1, verses 2 and 3 are translated in the second person singular in agreement with the personal address in verses 4–5. In the last verse the translation follows some versions that read "and I dwell," rather than the received Hebrew text, "and I return." Here the idea is not that of taking up residence permanently in the Temple, but rather, as in

---

* The poet refers to watering places where sheep find security and refreshment.

Psalm 15:1, being a guest or sojourner in Yhwh's "tent"—that is, frequently visiting the Temple, where God is present. In verse 4 the author has adopted the translation "reassure me" from the Jewish scholar, Julius Morgenstern. On oil as a symbol of festive joy (v. 5), see Psalm 45:7; 92:10–11; and 133:2.]

The major problem in interpreting this psalm is that it presents two images that are quite different. In verses 1–4, Yhwh is portrayed as the good shepherd who cares for the flock; in verses 5 and 6, on the other hand, Yhwh is the host who offers hospitality to a guest and protects the guest from enemies. In German it can be said, with a euphonious play on words, that Yhwh is *mein Hirt und mein Wirt* ("my shepherd and my host"), but in the poem itself the images do not seem to harmonize so nicely. What do the shepherd and the host really have to do with each other?

This problem begins to resolve itself when we project ourselves imaginatively out of our industrial milieu into the pastoral way of life that still prevails in some parts of the world. The shepherd can be portrayed from two standpoints. He is the protector of the sheep as they wander in search of grazing land. Yet he is also the protector of the traveler who finds hospitality in his tent from the dangers and enemies of the desert.[3] Even today the visitor to certain parts of the Middle East can see the scene that lies at the basis of the psalm: the black camel's hair tent where the traveler receives Bedouin hospitality, and the surrounding pastureland where the sheep graze under the protection of the shepherd. In Psalm 23, Yhwh is portrayed as the shepherd in both aspects of the shepherd's life: as the leader of the flock, and as the hospitable host.

By Still Waters

In the first part of the psalm, the psalmist likens personal trust in Yhwh to that of sheep who confidently follow the shepherd as he leads them to green pastures and by quiet waters. This image is found repeatedly in the Old Testament (Ps. 80:1; 95:7; 100:3; Isa. 40:11; 49:9–10; 63:14; Ezek. 34:10–31). It is recapitulated in the New Testament in the parable of the lost sheep (Luke 15:3–7) and in the Johannine picture of Jesus Christ as the good shepherd (John 10:1–18). The image is admirably suited to express the understanding that human beings are not the ultimate measure of things, the controller of their world, or the determiner of their destiny. Yhwh, the psalmist affirms, is Israel's maker; therefore the people belong to Yhwh, relying upon their God as sheep depend on their shepherd.

Know that the Lord is God,
    the God who made us, and to whom we belong;
    we are God's people, the sheep of his pasture.
               (Ps. 100:3, BWA cf. 95:6–7)

However, the image of the shepherd and his flock should not be under-stood in an idyllic sense. In the ancient Near East the king was regarded as the shepherd of his people. To address Yhwh as Shepherd was to af-firm that God comes to rule with majestic (kingly) power, achieving peace and justice.

Here is Lord Yahweh coming with power,
his arm maintains his authority,
his reward is with him
and his prize precedes him.
He is like a shepherd feeding his flock,
gathering lambs in his arms,
holding them against his breast
and leading to their rest the mother ewes.
               (Isa. 40:10–11, NJB)

This confidence that Yhwh is Israel's shepherd, which the psalmist personally appropriates by saying "my shepherd," leads immediately to the affirmation that nothing more is needful—a statement that sounds somewhat strange in our commercialized world where the media con-spire to prove how much we are lacking. The psalmist's thought is echoed in many other psalms—for example, the testimony that those who trust Yhwh "lack no good thing" (Ps. 34:8–10) or that Yhwh is one's "portion constantly" even though physical energies ebb (Ps. 73:25–26).

Having gone this far into the psalm, we now need to consider some-thing that may have escaped attention: the psalm has a superscription that associates it with David, "the shepherd of Israel." In the introduc-tory chapter it was pointed out that this title (*leDawid*) is ambiguous: it may mean "to David" (in dedication), "of David" (belonging to David), or "for David" (to be used by the Davidic king in worship). This prob-lem is resolved in the final form of the Psalter, in which David is pre-sented as the ideal king ("anointed one," messiah) who speaks for the people in expressing their faith in God.

In this representative role the Davidic king does not espouse a faint-hearted, otherworldly faith that turns away from the experiences of this life and seeks fulfillment in some higher realm. On the contrary, "David" testifies that his faith in God has repeatedly renewed his life at the very core of his being (the Hebrew *nefesh,* often translated "soul" at v. 3a, really means "self," "being"). He discerns a meaning flowing through his life, which he can account for only by saying that Yhwh, like a shepherd who guides his sheep into the right trails (the trails that are beneficial for the flock), has been directing his life along a course that leads toward fulfillment. The psalmist is aware of the threats to his existence (cf. Ps. 5:8); but even more, he is aware of God's saving action bestowed only for the sake of his divine honor, that is, because God's nature (name) is gracious (see the discussion of God's name in chapter 1). Just as the sheep do not always pasture in verdant meadows or drink at quiet waters but at times must walk precariously through the dark and narrow valley where wild beasts and other dangers lurk, so the psalmist affirms that God has guided him through experiences that put him under trial or brought him to the point of death. The familiar translation "the shadow of death" goes beyond the meaning of the Hebrew term, which signifies "deep darkness" (Amos 5:8; Isa. 9:2; Ps. 44:19). Yet this secondary interpretation is consistent with the original meaning, for in the view of the psalmists the power of death encroaches into a person's life when the vitality of bodily life is weakened (see the discussion of death in chapter 8).

A Table Prepared

In the second part of the psalm (vv. 5–6) the imagery shifts to the shepherd as host. According to the Bedouin law of hospitality, once a traveler is received into the shepherd's tent, and especially once his host has spread food before him, he is guaranteed immunity from enemies who may be attempting to overtake him.[4] In pastoral circles no human protection is greater than that afforded by the table hospitality of a Bedouin chief. So the psalmist expresses trust in the good shepherd by saying that in Yhwh's tent one finds a protecting and gracious welcome. This divine hospitality is not just a temporary reprieve but a limitless protection from the powers that threaten one's existence. The host's tent is none other than the Temple, as in Psalm 27:1–6 which closely parallels the thought of Psalm 23.

> For in the day of trouble
>   he will keep me safe in his dwelling;
> he will hide me in the shelter of his tabernacle
>   and set me high upon a rock.
>   (Ps. 27:5, NIV; cf. Ps. 61:4)

The psalmist declares that in Yhwh's house ("tabernacle") a table is prepared before him (perhaps a reference to a sacrificial meal in the Temple; see Ps. 22:26) and he is given the most cordial welcome—in full sight of his enemies (see Ps. 27:6 and the discussion of the enemies in chapter 3). Now it is no longer his enemies who pursue him; rather, it is Yhwh's grace and goodness that follow after him as long as he lives.

It has been suggested that the Shepherd's Psalm was composed by a person who in the maturity of life looked back across the years and traced the purpose of God through the whole story. One commentator writes:

> The sentiments of an almost childlike trust which the poet is able to express in this psalm are, however, by no means the product of a carefree unconcern characteristic of young people; on the contrary, they are the mature fruit of a heart which, having passed through many bitter experiences and having fought many battles (vv. 4, 5), had been allowed to find at the decline of life in its intimate communion with God (vv. 2, 6) the serenity of a contented spirit, peace of mind (v. 6) and, in all dangers, strength.[5]

Although this may claim too much for the psalm, it is true that the language has spoken to many people with increasing depth of meaning through the maturing years, which hasten toward the "deep darkness." And when the psalm is read from the standpoint of Christian faith, it speaks of a table graciously spread, not only in the presence of the hostile powers of this age but also in the presence of "the last enemy" (1 Cor. 15:26).

The Protecting Shadow

Trust in Yhwh finds its most powerful, and at the same time most problematic, expression in Psalm 91, another well-known song of trust. The psalm, however, is difficult to interpret. The difficulty arises in part from the question of how to understand the overall structure of the psalm and its three component parts. Who is the speaker and the one spoken to? What setting in worship is reflected? How does the climactic divine oracle (vv. 14–16) relate to the previous parts? Since these questions cannot be answered decisively, the psalm presents a challenge to the interpreter.

Refuge in God (Ps. 91:1–2)

In the introduction someone addresses a person who seeks shelter in the protecting care of God symbolized by the Temple (see also Ps. 27:5; 61:4).

> Whoever dwells in the shelter of Elyon,
> and tarries in the shadow of Shaddai,
> will say to Yhwh:
> "My refuge and my fortress, My God in whom I trust!"
>
> (vv. 1–2, BWA)

Possibly the psalmist has in mind the ancient view that a holy place was an asylum in which fugitives could find refuge or sanctuary from the hasty justice of their pursuers by grasping "the horns of the altar" (see 1 Kings 1:50–51). The asylum motif is suggested by the language in v. 1 ("shelter") and especially later in v. 4, where the poet refers to protection beneath the outspread wings of the cherubim in the Holy of Holies of the Temple (cf. 36:7; 99:1). This custom of granting asylum, as well as the location of the sacred Ark in the Temple, now provides the metaphorical imagery that enlarges the horizon of thought beyond the limitations of time and place. Any person within the community of faith may be addressed. Notice that epithets for deity, inherited from the pre-Israelite environment, are mentioned first: *'Elyon,* usually translated as "the Most High," and *Shaddai,* usually translated as "the Almighty"; however, these terms are subordinated to the worshiper's relationship to God known by the personal name Yhwh.

Instruction in Faith (Ps. 91:3–13)

In the next section the person addressed is informed about what trusting in Yhwh will mean in the stresses and strains of daily life. The identity of the speaker is not disclosed. Is it a priest who gives *torah* (instruction)? Is it a wisdom teacher who sets forth a traditional philosophy of life found, for instance, on the lips of one of Job's "pastoral counselors" (Job 5:17–27)? Or is it an ordinary person who "teaches" others out of the experience of help received from Yhwh?[6] In any case, the speaker sets forth a rather elementary view of God's protecting presence—a view that is unqualified by exceptions to glittering generalities, untouched by any notion that suffering may be divine discipline, and untroubled by jarring cries of expostulation often heard in psalms of lament. Faith grasps for the assurance that Yhwh's faithfulness is a sure defense in any extremity:

> For he will rescue you from the fowler's snare,
> from the fatal plague.
> With his pinions he will cover you,
> and under his wings you'll seek refuge.
> A shield and rampart is his faithfulness.
>
> (vv. 3–4, BWA)

The speaker goes on to say rather cavalierly that trust in God will protect one from hostile (perhaps demonic) attack (vv. 5–6), from pestilence that strikes people right and left (vv. 7–8), and from dangerous experiences (vv. 11–13). The sweeping promise is given that because Yhwh/Elyon is a "safe retreat" (v. 9),

> no disaster shall befall you,
> no calamity shall come near your tent.
>
> (v. 91:10, BWA)

Divine Oracle (Ps. 91:14–16)

As indicated by the grammatical shift from second to first person, the final verses are presented as an oracle from God, possibly spoken by a priest. The effect of the pronouncement is to endorse the *trust* of the person who has been addressed, though not necessarily to confirm all of the simplistic "teaching" given in the preceding part. Notice that the divine approval is given to one who "knows" Yhwh's name (identity), and thus stands in an I-thou relationship.*

> Because he clings to me, I will deliver him,
> I will protect him because he knows my name.
> When he invokes me [by name], I will answer him.
> I will be with him in distress,
> I will rescue him and give him honor.
> With a long life I will satisfy him,
> and let him see my salvation.
>
> (vv. 14–16, BWA)

The danger of this psalm is that it may encourage a one-sided and immature view of what divine protection means. In too much popular piety, faith in God offers an insurance against trouble, and prayer is a

---

* Recall our previous discussion of the name of God, chapter 1.

form of magic. It is significant that in the New Testament story of Jesus' temptations in the wilderness, one of Satan's tests is supported by quoting a passage from this psalm (vv. 11–12), which promises that God's angel will "guard you in all your ways" (see Matt. 4:6; Luke 4:10–11). Satan's test is insidious because it is based on a truth, not a falsehood; God's "faithfulness" is indeed "a shield and a rampart" (v. 4c). But this truth can easily be distorted, even by people of religious faith. It must be read in the larger theological context of Scripture which shows that, in ways past our understanding, God's purpose embraces all the ups and downs of human life and that "in everything God works for good with those who love him" (Rom. 8:28).

Meditations on the Good Life

In the Psalter we find a number of psalms that reflect the wisdom movement. This movement, as we know from archaeology and the study of ancient culture, was diffused throughout the whole ancient Near East—Egypt, Canaan, the fringes of Arabia, Asia Minor, Mesopotamia. Very early this movement made its impact on Israel, with the result that Solomon came to be regarded as the patron of wisdom, and important wisdom writings, such as Proverbs and Ecclesiastes, were attributed to him. In Israel, however, the wisdom movement developed a distinctive Israelite accent, evident in the proverb: "The fear of Yhwh is the beginning of wisdom" (Prov. 9:10; Job 28:28; Ps. 111:10). Israel's sages insisted that wisdom does not come just from observing human conduct or through rational reflection on the teachings handed down in the wisdom schools. Rather, the "beginning" (that is, the foundation or the premise) of wisdom is faith—faith in Yhwh, the God who is known and worshiped in Israel.

Wisdom motifs found their way into Israelite psalms at an early period. For instance, Psalm 78, one of the storytelling psalms to which we have alluded several times (e.g., in chapter 3), begins in the style of a wisdom poem (vv. 1–4). In verse 2 the recitation of Yhwh's deeds and the people's unfaithfulness is specifically called a wisdom utterance (Hebrew *mashal,* "parable"). The purpose of the psalm is to edify the congregation through the recollection of a shared history, so that the people may learn from the past how to live in the present and face the future. The introduction to this psalm is like the opening of Psalm 49, in which a wisdom meditation upon the transience of life is brought into the context of worship.

Hear this, all you peoples;
listen, all you inhabitants of the world,
both high and low,
rich and poor,
for the words that I have to speak are wise;
my thoughts provide understanding.
I listen with care to the parable [*mashal*]
and interpret a mystery to the music of the lyre.
(Ps. 49:1–4, REB)

These psalms show that the Israelite faith did not advocate "a sacrifice of the intellect" such as is made in some situations today when people "check" their minds, along with coats and hats, in the vestibule before entering the sanctuary! Rather, wisdom belongs in the context of worship, as attested by the presence of wisdom psalms in the Psalter.

Wisdom Psalms

36	"With thee is the fountain of life" (this psalm is a mixed composition, having elements of wisdom [vv. 1–4], hymn [vv. 5–9], and lament [vv. 10–21])
*37	"The mouth of the righteous utters wisdom"
*49	"My mouth shall speak wisdom"
*73	"Nevertheless I am continually with thee" (classification as a wisdom psalm is uncertain)
78	"I will open my mouth in a parable" (a narrative or storytelling psalm)
112	"Light arises in the darkness for the upright" (an alphabetical acrostic psalm)
127	"The fruit of the womb a reward"
128	"It shall be well with you"
133	"When brothers dwell in unity"

(See also Proverbs 8; Ecclesiasticus 14:2–15:10)

Characteristics of Wisdom Psalms

There is much difference of opinion about the criteria for determining wisdom psalms and about the number of psalms that should be included in this category. The influence of Israelite sages was so widespread that wisdom motifs were employed in narrative, prophetic speech and in various types of psalms (laments, thanksgivings, hymns).

Roland Murphy proposes that we should look for the following elements in deciding about the classification of wisdom psalms:[7]

- A sharp contrast between the righteous and the wicked
- Advice about conduct that results in either welfare or misfortune
- The premise that "the fear [reverence] of Yhwh" is the starting point of wisdom
- Comparisons and admonitions that are used to exhort one to good conduct
- Alphabetical acrostic pattern
- "Better than" sayings (cf. Prov. 17:1; 19:1)
- The address "my son," customary in wisdom schools
- The approving word "blessed" (happy, fortunate)

Not all these features would have to be found in every psalm to identify it as a wisdom type. However, a number of them are present in Psalms 37 and 49, which are generally agreed to be wisdom psalms.

Wisdom psalms are not immediately or essentially connected with specific acts of worship. Although they refer to going to the sanctuary (Ps. 73:17) or use the metaphor of finding refuge under Yhwh's wings (Ps. 36:7)—a reference to the wings of the cherubim outstretched over the ark in the Holy of Holies—they are essentially meditations on the good life. Often they begin with beatitudes ("blessed [happy] is the one who . . .") or contain admonitions against following evil and foolish ways. The ultimate background of this instruction is the ancient doctrine of the "two ways" as taught in wisdom circles: the way of life, which the wise pursue, and the way of destruction, which the foolish follow (cf. Matt. 7:13–14). According to Israel's teachers, however, this instruction does not have its source in human wisdom; rather, it is a divine gift. Yhwh teaches people to walk in "the right paths," the paths of salvation. Accordingly, in Israel's wisdom psalms true wisdom is identified with "the fear of Yhwh" and, even more specifically, with faithfulness to Yhwh's *torah* (teaching, instruction; often weakly translated "law"). One of the stanzas in Psalm 37, which is based on the alphabetical acrostic pattern, says:

> The mouth of the righteous man utters wisdom,
>   and his tongue speaks what is just.
> The law [*torah*] of his God is in his heart;
>   his feet do not slip.
>
> (Ps. 37:30–31, NIV)

Expressions of Delight in God's Teaching

Closely related to the wisdom psalms listed above are several psalms
that extol the *torah* of Yhwh as the medium through which the will of
God is known and hence the basis for true wisdom and happiness.

Torah Psalms

*1	"Like a tree planted by streams of water"
*19:7–14	"More to be desired than gold" (the first part of the psalm is a creation hymn)
119	"O how I love thy law!" (an alphabetical acrostic psalm)

As we have already noticed, our English word "law" is an inadequate translation of the Hebrew word *torah*. This usual translation,
which is also found in the New Testament (Greek, *nomos,* "law"), suggests an inhibiting legalism ("the bondage of the law") from which
persons need to be set free so that they may have life abundantly.
But the knowledge of Yhwh's *torah* is the occasion for the heart to rejoice, as one psalmist says (Ps. 19:8), and this kind of celebration still
takes place in the Jewish festival called Simchat Torah (Rejoicing in
the Torah).

The Hebrew word *torah* is rich with meaning. It may refer to the
story of Yhwh's actions to create a people and guide them into the future, as in the storytelling psalms (see chapter 3), or it may refer to the
obligations (i.e., precepts, commandments) that shape the lifestyle of a
people who tell and retell the story. These two dimensions—narration
and obligation or, in Jewish tradition, Haggadah and Halakkah—are so
inseparable that it is impossible to think of one without the other. Torah
in this twofold sense was mediated to the people through a chain of tradition that went back to Moses, the fountainhead. However, in the period of the exile and restoration, about the time of Nehemiah and Ezra,
the Torah was mediated in written form, as "scripture." The scriptural
Torah was identified preeminently with the first five books of the Bible,
the Pentateuch.

Delight in the Torah of the Lord

According to Psalm 1, the psalm that introduces the whole Psalter,
the wise person is the one who reads and meditates on the Torah day

and night. This psalm begins with a beatitude ("Blessed . . .") typical of a wisdom poem, as in Jeremiah 17:5–8, a wisdom utterance that may have influenced the psalmist. In both instances the wise person, who ponders the Torah, is likened to "a tree planted by waters" that bears fruit in its proper season in contrast to the foolish (wicked) who are like evanescent chaff, driven away by the wind. The psalm has a symmetrical structure in which contrasting positive and negative statements are balanced for the purpose of teaching.

Positive: Blessed are those who do not . . . [negative]

> Rather . . [positive]
> Result

Negative: Not so are the wicked. . .

> Rather
> Result

Summary: introduced by "for" (ki)

> Blessed are those who
>> do not follow the counsel of the wicked
>> do not stand in the way [lifestyle] of sinners,
>> and do not sit in the company of the insolent.
>
> Rather, in the Teaching of Yhwh they delight,
> and on God's Torah they ponder day and night.
> They are like a tree planted by a fresh stream,
>> that yields its fruit at the proper time,
>> and whose foliage never fades.
>
> Whatever they do comes to fruition!
> Not so are the wicked, not so.
>> Rather, they are like chaff the wind scatters.
>
> Hence, in the divine judgment the wicked will not stand,
>> nor sinners [stand] in the community of the righteous.
>
> For [*ki*] Yhwh recognizes the way of the righteous.
>> but the way of the wicked leads to naught.
>>
>> (Psalm 1, BWA)

Some may regard this as an "achievement" psalm: the wise person who lives by the Torah is successful, while the one who flouts it is a failure. But this simplistic view hardly does justice to the poem. Here the psalmist sharply contrasts two attitudes, or, as we would say today, two lifestyles. On the one hand, there are persons who humbly acknowledge their dependence on God and seek to know God's will by studying the Torah. They live by a personal relationship to God, striving constantly, and listening intently, for the word of God day and night. They may not be great persons as the world measures greatness, but they are blessed by a serene sense of the God-given meaning of life. On the other hand, there are persons who care nothing about the religious tradition, who are determined to live out of their own resources, and who are scornful of the devout life. Such persons belong in the category of the "fool" who says in his heart (mind), "There is no God" (Ps. 10:4; 14:1), that is, the practical atheist who supposes that a person can live as he or she pleases and get away with it because God is not to be taken seriously. These people, says the psalmist, are like the chaff that the wind blows away during a threshing of the wheat, for their existence lacks deep roots.

The Longest Psalm

The theme of seeking to know the will of God, which is developed with chaste simplicity in Psalm 1, is expanded to almost wearisome length in Psalm 119, the longest psalm in the Psalter. Various passages in this psalm show that it is a struggle to know and do God's will, a struggle that is waged in the face of adverse experiences and threats to one's existence (e.g., vv. 153–60).

The only unity that this long psalm has is provided by the Hebrew alphabet: each successive stanza begins with the next letter of the alphabet. The first eight-line stanza begins with the first letter (aleph), the second eight lines with the second letter (beth), and so on through the twenty-two letters of the alphabet. (The alphabetic arrangement is displayed in some translations, e.g., NIV.) This acrostic scheme was a convenient device for use in teaching or memorizing, but psalms of this kind seem to be far removed from poems that were actually shaped by traditional liturgy forms or by liturgical usage. Two of the psalms listed above as wisdom psalms are alphabetical acrostics (37 and 112), and this pattern is followed in other types of psalms too. Notice that the acrostic scheme may be used in any type of psalm: lament, hymn, thanksgiving.

Alphabetical Acrostic Psalms

| 9–10 | Individual lament |
| 25 | Individual lament |

34	Individual song of thanksgiving
37	Wisdom psalm
111	Hymn
112	Wisdom psalm
119	Torah psalm
145	Hymn

The Enigmas of Life

Wisdom and torah psalms agree on one premise: actions have consequences. The person whose lifestyle is based on the fear of Yhwh and the teachings of the Torah is "blessed" or "happy"; the person whose actions and attitudes have another foundation is denied this felicity. At first consideration it seems that this is a pragmatic philosophy, one that measures the truth of religious beliefs by their practical results. Admittedly, many people then as now were tempted by a simplistic view of the blessings that result from faith in God or the curses that may fall upon the disbeliever. At their depth, however, the biblical psalms do not express an easygoing pragmatism but rest, rather, upon a theology of creation. The action-consequence pattern is written into the very fabric of the universe that was created and ordered by God. Those who are wise strive to attune their actions to the cosmic order; those who are foolish violate this order and bring upon themselves the inevitable consequences. Israel's sages would have agreed with the statement of Paul that God is not to be mocked, "for whatever one sows, that will one reap" (Gal. 6:7).

In some wisdom circles, represented, for instance, by the book of Ecclesiastes, sages become pessimistic about the ability of human wisdom to penetrate the divine "secret" of the creation and to know the will of the Creator. However, the wisdom psalms of the Psalter are more optimistic, and the main reason for this is their conviction that God has revealed in the Torah the precepts that enable one to live in harmony with the Creator's will. Psalm 19, which we considered in chapter 7, shows the correspondence between the marvelous order of the cosmos (Psalm 19A) and the ordering will of God revealed through the Torah (Psalm 19B).

Hence these psalms give the assurance that those who fear Yhwh and obey the divine teaching will enjoy the good life—not in another world, but in this historical world, here and now. A faithful relationship with God will mean the enjoyment of God and, consequently, the tasting of life's goodness. Such a person will experience all that "salvation" involves: health, wholeness, welfare, the freedom to be, and the freedom to serve God, in the covenant community.

The Issue of Theodicy

It is this healthy, life-affirming attitude, however, that prompts the question with which these wisdom psalms wrestle: Why is it that things often work out so badly for the God-fearing person and so well for the one who is careless about, or defiant of, God? Three wisdom psalms, Psalms 37, 49, and 73, are especially concerned with this problem, which has plagued people of faith down through the centuries. Beyond the Psalter, the book of Job is preeminently addressed to this problem.[8]

The simple solution to the problem—the one advanced by friends of Job—was to say that life's imbalances are only temporary and will be rectified shortly. In the meantime, suffering is, at best, the chastening or correction of the Almighty (Job 5:17–27). Yet one has only to read Psalm 37 to realize that this kind of answer is a whistling in the dark. Here the psalmist goes all the way with the doctrine: just be patient and you will see the reward of the righteous and the retribution of the wicked. Indeed, at one point the poet blandly testifies:

> I was young and now I am old,
>   yet I have never seen the righteous forsaken
>   or their children begging bread.
>   (Ps. 37:25, NIV)

The appropriate response to this statement is that the psalmist either had not lived long enough, or that he must have lived someplace where he was sheltered from the hard realities of life! Furthermore, the possibility has to be reckoned with—as at the end of the book of Job—that suffering *may* be the occasion for a deeper understanding of one's relationship to God.

The Great Nevertheless

Psalm 73, the greatest of the wisdom psalms, grapples with this problem at the profoundest level in the whole Psalter, and in so doing comes closest to the testimony of Job. The psalmist begins by asserting the "orthodox" thesis:

> Assuredly God is good to the upright [Israel],*
> to those who are pure in heart!
>
> (Ps. 73:1, REB)

Then follows the crucial "but" (v. 2)—the adversative conjunction—which was dictated by the poet's own experience. When he considered the imbalances of life, so we read, his faith was almost destroyed (vv. 2–16). The only thing that restrained him from speaking out his doubts was concern for the effect that it would have on the younger generation!

Searching for an answer to this baffling problem was a "wearisome task." The poet, at the end of his rope, was about to surrender his faith.

> Until I went into God's sanctuary,
> where I saw clearly what their destiny would be.
> Indeed you place them on slippery ground
> and drive them headlong into utter ruin!
> In a moment they are destroyed,
> disasters making an end of them,
> like a dream when one awakes, Lord,
> like images dismissed when one rouses from sleep!
>
> (vv. 17–20, REB)

Like Job, the psalmist was ready to recant his presumptuous attempt to judge the ways of God from the limited standpoint of his experience (cf. Job 42:1–6). But, like Job, he too seemed to break through the limitations of his past understanding into a new apprehension of God's presence and power, which his theology, however orthodox, could not fully comprehend. The turning point in the psalm is indicated by another adversative conjunction—"the great *nevertheless*"—which stands at the beginning of v. 23:

> Nevertheless I am continually with you;
> you hold my right hand.
> You guide me with your counsel
> and afterward you will receive me with honor.
>
> (vv. 23–24, NRSV)

---

* The received Hebrew text reads "Israel"; by using Israel parallel to "pure in heart" the poet or editor may have viewed the community as representing the individual.

Unfortunately, the meaning of the last sentence, is obscure in the Hebrew. It may be, as some interpreters have insisted, one of the few
places in the Old Testament where there is an "intimation of immortality," that is, a hope for a breakthrough into a new form of existence in
which, as Paul put it, "the mortal puts on immortality" in a mystery that
is comprehended solely in God's wisdom (1 Cor. 15:42–58). But if it is
an intimation, it is no more. The psalmist is not really concerned with
what lies beyond the boundary of death, but with the solution to existential problems that *now* demand an answer if one is to live in faith—
and die in faith. A similar view, it seems, is expressed at one point in
another wisdom psalm:

> Such is the fate of the foolish
> and of those after them who approve their words.
> Like sheep they head for Sheol;
> with death as their shepherd,
> they go straight down to the grave.
> Their bodies, stripped of all honour,
> waste away in Sheol.
> But God will ransom my life [*nefesh*]
> and take me from the power of Sheol.
>   (Ps. 49:13–15, REB)

Psalm 73 speaks for us in our time, not because it gives a theological answer but because it portrays the situation in which new theological understanding must be found. Today we know, even more radically
than the wisdom psalmist, that theological formulations which were
satisfactory in a previous day no longer cope with the hard realities of
contemporary human experience. How can one talk about the "happiness" of the God-fearing in a world where six million Jews were burned
in Nazi ovens, where many people are doomed to live out their lives in
economic ghettos, where the threat of nuclear annihilation or biological
warfare hangs over every military adventure, where science is pushing
back our earthly horizons into the vast reaches of the cosmos? Theology that is vital stands on the boundary between the old theology,
which has been systematized, and the new theology, which must be for-
mulated. And if a person's intellect is to be brought into the sanctuary
of God, this standing on the boundary between the old and the new is
imperative.[9]

A Heart of Wisdom (Psalm 90)

It is appropriate to conclude this discussion with the well-known Psalm 90 which, though technically not a wisdom psalm, was profoundly influenced by the wisdom movement. In structure this psalm is a community lament occasioned by a situation of sore distress that threatens human welfare and security.

Address to God (Psalm 90:1–6)

The first part opens with an address to Yhwh, who existed before the creation and whose sovereignty transcends all the boundaries of time. Strikingly, here at the beginning, as well as at the end (v. 17), Yhwh is addressed as Adonai (Lord), a title of majesty (cf. Ps. 8:1).

> Lord, you have been our refuge
> from age to age.
>
> Before the mountains were born,
> before the earth and the world came to birth,
> from eternity to eternity you are God.
> (vv. 1–2, NJB)

In hymnic fashion this address is expanded in two "thou" strophes that ascribe praise to the almighty Sovereign, each of which contrasts human transience with God's eternity (vv. 3–4 and 5–6).

Lament in Distress (Psalm 90:7–12)

After the address to God comes a twofold description of human distress, a description that transcends any situation of Israel's lament and speaks to the human condition generally. First, human life is lived under the inescapable judgment (wrath) of God, from whose penetrating scrutiny there is no escape even in the innermost secrets of one's life (vv. 7–8, cf. Ps. 139:1–16, 23–24). Secondly, the wise person is the one who knows the limitations and transience of human life and acts accordingly in sober faith.

> All our days pass under your wrath,
> our lives are over like a sigh.
> The span of our life is seventy years—
> eighty for those who are strong—

> but their whole extent is anxiety and trouble,
> they are over in a moment and we are gone.
>
> (vv. 9–10, NJB)

This section concludes with a prayer (vv. 11–12) that God will bestow the gift of wisdom which recognizes human fallibility and mortality.

> Teach us to count up the days that are ours,
> and we shall come to the heart of wisdom.
>
> (v. 12, NJB)

Prayer for Help (Psalm 90:13–17)

The final movement of the psalm, consistent with the lament form (see chapter 4), is a petition introduced by the typical cry of lament, "How long?" (e.g., Ps. 13:1–3). Speaking for the community of faith, the psalmist prays that we may awake in the morning (cf. Ps. 139:18) filled with confidence in Yhwh's *hesed,* or covenant loyalty. Human trust is grounded in the God who, as announced at the opening of the psalm, transcends all times, whose sovereignty is "from everlasting to everlasting." Because our transient lives, from beginning to end, are embraced within the Creator's faithfulness, says the psalmist, we may rejoice all of our hastening days and may live and die in the confidence that "the work of our hands" will be conserved and enhanced in God's eternal purpose.

Human Grandeur and Misery

A rabbi observed that a person should carry in a pocket two stones, one inscribed with "For my sake the world was created," and the other with "I am but dust and ashes." And each stone should be pulled out, as the occasion requires, to remind us of who we are in God's creation.

This is a good illustration of the "wisdom" that is found in the Psalms. There are psalms that exalt human beings to a position of supremacy in God's creation and that endow them with the role of expressing the praise of the whole creation to the Creator (see the discussion of Psalm 8 in chapter 7). Human beings are called to be kings and queens in God's earthly estate. Though related to the *'adamah* ("soil"), like the animals, as portrayed in the paradise story (Genesis 2–3), human beings transcend the natural world and are objects of God's concern. The tremendous achievements in the fields of medicine, transportation, communication, space exploration, music, and the arts—to mention only a few—may be regarded as the exercise of the task that God has given to human beings to be agents of the divine rule. Against philosophies that reduce the human to the level of nature, Israel's psalmists enable one to say, "For my sake the world was created."

On the other hand, the high position of human beings in God's cosmic administration may tempt them to live like the "fool" who says, "There is no God" (Ps. 10:4; 14:1). When human beings attempt to "play God," as though they were running the show, their royal dominion over the earth leads to the picture portrayed in the primeval history (Genesis 2–11): violence that corrupts the earth, to the point that chaos threatens to return. Wisdom psalms humble us with the sober reminder that human life, in contrast to God's eternity, is evanescent, like the flash of a firefly in the night. Frail and earthly creatures we are, made from the dust and returning to the dust.

> You turn us back to dust,
>   and say "Turn back, you mortals."
>   (Ps. 90:3, NRSV)

In the wisdom perspective of Psalm 90, all our vaunted achievements, impressive as they are, mean nothing except for God's faithfulness (*hesed*), which overarches and undergirds human life from birth to death. So when we are tempted to think of ourselves more highly than we ought to think, Israel's sages teach us to say, "I am but dust and ashes."

More than Conquerors

Psalm 73, as we have noticed, reaches a turning point in "the great nevertheless." This is not an adversative that turns us away from the problems of existence; rather, it turns us toward the world with the confidence that God is present and at work there. In its simplest terms this faith affirms, "Nevertheless, I am continually with thee." On a profounder level this biblical faith joyfully announces that, because of God's victory in Jesus Christ,

> in all these things we are more than conquerors through him who loved us. For I am convinced that neither death nor life, neither angels nor demons, neither the present nor the future, nor any powers, neither height nor depth, nor anything else in all creation, will be able to separate us from the love of God that is in Christ Jesus our Lord. (Rom. 8:37–39, NIV)

10

Reading the Book
of Psalms as a Whole

In previous chapters we have considered the Psalter as a collection of literary types (laments, thanksgiving, hymns, songs of trust, etc.) and classifications (royal, wisdom, festival psalms, etc.). Many of these psalms reflect an orientation to the temple of Jerusalem, whether participating in its worship services or longing to go up to Zion where one could "contemplate the beauty of Yhwh" and "inquire in his temple" (Ps. 27:4).

The whole situation changed when the temple was destroyed in 587 B.C. and the people, most of them in exile, had to learn to pray to God away from Jerusalem. Even after the second temple was built in 515 B.C. many people learned to read or recite the psalms in a noncultic setting, perhaps in the synagogue, in wisdom schools, or in the home. Attention turned more and more to the Psalms as *scripture,* that is, sacred writing or a book.

The Psalms as Scripture

Around the beginning of the twentieth century, the great scholar Hermann Gunkel revolutionized the study of the Psalms by introducing the method known as form criticism: the study of individual texts according to their literary form or type. Since then, the form-critical approach, which we have been using in this study, has become the starting point and basis for scholarly work. Gunkel's approach was supplemented by the cult-functional (liturgical) approach of Sigmund Mowinckel, who sought to understand how these psalms actually functioned in services of worship, especially the great religious festival celebrated at New Year's (see chapter 8). Later Gerstenberger's sociological approach attempted to understand many of the psalms in the life setting of the family or tribes.

In recent years, however, scholars have been moving beyond form-critical and cult-functional approaches into a study of the shaping and editing of the Psalms as a book, a canonical whole. The concern is not just to understand the "situation in life" or the "setting in liturgy," but the "setting in the text."

This holistic approach to the book of Psalms does not invalidate or supersede the studies of individual psalms in their sociological (Gerstenberger), literary (Gunkel), or liturgical (Mowinckel) setting. Usually we do not read the book of Psalms as a whole, anymore than we study a hymnbook as a whole. Rarely does a person sit down to read the 150 psalms straight through from beginning to end. Usually we read the psalms one by one, perhaps in worship services (the so-called "responsive readings") or in private devotions. However, when we give our attention to the Psalms as a whole book, another dimension comes into view: the psalms serve as teaching or instruction (Hebrew, *torah*). As J. Clinton McCann Jr. observes, "Although [the psalms] may have originated primarily within the liturgical life of ancient Israel and Judah, [they] were finally appropriated, preserved, and transmitted as instruction to the faithful."[1] At this final stage, he says, the Psalter was a book "to be read rather than performed, meditated over rather than recited from."[2]

This shift from liturgical use to religious education corresponds to a profound institutional change that occurred in the pre-Christian centuries: from temple to synagogue. The psalms were regarded primarily as a book, as scripture in which one can discern the will of God or God's activity in the world. Recall the episode in Luke when, after the crucifixion, Jesus walked with two disciples on the road to Emmaus and how he "opened their minds to understand the scriptures," that is, he interpreted the torah of Moses, the message of the prophets, and the teaching of the Psalms (Luke 24:4–45).

The Psalms: A Five-Part Book

On glancing through the Psalter we discover that the 150 psalms are arranged into five parts or "books."

Book I	Psalms 1—41
	Concluding doxology: Ps. 41:13
Book II	Psalms 42—72
	Concluding doxology: Ps. 72:18–19

Book III	Psalms 73—89
	Concluding doxology: Ps. 89:52
Book IV	Psalms 90—106
	Concluding doxology: Ps. 106:48
Book V	Psalms 107—150
	Concluding doxology for entire Psalter: Psalm 150

Notice that each of the first four books concludes with a brief doxology that is not a literary part of the psalm with which it is associated. Psalm 150 not only fittingly concludes the last book, but rounds off the entire Psalter with a doxology in which all kinds of instruments praise God symphonically.

This fivefold arrangement of the Psalter was made relatively late in the Old Testament period and was undoubtedly patterned after the Torah (Pentateuch), the so-called "Five Books of Moses." In its present form the Psalter comes from the period of the second temple—the temple of Zerubbabel, which was rebuilt in 520–515 B.C., (the time of the prophets Haggai and Zechariah) and stood until it was superseded by the temple of King Herod (begun about 20 B.C.), the stones of which are visible in the famous Western Wall of Jerusalem. Sometimes the Psalter is spoken of as "the hymnbook of the second temple." This is proper insofar as the Psalter was given its final shape and was used in temple services during this period. Yet this was also the period when the synagogue was emerging as the focal point of prayer and interpretation of scripture. Therefore the Psalter may be called the prayer book of the synagogue with equal justification, especially since it opens with a psalm that reflects the piety based on the study of the Torah.

The rise of the synagogue was a major factor in keeping alive the faith and tradition of Israel in a time when Jewish colonies were springing up outside Palestine. Alexandria in Egypt came to be one of the major centers of the Jewish dispersion in the postexilic period. About 250 B.C. the Alexandrian Jews began to translate their sacred scriptures into the vernacular, which for them was the ordinary Greek of the Hellenistic world. This Greek version of the Old Testament (known as the Septuagint) contains a Psalter that differs in several interesting respects from the Hebrew tradition followed by the Protestant Reformers. For one thing, the Greek Old Testament—like the scriptures of the Dead Sea community of Qumran—contains an extra psalm (Ps. 151), which is attributed to David.[3] Also the Greek Bible differs somewhat in the determination of where a particular psalm begins and ends, for instance, what is regarded as one psalm in the Greek Bible may appear as two in the Hebrew Bible, as in Psalms 9—10 or 114—115. Further, in the Greek version thirteen more psalms are attributed to David than in the Hebrew original.[4]

The early Christian community, being Hellenistic in complexion, read its Old Testament in Greek. Accordingly, the structure of the Psalter in the Greek Bible has influenced Christian usage, as may be seen from translations used in the past in Roman Catholic and Eastern Orthodox communities. In this study, however, we have followed the numbering of the RSV, which has been accorded the status of "the common Bible" by Protestant, Roman Catholic, and Eastern Orthodox representatives. Even this numbering, however, has to be questioned at points, for some psalms, reckoned as two in the Hebrew Bible (and hence in the common Bible) actually constitute one literary unit (e.g., Psalms 42—43), and vice versa, a psalm that is considered as one may actually consist of two literary units (e.g., Psalm 27). In other words, the numerical determination of the psalms does not always coincide with the scope of the literary units, as we have seen again and again. (See the listing in appendix B.)

The Editing of the Book of Psalms

In addition to the fivefold organization (for the purpose of imitating the structure of the Torah) can anything more be said about the purpose of the final editing of the Psalms? Since these editors, in contrast to editors of modern hymnbooks, have not divulged their editorial plan, one must deduce it from the shape of the book.

A helpful attempt to understand the shaping of the book of Psalms is found in *Reading from the Beginning* by Nancy deClasse-Walford.[5] This intriguing title expresses her view that the best way to read any piece of literature is to follow the King's advice to the White Rabbit in Lewis Carroll's *Alice in Wonderland:* "Begin at the beginning, and go on till you come to the end: then stop." If we do this in the case of the book of Psalms, she maintains, we will find ourselves following a story line that gave the Israelite community a sense of identity and power of survival in a postexilic situation when the people had lost monarchy and nationhood.[6]

Clues of this story allegedly are found in the arrangement of and superscriptions to the psalms. Endorsing in her own way Gerald Wilson's view of the editing of the psalms (to be considered later), she writes:

> The Hebrew Psalter is a story of the rise of ancient Israel
> under the leadership of Kings David and Solomon (Books

One and Two); of the demise of ancient Israel, the destruction of Jerusalem at the hands of the Babylonians, and the Exile (Book Three); and of the return to the land and the time when Yahweh would restore the fortunes of ancient Israel (Books Four and Five).[7]

In this view, the book of Psalms reflects Israel's new sense of identity and new understanding of the sovereignty of God in a time when the whole question of kingship had to be reconsidered. There are two problems, however, with this creative proposal. For one thing, it is difficult if not impossible, as deClasse-Walford frankly admits, to penetrate the period when the Psalms were shaped editorially. We know something about the final formation of the Torah in the time of Ezra and Nehemiah (fifth century B.C.), but the time from 400 to the Maccabean revolution in 168 B.C. is almost a historical blank.

Secondly, this reading of the arrangement of the psalms in the light of a "story" and particularly the superscriptions to the various psalms is interesting, but rather subjective. It would be better to base our understanding of the final shape of the Psalter not upon a reconstruction of a historical situation, but upon the text of the fivefold book.

Themes Set Forth in Introductory Psalms

Let us, then, look at the text. When opening the book of Psalms, one is immediately struck by the fact that the first two psalms serve as an introduction to the fivefold Psalter. Unlike most of the psalms that follow in Book I, these psalms lack superscriptions that identify them with a Davidic collection. The compilers must have put them here to announce at the outset basic themes in Judaism: the revelation of God's will in the Torah (Ps. 1), the dominion of God manifest in a Davidic king (Ps. 2), Yhwh's Anointed One (Hebrew, *mashiach;* Greek, *christos;* Latin, *messias*). We can best understand the final editing of the Psalter by considering these two themes that run through the whole from beginning to end. They provide doors, as it were, through which the reader may gain entrance into the finished edifice.

The Psalms as a Book of Teaching

As we have noticed repeatedly, the familiar translation of Hebrew *torah* as "law" (New Testament Greek, *nomos*) is inadequate. Jewish scholars point out that the term can have a very broad meaning, including the tradition handed down by teacher, cosmic law (cf. Ps. 19A) or "unmediated divine teaching."[8] Frequently the best translation is "teaching," as in Psalm 1:

> The teaching of the Lord is his delight,
> and he studies that teaching day and night.
>
> (Ps. 1:2, NJPS)

Here the psalmist seems to refer primarily to the heart of Torah, the Pentateuch, but this does not preclude meditation on God's torah that is given in other places, including the book of Psalms itself.

Besides this lead psalm, other torah psalms are scattered throughout the Psalter (e.g., 19, 119), strengthening the impression that the Psalter as a whole had an instructional purpose. In their final form, McCann observes, joining his voice with other scholars, "the Psalms are not only to be prayed and sung, but they are to be taught, learned from, and proclaimed."[9]

The teaching purpose of the book of Psalms would be further evident if, as Claus Westermann proposes, the book originally concluded with Psalm 119, the longest psalm in the Psalter.[10] In that case, the whole book would be clasped within a torah psalm at the beginning and one at the end. Moreover, there is a very fine line between torah and wisdom. As we have seen in chapter 9, the Psalter includes numerous psalms that stress gaining wisdom. The sage is the person who studies the torah day and night and seeks to live by its teaching, as in the case of Daniel in the Persian court (see Daniel 1).

This view of the Psalms as teaching is not really new; it prevailed in the period before the rise of the form-critical and cult-functional approaches. Clinton McCann, who makes this point, calls our attention to what Calvin said in the preface to his commentary on the Psalms. The book of Psalms, said Calvin, wants "to teach us the true method of praying aright"; moreover, "there is no other book in which we are more perfectly taught in the right manner of praising God."[11]

The Dominion of God

The second prefatory psalm, the royal Psalm 2, introduces another line that runs through the book of Psalms when considered as a whole. It is the theme of the kingdom or dominion of God, which is manifest through the Davidic king (God's anointed one) and which will ultimately come fully "on earth as it is in heaven," to use the familiar language of the Lord's Prayer. God is the cosmic creator and king, before whom not only Israel but all peoples should kneel in praise and adoration. The Psalms invite us into a God-centered world, the dominion of God, which was, which is, and is to come.

The theme of God's kingship is rooted primarily in royal covenant theology, which moves beyond the confines of Israel's Mosaic covenant theology into a universal and cosmic dimension. In this view, God made "an everlasting covenant" with the Davidic dynasty, assuring David and his successors that God would not go back on the "promises of grace" made to David.[12] It is significant that the Psalter contains a number of royal psalms, as we have seen, and that the book of Psalms as a completed whole is ascribed to David, the prototype of Yhwh's Anointed.

From Lament to Praise

Let us turn briefly to the headings to the Psalms, restricting our attention to the superscriptions that relate to an event in David's life. When we examine these, several things come to attention. First of all, each of these superscriptions relates to a period of trouble in David's life, especially the time of David's guerrilla war with Saul (Psalms 52; 54; 57; 59; 63; 142). Obsessed with the upstart warrior in his court, the powerful King Saul hounded David throughout the Judean desert. Other enemies of David are specifically mentioned: Cush (Psalm 7), Abimelech (Psalm 34), Philistines (Psalm 56). Besides enemies, David also had to face his own moral failure (Psalm 51).

One infers from these narrative superscriptions that the basis of Davidic prayers is not strength, but weakness. In other psalms David is portrayed in grand terms—king, servant of the Lord, chosen one, the anointed—but here David speaks as one in need, one who is completely dependent on God. This seems to suggest that in the final edition of the book of Psalms David is regarded as a model of a "perfect" worshiper, a devotee of Yhwh (*tzaddiq,* "righteous one").

Notice also that after the two introductory psalms the next psalm carries a narrative superscription: "A psalm of David when he fled from his son Absalom." The tragic story of Absalom (2 Samuel 17–19) strikes themes that reflect the brokenness of our world: betrayal, greed, vengeance, lust, family estrangement, oppression. Surely there is no scene in David's life more tragic and moving than his flight from Jerusalem before the army of Absalom and his overwhelming sorrow on hearing the news of Absalom's death. (A powerful modern portrayal of the haunting scene of the death of David's son is given by William Faulkner in *Absalom! Absalom!* [1936].)

These superscriptions, then, present David as a metaphorical "type," a poetic "figure" who moves with the people from grief to consolation, from suffering to trust in God.[13] It is significant that the Psalter begins, after the two introductory psalms, with a song of weakness and betrayal. From this lowly situation of distress Davidic prayer rises to the level of thanksgiving and praise. This portrayal of David, a man of the people and also a man of faith, supports the view that the Psalter in its final form begins with prayer "out of the depths" and rises to praise that is grounded in the sovereignty of God and God's "everlasting covenant" with the Davidic dynasty.

The Failure of the Davidic Covenant

The covenant with David, however, was called into question by tragic historical events and prompted the powerful lament with which Psalm 89 concludes:

> Lord, where is your steadfast love of old,
>   which by your faithfulness you swore to David?
>
>   (Ps. 89:49, NRSV)

In this important royal psalm, there is no attempt to cover up the historical experience of disillusionment and despair. The Davidic covenant was tried by fire, and found wanting.

In a book on editing the Psalms, Gerald H. Wilson has proposed that the editors' purpose in the final edition of the book was to cope with the failure of royal covenant theology based on the promises of grace to David.[14] He finds the evidence for this in the "seams" of the five books, that is, the places where one book of psalms is joined to another. Book I begins with a royal psalm (Ps. 2) and ends with what may be regarded as a royal psalm (Ps. 42). Book II ends with a royal psalm (Ps. 72), as does Book III (Ps. 89). The psalm that concludes Book III (89), however, marks a turning point. It begins with hymnic praise to God for promises of grace to David (referring to Nathan's oracle in 2 Samuel 7); it ends with a poignant lament (vv. 38–51) over the failure of those promises.

In Wilson's view, the problem of the breakdown of Davidic theology is overcome in Book IV, "the editorial center of the final form of the Hebrew Psalter." At this point editors have placed the hymns celebrating Yhwh's accession as cosmic king and ruler of the nations (Psalms 93, 95–99). These psalms, coming after the failure of the Davidic covenant, have the effect of lifting sovereignty from the level of princes and kings to the cosmic level of God's eternal dominion.

This is an attractive, even tempting, hypothesis. It breaks down, however, on the text of the book of Psalms itself. The Achilles' heel is Psalm 132, which comes after the psalms of God's enthronement. Here we find a restatement of the tenets of Davidic theology: the election of the Davidic king to a role in God's cosmic administration, and the choice of the temple of Zion as God's "dwelling-place."[15] And the other royal psalms, chiefly Psalm 110 which exalts the Davidic "messiah" to a position at the right hand of God's celestial throne, are found in the latter part of the book of Psalms. The truth is that Israelite interpreters, even in the face of harsh realities of history, never surrendered the hope for a coming monarch of the Davidic line who would rule as God's vicegerent, as portrayed in a well-known prophecy of Isaiah:

> His authority shall grow continually,
>   and there shall be endless peace
> for the throne of David and his kingdom.
>   He will establish and uphold it
> with justice and with righteousness
>   from this time onward and forevermore.
>   (Isa. 9:7, NRSV)

The Center of the Book of Psalms

Nevertheless, this proposal draws our attention to an important aspect of the Psalms as an edited whole. As we have seen, the book begins with laments "out of the depths" and moves to a great climax with hymns that celebrate God's dominion. These psalms, ending with "Old Hundredth" (Psalms 93, 95–100), may not be the center of the Psalter exactly, but they are certainly the doxological goal toward which the book moves. To be sure, there are hymns of praise along the way, such as the magnificent Eighth Psalm ("What are human beings that you are mindful of them?") and there are laments after the doxological climax, such as Psalm 130 ("Out of the depths"), but by and large the movement of the book of Psalms is from laments, which abound in the first part, to hymns of praise to God the Creator and King in the last part.

This arrangement tells us something important about our worship of God. The Psalter does not teach us that life before and with God is a falling away from a high plateau of serenity and order into a dark valley of despondency and disorder and then a regaining of those sublime heights. This pattern has been suggested by Walter Brueggemann in the "grid" that he uses for the classification of the psalms: psalms of orientation, disorientation, and new orientation.[16] But in the kind of world we live in everyday, I suspect that most people begin their worship of God with a sense of the brokenness of human life, manifest in family tensions, random violence, oppression of the helpless, and injustice that takes many forms. Perhaps people of the middle class want to persuade themselves that "God's in his heaven and all's right with the world," but if they are honest this is not so. Therefore, the shape of the book of Psalms is appealingly realistic. Here we see that prayer and worship move from the human depths of distress, godforsakenness, and guilt, to the heights of thanksgiving and praise. But these heights we cannot keep. The movement from lament, to thanksgiving, to hymnic praise occurs throughout life. Perhaps our lectionary and even our form of public worship should be brought more into line with the shape of the Psalter.

In summary, the book of Psalms is structured in such a way as to invite us to begin at the beginning with Psalms 1 and 2 and follow the symphony of praise until it ends with the mighty hallelujah chorus of Psalm 150. We ought to learn to follow this symphony as it develops, movement by movement, book by book. This would be a therapeutic procedure for pastoral counseling and for individual devotions, whether at bedtime, in the hospital, even on vacation! There is an old Jewish prescription for help in time of trouble: drink a warm glass of milk and read the Psalms, beginning at the beginning and taking them as they come.

Reading the Psalms in the Christ Context

At the end of our study we return to the question that was raised at the outset. In what sense does the Psalter speak to us of Jesus Christ?

Today we can say with greater clarity than ever before that the whole story of Israel, from the oppression in Egypt and on, was a passion story in which Israel experienced the reality of God in the midst of suffering and waited in hope for the coming of God's kingdom. This was the vision of the prophet Isaiah:

> The LORD is the everlasting God,
>   the Creator of the ends of the earth.

He does not faint or grow weary;
  his understanding is unsearchable.
He gives power to the faint,
  and strengthens the powerless.
Even youths will faint and be weary,
  and the young will fall exhausted;
but those who wait for the LORD
  shall renew their strength,
  they shall mount up with wings like eagles,
they shall run and not be weary,
  they shall walk and not faint.
                    (Isa. 40:28–31, NRSV)

In this prophetic view, Israel is the servant, called by God to share the good news of the coming of God's kingdom with the nations of the world.

As interpreted in the New Testament, the psalms not only anticipate the advent of the King who would inaugurate God's kingdom, but portray the passion and struggle he would undergo in fulfilling his task as God's anointed. To the Christian community the Psalms show, as Christoph Barth observes, that "Jesus and Israel belong together, and that their respective histories cannot be understood apart from each other."[17] From a Christian point of view, the story of Jesus and the story of Israel constitute one story: a story in which God is involved personally and redemptively in the historical experiences of "the people of God" to open a way into the coming dominion of God in which all peoples ultimately will find true unity and community (Isa. 2:2–4). In this perspective, Christians pray the Psalms "in Christ," the anointed one, who stands in the line of David but is far greater than he.

Appendix A

Outline of Psalms Considered in This Study

(Asterisks mark psalms recommended for special reading. Some psalms are listed in more than one place.)

Chapter 3: Narrative or Storytelling Psalms

*78	135
*105	*136
106	

Chapter 4: Laments

Community Laments

*12	89:38–51 (royal lament)
*44	*90
58	*94
60	123
74	126
79	129
*80	137
83	Lamentations 5
*85	

Individual Laments

*3	54
*4 (song of trust?)	55

5	56
7	*57
9–10	59
*13	61
14 (= 53)	63
17	64
*22	*69
25	70 (=40:13–17)
26	*71
27:7–14	*77
28	86
*31	*88
35	109
36	120
*39	139
40:11–17	140
41	141
*42–43	142
52	Lamentations 3
53 (= 14)	

Chapter 5: Penitential Psalms

6	*102
*32 (song of thanksgiving)	*130
38	*139 (individual lament?)
*51	143

Chapter 6: Songs of Thanksgiving

Community Songs of Thanksgiving

65 (hymn?)	*124
67 (hymn?)	136 (hymn?)
75	1 Samuel 2:1–10
*107	

Individual Songs of Thanksgiving

18 (= 2 Sam. 22)	*103 (probably a hymn)
(royal thanksgiving)	108 (=57:7–11; 60:5–12)
21 (royal thanksgiving)	

30
*32 (penitential psalm)
*34
40:1–11
66:13–20
*92

*116
*118 (royal thanksgiving)
*138
Isaiah 38:9–20
Jonah 2:2–9

Chapter 7: Hymns of Praise

Hymns to God, Who Created (Redeemed) Israel

66:1–12
*100
111
*114
149

*Exodus 15:1–18
Deuteronomy 32:1–43
Habakkuk 3:2–19
Isaiah 52:7–10

Hymns to God, Who Created the World

*8
*19:1–6
95:1–7a

*104
*148
See also 74:12–17; 89:5–18

Hymns to the Creator and Ruler of History

*33
*103 (song of thanksgiving?)
113
117

*145
*146
*147
150 (a doxology that
concludes the Psalter)

(See also "Enthronement Psalms" and "Songs of Zion,"
chapter 8)

Chapter 8: Festival Songs and Liturgies

Covenant Renewal Liturgies

50
*81

Enthronement Psalms

24 (entrance liturgy)
29

*96
97

*47   *98
93   *99
*95

Psalms of the Davidic Covenant

*78 (storytelling psalm)
*89 (royal hymn and lament psalm)
*132

Royal Psalms

*2   45
*18 (royal thanksgiving)   72
20   101
21   *110
144:1–11 (royal lament)

Songs of Zion

*46   87
48   *121
76   *122
*84

Chapter 9: Songs of Trust and Meditation

Songs of Trust

11   *63 (individual lament)
16   *91
*23   *121
*27:1–6   125 (community lament?)
62   131

Wisdom Psalms

36 (mixed type)   127
*37   128
*49   133
*73   Proverbs 8
78 (storytelling psalm)   Sirach 14:2–15:10
112

Torah Psalms

*1
*19:7–14
 119

Liturgies

15 (compare Ps. 24)
68
82
115
134

Appendix B

Index of Psalms according to Type

The following is presented only as a working basis for the study of the Psalms. There are too many uncertainties to permit an exact and rigid classification according to type.

PSALM	TYPE

Book I

PSALM	TYPE
1	Torah (wisdom) psalm
2	Royal psalm
3	Individual lament
4	Individual lament (psalm of trust?)
5	Individual lament
6	Individual lament (penitential psalm)
7	Individual lament
8	Hymn
9–10	Individual lament? (alphabetical acrostic)
11	Song of trust
12	Community lament
13	Individual lament
14	(=53) Individual lament
15	Liturgy for admission to the cult
16	Song of trust
17	Individual lament
18	(=2 Sam. 22) Individual thanksgiving (royal)

PSALM	TYPE
19:1–6	Hymn
19:7–14	Torah (wisdom) psalm
20	Royal psalm
21	Royal psalm (thanksgiving)
22	Individual lament
23	Song of trust
24	Temple entrance liturgy
25	Individual lament (alphabetical acrostic)
26	Individual lament
27:1–6	Song of trust
27:7–14	Individual lament
28	Individual lament
29	Hymn
30	Individual song of thanksgiving
31	Individual lament
32	Individual song of thanksgiving (penitential psalm with wisdom elements)
33	Hymn
34	Individual song of thanksgiving (alphabetical acrostic with wisdom elements)
35	Individual lament
36	Mixed type, including wisdom, hymn, lament
37	Wisdom psalm (alphabetical acrostic)
38	Individual lament (penitential psalm)
39	Individual lament
40:1–11	Individual song of thanksgiving
40:12–17	Individual lament
41	Individual lament

Book II

42–43	Individual lament
44	Community lament
45	Royal psalm
46	Hymn (song of Zion)
47	Hymn (enthronement psalm)

PSALM	TYPE
48	Hymn (song of Zion)
49	Wisdom psalm
50	Covenant renewal liturgy
51	Individual lament (penitential psalm)
52	Individual lament (mixture of types)
53	(= 14) Individual lament
54	Individual lament
55	Individual lament
56	Individual lament
57	Individual lament
58	Community lament
59	Individual lament
60	Community lament
61	Individual lament
62	Song of trust
63	Song of trust (or individual lament)
64	Individual lament
65	Community song of thanksgiving (hymn?)
66:1–12	Hymn
66:13–20	Individual song of thanksgiving
67	Community song of thanksgiving (hymn?)
68	Zion liturgy ? (almost impossible to classify)
69	Individual lament
70	(=40:13–17) Individual lament
71	Individual lament
72	Royal psalm

Book III

73	Wisdom psalm
74	Community lament
75	Community song of thanksgiving?
76	Hymn (song of Zion)
77	Individual lament
78	Storytelling psalm based on the Davidic covenant
79	Community lament
80	Community lament
81	Covenant renewal liturgy

PSALM	TYPE
82	Liturgy
83	Community lament
84	Hymn (song of Zion)
85	Community lament
86	Individual lament
87	Hymn (song of Zion)
88	Individual lament
89	Royal psalm based on the Davidic covenant
89:1–37	Hymn
89:38–51	Lament

Book IV

90	Community lament
91	Song of trust (including an oracle of protection)
92	Individual song of thanksgiving
93	Hymn (enthronement psalm)
94	Community lament
95	Hymn
96	Hymn
97	Hymn (enthronement psalm)
98	Hymn
99	Hymn
100	Hymn
101	Royal psalm
102	Individual lament including hymnic elements (penitential)
103	Hymn
104	Hymn
105	Storytelling psalm (in mood of hymnic praise)
106	Storytelling psalm (in penitential mood)

Book V

107	Community song of thanksgiving
108	(=57:7–11; 60:5–12) Mixed type

PSALM	TYPE
109	Individual lament
110	Royal psalm
111	Hymn (alphabetical acrostic)
112	Wisdom psalm (alphabetical acrostic)
113	Hymn
114	Hymn
115	Liturgy
116	Individual song
117	Hymn
118	Individual song of thanksgiving (royal)
119	Torah (wisdom) psalm (alphabetical acrostic)
120	Individual lament
121	Song of trust
122	Song of Zion
123	Community lament
124	Community song of thanksgiving
125	Song of trust (community lament?)
126	Community lament?
127	Wisdom psalm
128	Wisdom psalm
129	Community lament?
130	Individual lament (penitential psalm)
131	Song of trust
132	Royal psalm based on the Davidic covenant
133	Wisdom psalm
134	Liturgy
135	Storytelling psalm (hymnic praise)
136	Storytelling psalm (hymnic praise)
137	Community lament
138	Individual song of thanksgiving
139	Individual lament (wisdom psalm?)
140	Individual lament
141	Individual lament
142	Individual lament
143	Individual lament
144:1–11	Royal psalm
145	Hymn (alphabetical acrostic)

Appendix B

PSALM	**TYPE**
146	Hymn
147	Hymn
148	Hymn
149	Hymn
150	Hymn (doxology to conclude the Psalter of thanksgiving)

Appendix C

Quotations from
Old Testament Psalms in the New Testament

Echoes of Old Testament psalms are heard in more New Testament passages than those included in this list, which is confined for the most part to direct quotations or specific allusions.

Old Testament Psalm	*New Testament Context*
Ex. 15:1–18	Rev. 15:3
Deut. 32:35–36	Rom. 12:19; Heb. 10:30
Ps. 2:1–2	Acts 4:25–26
2:1, 5	Rev. 11:18
2:7	Acts 13:33; Heb. 1:5; 5:5
2:8–9	Rev. 2:26–27; 12:5; 19:15
Ps. 4:4	Eph. 4:26
Ps. 5:9	Rom. 3:13
Ps. 6:8	Matt. 7:23; Luke 13:27
Ps. 8:2	Matt. 21:16
8:4–6	Heb. 2:6–8
8:6	1 Cor. 15:27; Eph. 1:22
Ps. 10:7	Rom. 3:14
Ps. 14:1–2	Rom. 3:10–12
Ps. 16:8–11	Acts 2:25–28, 31
16:10	Acts 2:31; 13:35
Ps. 18:49	Rom. 15:9
Ps. 19:4	Rom. 10:18

Old Testament Psalm	*New Testament Context*
19:9	Rev. 16:7; 19:2
Ps. 22:1	Matt. 27:46; Mark 15:34
22:7–8	Matt. 27:39; Mark 15:29; Luke 23:35
22:8	Matt. 27:43
22:13	1 Pet. 5:8
22:16(cf. 69:21)	John 19:28
22:18	Matt. 27:35; Mark 15:24; Luke 23:34; John 19:24
22:21	2 Tim. 4:17
22:22	Heb. 2:12, 17
Ps. 23:1–2	Rev. 7:17
Ps. 24:1(cf. 50:12)	1 Cor. 10:26
Ps. 31:5	Luke 23:46
Ps. 32:1–2	Rom. 4:7–8
Ps. 33:3	Rev. 5:9; 14:3
Ps. 34:8	1 Pet. 2:3
34:12–16	1 Pet. 3:10–12
34:20	John 19:36
Ps. 35:19	John 15:25
Ps. 36:1	Rom. 3:18
Ps. 37:11	Matt. 5:5
Ps. 40:6–8	Heb. 10:5–7, 8–10
Ps. 41:9	John 13:18
Ps. 42:6, 12; 43:5	Matt. 26:38; Mark 14:34
Ps. 44:22	Rom. 8:36
Ps. 45:6–7	Heb. 1:8–9
Ps. 48:2	Matt. 5:35
Ps. 50:12(cf. 24:1)	1 Cor. 10:26
50:14, 23	Matt. 5:33; Heb. 13:15
Ps. 51:4	Rom. 3:4
Ps. 53:1–2	Rom. 3:10–12
Ps. 55:22	1 Pet. 5:7
Ps. 68:18	Eph. 4:8
Ps. 69:4	John 15:25
69:9	John 2:17; Rom. 15:3
69:21	Matt. 27:34, 48; Mark 15:36; Luke 23:36; John 19:28
69:22–23	Rom. 11:9–10
69:25	Acts 1:20
69:28	Rev. 3:5; 17:8; 20:12; 21:27

Old Testament Psalm	*New Testament Context*
Ps. 75:8	Rev. 14:10
Ps. 78:2	Matt. 13:35
78:24(cf. 105:40)	John 6:31
Ps. 82:6	John 10:34
Ps. 86:8–10	Rev. 3:9; 15:4
Ps. 89:3–4	Acts 2:30
89:26–27(cf. 2 Sam. 7:14)	Heb. 1:5b
89:27	Rev. 1:5
Ps. 90:4	2 Pet. 3:8
Ps. 91:11–12	Matt. 4:6; Luke 4:10–11
91:13	Luke 10:19
Ps. 94:11	1 Cor. 3:20
94:14	Rom. 11:1–2
Ps. 95:7–8	Heb. 4:7
95:7–11	Heb. 3:7–11
95:11	Heb. 4:3
Ps. 97:7	Heb. 1:6
Ps. 102:25–27	Heb. 1:10–12
Ps. 103:8(cf. 111:4)	James 5:11
Ps. 104:4	Heb. 1:7
Ps. 105:40(cf. 78:24)	John 6:31
Ps. 106:20	Rom. 1:23
Ps. 109:8	Acts 1:20
109:25	Matt. 27:39; Mark 15:29
Ps. 110:1	Matt. 22:44; 26:64; Mark 12:36; 14:62; 16:19; Luke 20:42–43; 22:69; Acts 2:34–35; 1 Cor. 15:25; Eph. 1:20; Col. 3:1; Heb. 1:13; 8:1; 10:12–13; 12:2
110:4	Heb. 5:6; 7:17; 7:21
Ps. 112:9	2 Cor. 9:9
Ps. 115:4–7	Rev. 9:20
115:13	Rev. 11:18; 19:5
Ps. 116:10	2 Cor. 4:13
Ps. 117:1	Rom. 15:11
Ps. 118:6	Heb. 13:6
118:22–23	Matt. 21:42; Mark 12:10; Luke 20:17; Acts 4:11; 1 Peter 2:7
118:25–26	Matt. 21:9, 15; Mark 11:9–10; John 12:13
118:26	Matt. 23:39; Luke 13:35; 19:38

Old Testament Psalm	**New Testament Context**
Ps. 132:5	Acts 7:46
132:11	Acts 2:30
Ps. 135:15–17	Rev. 9:20
Ps. 137:8	Rev. 18:6
137:9	Luke 19:44
Ps. 140:3	Rom. 3:13
Ps. 143:2	Rom. 3:20; Gal. 2:16
Ps. 146:6	Acts 2:24; 14:15; Rev. 10:6

Notes

Preface Notes

1. See the Service Book (Ontario: United Church of Canada, 1969, 45.

1. Songs of a Pilgrim People

1. Natan Sharansky, *Fear No Evil,* trans. Stefani Hoffman (New York: Vintage Books, 1988), 407–8.
2. See John D. Godsey, *The Theology of Dietrich Bonhoeffer* (Philadelphia: Westminster Press, 1960).
3. Dietrich Bonhoeffer, *Psalms: The Prayer Book of the Bible,* 2d ed., trans. J. H. Burtness (Minneapolis: Augsburg Publishing House, 1970).
4. Amos N. Wilder, *The Language of the Gospel* (New York: Harper & Row, 1964), chap. 1, esp. p. 24.
5. On the use of the psalms in the history of Christian worship, see chapter 10.
6. W. T. Davison: "More than any other book of the Old Testament it [the Psalter] has been baptized into Christ." Quoted in John Paterson, *The Praises of Israel* (New York: Charles Scribner's Sons, 1950), 7.
7. H. Richard Niebuhr, *The Meaning of Revelation* (New York: Macmillan Co., 1941), chap. 2.
8. See, for instance, Theodor H. Gaster, ed. and trans., *The Dead Sea Scriptures in English Translation* (Doubleday & Co., Anchor Books, 1956), 123–202. The archaeological discovery of the Qumran library began in 1947.
9. See further John H. Wheeler, "The Hebrew Old Testament as a Vocal Score," *The Hymn* 44, no. 3 (July 1993): 10–15. Suzanne Haïk-Vantoura, *The Music of the Bible Revealed,* trans. Dennis Weber, ed. John Wheeler (San Francisco: BIBAL Press/King David's Harp, Inc., 1991) is a difficult translation of her work. More accessible to the general reader

is the recording of her work, *La musique de l'a Bible révélée* (Harmonia Mundi France), cassette (HMA 43989), CD (HMA 190989).

10. Erhard S. Gerstenberger, *Psalms Part I, with an Introduction to Cultic Poetry,* Forms of the Old Testament Literature, vol. 14 (Grand Rapids: Wm. B. Eerdmans Publishing Co., 1988).

11. Deviations from the Hebrew numerical tradition of the Psalter are discussed by J. A. Sanders, *The Dead Sea Psalms Scroll* (Ithaca, N.Y.: Cornell University Press, 1967).

12. For further discussion of the divine name, see my *Contours of Old Testament Theology* (Minneapolis: Augsburg Fortress Press, 1999).

13. Artur Weiser, *The Psalms: A Commentary,* trans. Herbert Hartwell, Old Testament Library (Philadelphia: Westminster Press, 1962), 96.

14. Peter R. Ackroyd observes that spaces were left in ancient Hebrew manuscripts of the books of Samuel so that, at that point, readers could consider a psalm that was relevant to the career of David. (*Doors of Perception: A Guide to Reading the Psalms* [London: SCM Press, 1978], 35–36, 74–76).

15. Christoph Barth, *Introduction to the Psalms,* trans. R. A. Wilson (New York: Charles Scribner's Sons, 1966), 64–65.

16. One of the great contributions to twentieth-century Psalms research was that of the Scandinavian scholar, Sigmund Mowinckel, in which he attempted to connect many of the psalms with a New Year's festival at the Jerusalem temple. See *The Psalms in Israel's Worship,* vols. 1 and 2, trans. D. R. Ap-Thomas (Nashville: Abingdon Press, 1962).

17. Walter Brueggemann, *Abiding Astonishment: Psalms, Modernity, and the Making of History,* Literary Currents in Biblical Interpretation (Louisville, Ky.: Westminster/John Knox Press, 1991), 21. See also his *Israel's Praises* (Philadelphia: Fortress Press, 1988).

18. See Wordsworth's "Ode" on the intimations of immortality and "The World Is Too Much with Us," William Wordsworth, *Selected Poetry* (New York: Oxford University Press, 1998), 140–45 and 132–33.

19. Roland E. Murphy, *The Psalms, Job,* Proclamation Commentaries (Philadelphia: Fortress Press, 1977), 12–13.

2. The Poetry of Prayer and Praise

1. C. S. Lewis, *Reflections on the Psalms* (London: G. Bles, 1958), 31.

2. Ibid, 5.

3. See Robert Alter, *The Art of Biblical Narrative* (New York: Basic Books, 1981).

4. For an overview of these studies, see J. Kenneth Kuntz, "Recent Perspectives on Biblical Poetry," in *Religious Studies Review* 19, no. 4 (October 1993).

5. See Harold Fisch, *Poetry with a Purpose: Biblical Poetics and Interpretation* (Bloomington, Ind.: Indiana University Press, 1988).

6. See Robert Alter, *The Art of Biblical Poetry* (New York: Basic Books, 1985).

7. James L. Kugel, *The Idea of Biblical Poetry* (New Haven, Conn.: Yale University Press, 1981), 51–52.

8. Adele Berlin, *The Dynamics of Biblical Parallelism* (Bloomington, Ind.: Indiana University Press, 1985).

9. The translation of *The Song of Songs* by Ariel Bloch and Chana Bloch (New York: Random House, 1995) comes close to doing this.

10. For a fuller treatment of the characteristics of biblical poetry, see Adele Berlin, "Introduction to Hebrew Poetry" in *The New Interpreters Bible,* vol. 4 (Nashville: Abingdon Press, 1996), 301–15.

11. Mitchell Dahood, *Psalms,* vols. 1–3, Anchor Bible (Garden City, N.Y.: Doubleday & Co., 1965, 1968, 1970).

12. See Adrian H. W. Curtis, "The Psalms since Dahood," in *Ugarit and the Bible: Proceedings of the International Symposium on Ugarit and the Bible,* ed. George J. Brooke, Adrian H. W. Curtis, and John F. Healey (Munter Germany: Ugarit-Verlag, 1994), 1–10.

13. Translated by Mark S. Smith in *Ugaritic Narrative Poetry,* ed. Simon B. Parker, SBL Writings from the Ancient World Series (Atlanta: Scholars Press, 1997), 141.

14. The Revised English Bible takes the liberty of translating "sea" (*yam*) in verse twelve as "sea monster." Through the intensification and specification discussed earlier in this chapter, we would understand the "sea" to refer to Leviathan without an explicit translation. The Hebrew is brilliant here because the sea is "split" by Yhwh and so makes us think also of the parting of the Reed Sea. But other translations that keep *yam* as "sea" over-reach the play of meaning by translating "split" as "drove back" (NJPS) or, to a lesser extent, "divided" (NRSV). The verbs used to describe the destruction of the sea monster are "split," "broke," and "crushed." This illustrates the escalating particularity and vividness of biblical parallelism.

15. See my chapter, "The Slaying of the Fleeing, Twisting Serpent: Isaiah 27:1 in Context," in *From Creation to New Creation,* Overtures to Biblical Theology (Minneapolis: Fortress Press, 1994).

16. "Hymn to the Moon-God," trans. Ferris J. Stephens, in James B. Pritchard, ed., *Ancient Near Eastern Texts Relating to the Old Testament,* 3d ed. (Princeton, N.J.: Princeton University Press, 1969), 385–86.

17. "Hymn to the Aton," trans. John A. Wilson in Pritchard, *Ancient Near Eastern Texts,* 369–73.

18. *The Confessions of St. Augustine,* trans. J. G. Pilkington (New York: Liveright Publishing Corp., 1943), book 1, chap. 1.

3. Narrative Praise

1. See the insightful discussion by Amos N. Wilder, "Story and Story-World," *Interpretation* 37 (1983): 353–64.

2. Emil Fackenheim, a Jewish philosopher, points out that all Jewish tradition rests upon two fundamental experiences: "the saving experience" (exodus) and "the commanding experience" (Sinai covenant). See his *God's Presence in History: Jewish Affirmations and Philosophical Reflections* (New York: New York University Press, 1970).

3. Possibly translate "the people whom you created." On the creation of a people, see, for instance, Ps. 95:6 and Isa. 43:1.

4. Michael Goldberg, *Jews and Christians Getting Our Stories Straight* (Nashville: Abingdon Press, 1985), 13.

5. David and Tamar de Sola Pool, eds., *The Haggadah of the Passover* (New York: Bloch Publishing Co., 1953), 51.

6. See Gerhard von Rad, "The Form-Critical Problem of the Hexateuch," in *The Problem of the Hexateuch and Other Essays,* trans. E. W. T. Dicken (New York: McGraw-Hill Book Co., 1966), 1–78. Von Rad's view is summarized in *Genesis: A Commentary,* rev. ed., Old Testament Library (Philadelphia: Westminster Press, 1973), 13–23.

7. See Bertil Albrektson, *History and the Gods: An Essay on the Idea of Historical Events as Divine Manifestations in the Ancient Near East and in Israel* (Lund, Sweden: C. W. K. Gleerup, 1967). At the end of his study, Albrektson notes the peculiar way that Yhwh's acts in history were remembered and celebrated in the Israelite cult.

8. Amos N. Wilder, *The Language of the Gospel* (New York: Harper & Row, 1964), 64–65.

9. On the relationship between history, theology, and language see my *Contours of Old Testament Theology* (Minneapolis: Fortress Press, 1999).

10. H. Richard Niebuhr, *The Meaning of Revelation* (New York: Macmillan Co., 1941), 48.

11. The current emphasis on storytelling theology is discussed, e.g., in George W. Stroup, *The Promise of Narrative Theology* (Atlanta: John Knox Press, 1981) and Michael Goldberg, *Theology and Narrative: A Critical Introduction* (Nashville: Abingdon Press, 1982). For a collection of essays by some of the seminal thinkers in the narrative theology discussion see Stanley Hauerwas and L. Gregory Jones, eds., *Why Narrative? Readings in Narrative Theology* (Grand Rapids: Wm. B. Eerdmans Publishing Co., 1988).

12. Robert Alter, *The Art of Biblical Narrative* (New York: Basic Books, 1981), 155.

13. Helmer Ringgren, *The Faith of the Psalmists* (Philadelphia: Fortress Press, 1963), 35.

14. For a thorough, illuminating discussion of this important Hebrew term, see Katharine D. Sakenfeld, *The Meaning of Hesed in the Hebrew Bible,* Harvard Semitic Monographs 17 (Missoula, Mont.: Scholars Press, 1978). See further her *Faithfulness in Action: Loyalty in Biblical Perspective,* Overture Series (Philadelphia: Fortress Press, 1985).

15. For a thorough study of laments in the Old Testament, see Patrick D. Miller, *They Cried to the Lord: The Form and Theology of Biblical Prayer* (Minneapolis: Fortress Press, 1994).

4. The Trials of Faith

1. Claus Westermann, *The Praise of God in the Psalms,* 2d ed., trans. Keith R. Crim (Richmond: John Knox Press, 1965), 37.
2. See the discussion of Jeremiah's complaints in my *Understanding the Old Testament,* 4th ed., abridged (Upper Saddle River, N.J.: Prentice-Hall, 1998), 363–68.
3. On the distinction between a dirge and a lament, see Claus Westermann, "Lamentations," in *The Books of the Bible,* ed. Bernhard W. Anderson (New York: Charles Scribner's Sons, 1989).
4. Translated by Ferris J. Stephens in James B. Pritchard, ed., *Ancient Near Eastern Texts Relating to the Old Testament,* 3d ed. (Princeton, N.J.: Princeton University Press, 1969), 383–85.
5. Theodor H. Gaster, *The Dead Sea Scriptures in English Translation* (Garden City, N.Y.: Doubleday & Co., Anchor Books, 1956), 112. Gaster objects to the prosaic interpretation of the enemies in these psalms ("the company of Belial," "the men of corruption") as adversaries escaped or overcome in warfare. Such a view, he remarks, "confuses the 'sling and arrows of outrageous fortune' with concrete bazookas and guided missiles." A brief and informative summary of the Dead Sea scriptures can be found in William L. Holladay, *The Psalms through Three Thousand Years: Prayerbook of a Cloud of Witnesses* (Minneapolis: Fortress Press, 1993), 98–110.
6. See J. Paul Sampley, *Walking Between the Times: Paul's Moral Reasoning* (Minneapolis: Fortress Press, 1991), especially chap. 1.
7. See the helpful discussion of the book of Joel by Theodore Hiebert in Anderson, *Books of the Bible.*
8. The so-called penitential psalms are treated in chapter 5.
9. The classification is uncertain. Some regard this psalm as the lament of an accused person who casts himself upon the mercy of God, the Highest Judge who knows him intimately.
10. Erhard Gerstenberger, "Jeremiah's Complaints," *Journal of Biblical Literature* 82 (1963): 50n. In this study, Gerstenberger proposes that instead of "lament," which "bemoans a tragedy which cannot be reversed," we use the word "complaint," which implores God to reverse the situation. But the word "complaint" has difficulties too. Claus Westermann suggests that we make a distinction between "the lament of affliction" and "the lament of the dead." "The lament of the dead," he writes, "looks backward, the lament of affliction looks forward." ("The Role of the Lament in the Theology of the Old Testament," *Interpretation,* 28 [1974], 22)

11. Roland E. Murphy, *The Psalms, Job,* Proclamation Commentaries (Philadelphia: Fortress Press, 1977), 41.

12. Walter Brueggemann puts the psalms of lament under the rubric of disorientation; see his *The Message of the Psalms: A Theological Commentary* (Minneapolis: Augsburg Press, 1984).

13. In the ancient way of thinking, Sheol is the underground land of the dead to which the "shade" goes, the shadow of one's former self. In this shadowy existence, there is no real life—no memory, no community, hence no praise of God. "The shadow existence is dismal; eternal silence and darkness surrounds the disembodied shadows, whose presence there can only be recognised so long as their names are remembered in the Land of the Living." (Klaus Seybold, *Introducing the Psalms* [Edinburgh: T. & T. Clark, 1990], 169)

14. The remaining verses, 29–31, are not included in this translation. The Hebrew text is uncertain at points, but the psalmist continues on a note of praise.

15. Abraham J. Heschel, *The Prophets* (New York: Harper & Row, 1965), esp. chaps. 12–18.

16. For an overview of the debate on this question, see Gerald T. Sheppard " 'Enemies' and the Politics of Prayer in the Book of Psalms," in *The Bible and the Politics of Exegesis,* ed. David Jobling, et al., (Cleveland: Pilgrim Press, 1991), 61–82.

17. In this psalm, which opens the Elohistic Psalter (Psalms 42–83), editors have substituted the general name for deity (Elohim) for the personal name of God (Yhwh).

18. See the discussion of death in chapter 5; also "Life, Death, and Resurrection" in my *Contours of Old Testament Theology* (Minneapolis: Fortress Press, 1999).

19. This view has been advanced by Hans Schmidt, *Die Psalmen,* Handbuch zum Alten Testament 15 (Tubingen: J. C. B. Mohr, 1934).

20. Helmer Ringgren's brief discussion of "The Psalms and Comparative Religion" in *The Faith of the Psalmists* (Philadelphia: Fortress Press, 1963), 115–21, is helpful in this connection.

21. In the category of individual laments: Psalms 35, 59, 69, 70, 109, 139, 140; communal laments: Psalms 12, 58, 83.

22. *A Translation of the Psalms of David Attempted in the Spirit of Christianity and Adapted to the Divine Service* (London: Dryden Leach, 1765), 141.

23. Burtness (Minneapolis: Augsburg Publishing House, 1970). Bonhoeffer's view is discussed by John D. Godsey in *The Theology of Dietrich Bonhoeffer* (Philadelphia: Westminster Press, 1960), 191.

24. Christoph Barth, *Introduction to the Psalms,* trans. R. A. Wilson (New York: Charles Scribner's Sons, 1966), 43.

25. In particular, see Walter Brueggemann, "Psalm 109: Steadfast Love as Social Solidarity" in *The Psalms and the Life of Faith,* ed. Patrick D. Miller (Minneapolis: Fortress Press, 1995), 268–82, and Erich Zenger, "Toward a Hermeneutic of the Psalms of Enmity and Vengeance" in *A God of Vengeance? Understanding the Psalms of Divine Wrath,* trans. Linda M. Maloney (Louisville, Ky.: Westminster John Knox Press, 1996), 63–86.
26. The late reggae musician Bob Marley used Psalm 137 to inspire a spirit of protest in his listeners.
27. Gerald H. Wilson, "Songs for the City: Interpreting Biblical Psalms in an Urban Context," presented at the Psalms and Practice Conference, Austin, Texas, May 25–27, 1999.
28. Zenger, *God of Vengeance?*
29. In *The Faith of the Psalmists,* Helmer Ringgren asserts that "The imagery being mythological, the enemies are taken to be more than human; they become the representatives of all evil forces that threaten life and order in the world"—the order that the Creator continues to uphold against all the threatening powers of chaos. But this assertion goes too far. For a further discussion of this theme see my chapter, "Creation and Conflict," in *Creation versus Chaos* (Philadelphia: Fortress Press, 1987).
30. This contemporary experience is discussed by M. Scott Peck, *The People of the Lie* (New York: Simon & Schuster, 1983).
31. This phrase is quoted by James H. Smylie in his article, "On Jesus, Pharaoh, and the Chosen People: Martin Luther King as Biblical Interpreter and Humanist," *Interpretation* 24 (1970): 78.
32. For more on the "oppressive pharaoh" and his significance to Israelite theology, see my *Understanding the Old Testament,* 4th ed., abridged (Upper Saddle River, N.J.: Prentice-Hall, 1998), 49ff.
33. This phrase comes from Patrick D. Miller Jr., "Trouble and Woe: Interpreting the Biblical Laments," *Interpretation* 37 (January 1983): 32–45. This helpful essay demonstrates the value of paying attention to language along with a concern for narrative and historical contexts.
34. G. Ernest Wright, "Reflections Concerning Old Testament Theology," in *Studia Biblica et Semitica,* ed. Theodorus C. Vriezen (Wangeningen, Netherlands: H. Veeman & Zonen, 1966), 387.
35. Claus Westermann, *A Thousand Years and a Day* (Philadelphia: Fortress Press, 1962). See also Ringgren, *Faith of the Psalmists,* 31–32.
36. Zenger, *God of Vengeance?,* 77.

5. Psalms of a Broken and Contrite Heart

1. T. S. Eliot, *The Cocktail Party,* Centenary Edition (San Diego, New York, London: Harvests Books, Harcourt Brace & Co., 1950, 1973), 136–37.
2. John Fisher, *The English Works of John Fisher, Bishop of Rochester,* Early English Text Society 27 (London: N. Trubnor & Co., 1876), 70.

3. *The Seven Psalms: A Commentary on the Penitential Psalms, translated from French into English by Dame Eleanor Hull,* ed. Alexandra Barratt. Early English Text Society 307 (Oxford: Oxford University Press, 1995).

4. See the brief but helpful commentary on "The Seven Psalms," by Walter Brueggemann, in *The Message of the Psalms: A Theological Commentary* (Minneapolis: Augsburg Publishing House, 1984), 94–106.

5. A notable musical work based on this psalm was composed by Gregorio Allegri (1582–1652). It is said that Mozart heard the piece when he was fourteen years old, then went home and reproduced the score from memory. This is testimony not only to Mozart's genius but to the beauty and simplicity of Allegri's composition. It has been sung in the Sistine Chapel during Holy Week every year since it was composed.

6. See chapter 1.

7. Brueggemann, *Message of the Psalms,* 100.

8. Blaise Pascal, "Meditations," VI, 5, *Pensées et Opuscules,* ed. J. Roger Charbonel, Classiques Larousse (Sorbonne: Librairie Larousse, [n.d.]), 65. "Le coeur a ses raisons, que la raison ne connait point . . ."

9. John Calvin, *Commentary on the Book of Psalms,* vol. 2, trans. James Anderson (Grand Rapids: Wm. B. Eerdmans Publishing Co. 1949), 290. "The passage affords a striking testimony in proof of original sin entailed by Adam upon the whole human family."

10. Fisher, *English Works of John Fisher,* 207.

11. Dietrich Bonhoeffer, according to John D. Godsey, *The Theology of Dietrich Bonhoeffer* (Philadelphia: Westminster Press, 1960), 193.

12. Christoph Barth, *Introduction to the Psalms* (New York: Charles Scribner's Sons, 1966), 42.

13. Francis Thompson, *Hound of Heaven* (New York: Dodd, Mead & Co., 1922).

6. Singing a New Song

1. Walter Brueggemann, "From Hurt to Joy, From Death to Life," *Interpretation* 28 (1974): 3–19.

2. See the portrayal of the mythical view of the cosmos and the dynamic view of life and death expressed in this poetic idiom on p. 112.

3. James M. Robinson discusses the genre of the "thanksgiving" and the "blessing," both of which appear prominently in the psalms of Qumran (Dead Sea Scrolls), in his essay in *The Old Testament and Christian Faith,* ed. Bernhard W. Anderson (New York: Herder & Herder, 1969), esp. 131ff.

4. Otto Eissfeldt, *The Old Testament: An Introduction* (New York: Harper & Row, 1965), 122. He concludes: "Thus the Phoenician cultus, too, was familiar with the gesture of thanksgiving which the psalm passage attests [Ps. 116:13], and the words quoted from the inscription lead to the surmise that there existed there, too, songs of thanksgiving similar to those of the

Old Testament, as we have similar ones in Egypt in fair numbers and in fact from a very early date."

5. See the monograph by Aubrey R. Johnson, *The Vitality of the Individual in the Thought of Ancient Israel* (Cardiff: University of Wales Press, 1949).

6. John Calvin, *Commentary on Genesis 2:2,* quoted by William C. Placher, "Being Postliberal," *The Christian Century* 116, no. 11 (April 7, 1999), 391.

7. See further my *Creation versus Chaos* (Philadelphia: Fortress Press, 1987), 93–99.

8. In this connection see the penetrating discussion by Christoph Barth, "The Power and Overthrow of Death," in *Introduction to the Psalms,* trans. R. A. Wilson (New York: Charles Scribner's Sons, 1966), 49–55. See further Lloyd R. Bailey Sr., *Biblical Perspectives on Death* (Philadelphia: Fortress Press, 1979).

9. James Barr in *The Garden of Eden and the Hope of Immortality* (Minneapolis: Fortress Press, 1992) argues for intimations of immortality in the Old and New Testaments. The intimations, though, are not entirely convincing and must be teased out of the text.

10. See my *Contours of Old Testament Theology* (Minneapolis: Fortress Press, 1999), chap. 34.

11. Barth, *Introduction to the Psalms,* 50–51, 54–55. In this context he observes: " 'Life' for the psalms means the historical formation and appearance of the people of God, while 'death' means their sinking back into the natural existence of the heathen, fundamentally without history."

12. *The New Oxford Annotated Bible,* New Revised Standard Version, ed. Bruce M. Metzger and Roland E. Murphy (New York: Oxford University Press, 1991), 761n.

13. Many commentators concur on this point. See Hans-Joachim Kraus, *Psalms 60–150: A Commentary,* trans. Hilton C. Oswald (Minneapolis: Augsburg Publishing House, 1989), 289–90.

14. Dietrich Bonhoeffer, *Prisoner for God: Letters and Papers from Prison* (New York: Macmillan Co., 1953), 79. See also Martin Kuske, *The Old Testament as the Book of Christ: An Appraisal of Bonhoeffer's Interpretation,* trans. S. T. Kimbrough Jr. (Philadelphia: Westminster Press, 1976), 96ff.

7. The Wonder of God's Creation

1. Otto Eissfeldt, *The Old Testament: An Introduction* (New York: Harper & Row, 1965), 105–6.

2. Helmer Ringgren, in *The Faith of the Psalmists* (Philadelphia: Fortress Press, 1963), emphasizes this aspect of visual participation in the ritual drama: "The creation and the exodus from Egypt were not only great and precious memories treasured by the faithful and now and then recollected

or commemorated. They were events that were actualized and reexperienced whenever the great festivals were celebrated in the temple" (p. 90).

3. Some of these ancient hymns are found in James B. Pritchard, ed., *Ancient Near Eastern Texts Relating to the Old Testament,* 3d ed. (Princeton, N. J.: Princeton University Press, 1969), 365–401.

4. See the previous discussion in chapter 1. Also, "The Name of God" in my *Contours of Old Testament Theology* (Minneapolis: Fortress Press, 1999), 48–55.

5. See the discussion of "Name" in Johannes Pedersen, *Israel: Its Life and Culture,* vol. 1–2 (London: Oxford University Press, 1926, 1959), 1:245–59.

6. Gerhard von Rad, *Old Testament Theology,* vol. 1, trans. D. M. G. Stalker (New York: Harper & Row, 1962), 362.

7. Blaise Pascal, *Pensees,* The Modern Library (New York: Random House, 1941), fragment 229.

8. Here the verb *qana* is translated as "create" rather than "purchase." See Frank M. Cross, "The Song of the Sea and Canaanite Myth," in *Canaanite Myth and Hebrew Epic* (Cambridge, Mass.: Harvard University Press, 1973).

9. J. Clinton McCann Jr., *A Theological Introduction to the Book of Psalms: The Psalms as Torah* (Nashville: Abingdon Press, 1993), 59.

10. For a fuller treatment of this subject, see my chapter, "Creation and the Noachic Covenant," in *Contours of Old Testament Theology* (Minneapolis: Fortress Press, 1999).

11. See the discussion of this hymn in chapter 2.

12. On the reinterpretation of mythical symbolism in hymns of creation, see my *Creation versus Chaos* (Philadelphia: Fortress Press, 1987), chap. 3. A basic work on the mythical view of reality is Mircea Eliade, *Cosmos and History: The Myth of the Eternal Return,* trans. Willard R. Trask (New York: Harper & Brothers, 1959).

13. On postmodernism, see Stanley J. Grenz, *A Primer on Postmodernism* (Grand Rapids: Wm. B. Eerdmans Publishing Co., 1996).

14. W. H. Auden, "New Year Letter" (January 1, 1940) in *Collected Poems,* ed. Edward Mendelson (New York: Random House, 1976), 174.

8. Zion, the City of God

1. See chapter 1, "The Cultic Element," in Helmer Ringgren, *The Faith of the Psalmists* (Philadelphia: Fortress Press, 1963). He writes: "The psalms were not written for private use—at least, not originally, but for use in the cult of the Yhwh community, and in most cases the cult of the preexilic community" (p. 1).

2. Roland Murphy observes that "a liturgical mime" must have accompanied a poem such as Psalm 46; the invitation to "behold the works of the Lord"

suggests that "some activity accompanied the poem" (*The Psalms, Job,* Proclamation Commentaries [Philadelphia: Fortress Press, 1977], 13).

3. This service is discussed in the commentaries of Artur Weiser, *The Psalms: A Commentary,* trans. Herbert Hartwell, Old Testament Library (Philadelphia: Westminster Press, 1962) and Hans-Joachim Kraus, *Psalms 1–59: A Commentary* and *Psalms 60–150: A Commentary,* trans. Hilton C. Oswald (Minneapolis: Augsburg Publishing House, 1988 and 1989).

4. Weiser, *Psalms.*

5. See the discussion of the Mosaic covenant in my *Contours of Old Testament Theology* (Minneapolis: Fortress Press, 1999), part 2B.

6. See *The United Methodist Book of Worship* (1992).

7. See Frank M. Cross, "The Priestly Work," in *Canaanite Myth and Hebrew Epic* (Cambridge, Mass.: Harvard University Press, 1973), 299.

8. In the final form of the Psalter this cluster of psalms addresses the theological crisis brought on by exile. This collection of psalms "became the theological 'heart' of the expanded final Psalter" (Gerald Wilson, "The Use of the Royal Psalms at the 'Seams' of the Hebrew Psalter," *Journal for the Study of the Old Testament* 35 [1986]: 92).

9. Sigmund Mowinckel, *The Psalms in Israel's Worship,* trans. D. R. Ap-Thomas, vol. 1 (Nashville: Abingdon Press, 1962).

10. See my *Contours of Old Testament Theology* for an expanded discussion.

11. Mowinckel, 2: 15–22. This work first appeared in German as *Psalmenstudien, vol. 2: Das Thronbesteigungsfest Jawas und der Ursprung der Eschatologie* (Amsterdam: Schippers, 1961), 21ff.

12. See the illuminating paper by Harry P. Nasuti presented at the Psalms and Practice Conference, Austin, Texas, May 25–27, 1999, "The Sacramental Function of the Psalms in Liturgical Practice and Contemporary Scholarship." The words quoted are from his summary of the view of St. Athanasius (293–373), who introduced this sacramental view in his *Letter to Marcellinus.*

13. Walter Brueggemann, *The Message of the Psalms: A Theological Commentary* (Minneapolis: Augsburg Publishing House, 1984), 144, 145. This view is also presented in his *Israel's Praise: Doxology against Idolatry* (Minneapolis: Fortress Press, 1988).

14. James L. Mays, *The Lord Reigns: A Theological Handbook to the Psalms* (Louisville, Ky.: Westminster John Knox Press, 1994), 40–41.

15. The Sumerian king list, dating back to the third millennium B.C., is found in James B. Pritchard, ed., *Ancient Near Eastern Texts Relating to the Old Testament,* 3d ed. (Princeton, N.J.: Princeton University Press, 1969), 265.

16. See Gerhard von Rad, *Old Testament Theology,* vol. 1, trans. D. M. C. Stalker (New York: Harper & Row, 1962), 318–20.

17. Ibid., 324.

18. See Mircea Eliade's discussion of "The Symbolism of the Center" in *Cosmos and History: The Myth of the Eternal Return,* trans. Willard R. Trask (New York: Harper & Brothers, 1959), 12–17.

19. See my discussion of Isaiah's message in *Contours of Old Testament Theology,* chap. 26.

9. Like a Tree Planted by Waters

1. Artur Weiser, *The Psalms: A Commentary,* trans. Herbert Hartwell, Old Testament Library (Philadelphia: Westminster Press, 1962), 248.
2. Kathleen A. Farmer, "Psalms" in *The Women's Bible Commentary,* ed. Carol A. Newsom and Sharon H. Ringe (Louisville, Ky.: Westminster/John Knox Press, 1992), 137–44. Others have emphasized this psalm as reflecting the maternal characteristics of God; see Irene Nowell, *Sing a New Song: The Psalms in the Sunday Lectionary* (Collegeville, Minn.: Liturgical Press, 1993), 148–49.
3. This interpretation is influenced by John Paterson's exposition of Psalm 23 in *The Praises of Israel* (New York: Charles Scribner's Sons, 1950), 108–15, which, in turn, depends upon a study by George Adam Smith.
4. Klaus Seybold, *Introducing the Psalms* (Edinburgh: T. & T. Clark, 1990), 150, states that this imagery represents the rites of judicial acquittal.
5. Weiser, *Psalms,* 227.
6. This is the view of Hans-Joachim Kraus, *Psalms 60–150: A Commentary,* trans. Hilton C. Oswald (Minneapolis: Augsburg Publishing House, 1989), 219–25, who draws attention to the parallel in Psalm 34, where a person in a situation of thanksgiving teaches others out of personal experience.
7. Roland E. Murphy, *The Psalms, Job,* Proclamation Commentaries (Philadelphia: Fortress Press, 1977). See also "Psalms," in *The Jerome Biblical Commentary* (Englewood Cliffs, N.J.: Prentice-Hall, 1969), 569–602.
8. See the discussion of this problem in my *Contours of Old Testament Theology* (Minneapolis: Fortress Press, 1999), 242–49, 276–82, 302–11.
9. See the illuminating essay by Martin Buber, "The Heart Determines: Psalm 73," in *Theodicy in the Old Testament,* ed. James L. Crenshaw (Philadelphia: Fortress Press, 1983), 109–18.

10. Reading the Book of Psalms as a Whole

1. J. Clinton McCann Jr., "The Psalms as Instruction," *Interpretation* 46: 118.
2. Gerald H. Wilson, *The Editing of the Hebrew Psalter,* SBL Dissertation Series 76 (Chico, Calif.: Scholars Press, 1985), 207.
3. See James A. Sanders, *The Dead Sea Psalms Scroll* (Ithaca, N.Y.: Cornell University Press, 1967).
4. These and other variations are discussed by Mark S. Smith, "Taking Inspiration: Authorship, Revelation, and the Book of Psalms," a paper pre-

sented to the Psalms and Practice Conference, Austin, Texas, May 25–27, 1999.

5. Nancy L. deClasse-Walford, *Reading from the Beginning: The Shaping of the Hebrew Psalter* (Macon, Ga.: Mercer University Press, 1997).

6. She acknowledges indebtedness to Brevard Childs's emphasis upon the final canonical text in his "Reflections on the Modern Study of the Psalms," in *Magnalia Dei: The Mighty Acts of God—Essays on the Bible and Archaeology in Memory of G. Ernest Wright,* ed. F. M. Cross, W. E. Lemke, and P. D. Miller (Garden City, N.Y.: Doubleday, 1976), 377–88, to Gerald Wilson's *The Editing of the Hebrew Psalter,* SBL Dissertation Series 76 (Chico, Calif.: Scholars Press, 1985), and especially to James A. Sanders's style of canonical criticism advocated in "Adaptable for Life" in Cross, et al., *Magnalia Dei,* 531–60.

7. DeClasse-Walford, *Reading from the Beginning* (Macon, Ga.: Mercer University Press, 1997), 34.

8. Jon Levenson, "The Source of Torah: Psalm 119 and the modes of Revelation in Second Temple Judaism" in *Ancient Israelite Religion,* ed. P. D. Miller, Jr., et al. (Philadelphia: Fortress Press, 1987), 570.

9. J. Clinton McCann Jr., "Thus Says the Lord: 'Thou Shalt Preach on the Psalms,' " paper presented to the Psalms and Practice Conference, Austin, Texas May 25–27, 1999.

10. Claus Westermann, *Praise and Lament in the Psalms,* trans. K. R. Crim and R. N. Soulen (Atlanta: John Knox Press, 1981), 253.

11. Quoted in C. McCann, "The Psalms as Instruction," 121. From John Calvin, Preface to *A Commentary on the Book of Psalms* (1571), trans. James Anderson (Grand Rapids: Wm. B. Eerdmans Publishing Co., 1949). See further James Mays, "The Place of the Torah-Psalms in the Psalter," *Journal of Biblical Literature* 106 (1987): 3–12.

12. See above, chapter 8; further my *Contours of Old Testament Theology,* chap. 23.

13. See James Luther Mays, "The David of the Psalms," *Interpretation* 40, no. 2 (1986): 143–55.

14. Gerald H. Wilson, *The Editing of the Hebrew Psalter,* SBL Dissertation Series 76 (Chico, Calif.: Scholars Press, 1985).

15. DeClasse-Walford, *Reading from the Beginning,* agrees that the postexilic community of Israel (as reflected in the final editing of the Psalms) moved beyond the "nationhood" signified by Davidic king and temple. Strangely, she completely ignores Psalm 132 and its location in the final book of the Psalter.

16. Walter Brueggemann, *The Message of the Psalms* (Minneapolis: Augsburg Publishing House, 1984), see especially the introduction, 1–23.

17. Christoph Barth, *Introduction to the Psalms,* trans. R. A. Wilson (New York: Charles Scribner's Sons, 1966), 64–65.

Selected Bibliography

Commentaries on the Psalms

Anderson, Arnold A. *The Psalms*. 2 vols. New Century Bible. London: Oliphants, 1972.

Bellinger, William H., Jr. *Psalms: Reading and Studying the Book of Praises*. Peabody, Mass.: Hendrickson Publishers, 1990.

Brueggemann, Walter. *The Message of the Psalms: A Theological Commentary*. Augsburg Old Testament Studies. Minneapolis: Augsburg Publishing House, 1984.

Eaton, John H. *Psalms: Introduction and Commentary*. Torch Bible Commentaries. London: SCM Press, 1967.

Kidner, Derek. *The Psalms*. 2 vols. Tyndale Old Testament Commentaries. London: Inter-Varsity Press, 1973 and 1975.

Kraus, Hans-Joachim. *Psalms 1–59: A Commentary* and *Psalms 60–150: A Commentary*. Translated by H. C. Oswald. Minneapolis: Augsburg Publishing House, 1988 and 1989.

Mays, James Luther. *Psalms*. Interpretation: A Bible Commentary for Teaching and Preaching. Louisville, Ky.: Westminster John Knox Press, 1994.

McCann, J. Clinton, Jr. "The Psalms." *The New Interpreter's Bible*. Vol. 4. Nashville: Abingdon Press, 1996.

Murphy, Roland E. "Psalms." *The Jerome Biblical Commentary*. Englewood Cliffs, N.J.: Prentice-Hall, 1969.

Rogerson, J. W., and McKay, J. W., eds. *The Psalms*. 3 vols. Cambridge Bible Commentary. Cambridge: Cambridge University Press, 1977.

Tate, Marvin E. *Psalms 51–100*. Word Biblical Commentary 20. Dallas: Word Books, 1990.

Weiser, Artur. *The Psalms: A Commentary*. Translated by Herbert Hartwell. Old Testament Library. Philadelphia: Westminster Press, 1962.

General Writings on the Psalms

Ackroyd, Peter R. *Doors of Perception: A Guide to Reading the Psalms.* London: SCM Press, 1978.

Barth, Christoph. *Introduction to the Psalms.* Translated by R. A. Wilson. New York: Charles Scribner's Sons, 1966.

Bonhoeffer, Dietrich. *Psalms: The Prayer Book of the Bible.* Vol. 5 of *Dietrich Bonhoeffer Works.* English edition. Edited by Geffrey B. Kelly. Translated by Daniel W. Bloesch and James H. Burtness. Minneapolis: Fortress Press, 1996.

Brueggemann, Walter. "From Hurt to Joy, From Death to Life." *Interpretation* 28 (1974): 3–19.

———. *The Psalms and the Life of Faith.* Edited by Patrick D. Miller. Minneapolis: Fortress Press, 1995.

Eaton, John H. *Kingship and the Psalms.* London: SCM Press, 1976.

Gerstenberger, Erhard S. *Psalms: Part 1, with an Introduction to Cultic Poetry.* Forms of Old Testament Literature 14. Grand Rapids: Wm. B. Eerdmans Publishing Co., 1988.

Holladay, William L. *The Psalms through Three Thousand Years: Prayerbook of a Cloud of Witnesses.* Minneapolis: Fortress Press, 1993.

Lewis, C. S. *Reflections on the Psalms.* London: William Collins Sons & Co., 1960.

Mays, James Luther. *The Lord Reigns: A Theological Handbook to the Psalms.* Louisville, Ky.: Westminster John Knox Press, 1994.

McCann, J. Clinton, Jr., ed. *The Shape and Shaping of the Psalter.* JSOT Supplement Series 159. Sheffield: Sheffield Academic Press, 1993.

———. *A Theological Introduction to the Book of Psalms: The Psalms as Torah.* Nashville: Abingdon Press, 1993.

Miller, Patrick D., Jr. "Trouble and Woe: Interpreting the Biblical Laments." *Interpretation* 37 (1983): 32–45.

Murphy, Roland E. "The Faith of the Psalmist." *Interpretation* 34 (1980): 229–39.

———. *The Psalms, Job.* Proclamation Commentaries. Minneapolis: Fortress Press, 1977.

Ringgren, Helmer. *The Faith of the Psalmists.* Minneapolis: Fortress Press, 1963.

Seybold, Klaus. *Introducing the Psalms.* Edinburgh: T. & T. Clark, 1990.

Terrien, Samuel. *The Psalms and Their Meaning for Today.* Indianapolis: Bobbs-Merrill Co., 1952.

Westermann, Claus. *The Praise of God in the Psalms.* Translated by Keith R. Crim. 2d ed. Richmond: John Knox Press, 1965.

———. *Praise and Lament in the Psalms.* Translated by Keith R. Crim and Richard N. Soulen. Atlanta: John Knox Press, 1981.

———. "The Role of the Lament in the Theology of the Old Testament." *Interpretation* 28 (1974): 20–38.

Wilson, Gerald H. *The Editing of the Hebrew Psalter.* SBL Dissertation Series 76. Edited by J. J. M. Roberts. Chico, Calif.: Scholars Press, 1985.

Zenger, Erich. *A God of Vengeance? Understanding the Psalms of Divine Wrath.* Louisville, Ky.: Westminster John Knox Press, 1996.

Special Studies on the Psalms and Worship

Anderson, Bernhard W. *Creation versus Chaos: The Reinterpretation of Mythical Symbolism in the Bible.* Minneapolis: Fortress Press, 1987. See especially chapter 3, "Creation and Worship."

Clements, Ronald F. *God and Temple.* Philadelphia: Fortress Press, 1965.

Eaton, John H. *The Psalms Come Alive.* London: Mowbray, 1984.

Kraus, Hans-Joachim. *Worship in Israel: A Cultic History of the Old Testament.* Translated by Geoffrey Buswell. Rev. and enlarged ed. Richmond: John Knox Press, 1966.

Miller, Patrick D. *They Cried to the Lord: The Form and Theology of Biblical Prayer.* Minneapolis: Fortress Press, 1994.

Nowell, Irene. *Sing a New Song: The Psalms in the Sunday Lectionary.* Collegeville, Minn.: Liturgical Press, 1993.

Shepherd, Massey H. *The Psalms in Christian Worship.* Minneapolis: Augsburg Publishing House, 1976.

Werner, Eric. *The Sacred Bridge: The Interdependence of Liturgy and Music in Synagogue and Church during the First Millennium.* New York: Columbia University Press, 1959.

Index of Biblical Passages